T0288551

After the Crusade

After the Crusade

American Foreign Policy for
the Post-Superpower Age

Jonathan Clarke
and
James Clad

Foreword by James R. Schlesinger

Madison Books
Lanham • New York • London

Published by Madison Books
4720 Boston Way, Lanham, Maryland 20706

3 Henrietta Street
London, WC2E 8LU, England

Distributed by National Book Network

The paper used in this publication meets the minimum
requirements of American National Standard for
Information Sciences—Permanence of Paper for
Printed Library Materials, ANSI Z39.48–1984. ∞™

Library of Congress Cataloging-in-Publication Data

Clarke, Jonathan, 1947–
After the crusade : American foreign policy for the post
-superpower age / Jonathan Clarke and James Clad.
p. cm.
Includes bibliographical references (p.   ) and index.
1. United States—Foreign relations—1989–   I. Clad, James.
II. Title.
E881.C6 1995 327.73—dc20 94–47399 CIP

ISBN 1–56833–051–0 (cloth : alk. paper)

British Cataloging in Publication Information Available

Contents

Foreword

With the end of the Soviet empire in Eastern Europe, the collapse of the Warsaw Pact, and the subsequent demise of the Soviet Union itself, a kind of euphoria swept over much of the industrial world. The euphoria was perhaps understandable, indeed inevitable, for the Soviet threat had largely disappeared. That euphoria was best embodied in President Bush's phrase *The New World Order*. It was buttressed by the coalition's success in the Gulf War and by the prospect of continuing Russian–American cooperation. The post–Cold War order would be reasonably peaceful. Actions that the United States or other members of the "international community" found offensive would be punished through sanctions or suppressed. The world would enjoy a tranquillity that it had not hitherto known.

America's role, in our own view and in the view of many of our allies, would be substantial and critical. The United States would be the leader, presumably supported by the permanent members of the Security Council. The United States would take the lead in determining when sanctions needed to be imposed, aggression resisted, or internal peace imposed. She would organize the international coalitions, either through or outside the United Nations—which assumed the availability of willing partners. And in the view of some in the United States, in light of our budget difficulties, there was an additional assumption that perhaps others would be happy to pay, particularly for the American role in maintaining international order.

This was not to be. The vision was based upon presuppositions that were unsound and hopes that were unfounded. The post–Cold War world turned out to be quite disorderly. Passions that had been contained or disguised by the disciplines of the Cold War began to break out, as those disciplines ceased to restrain the actions of nations and ethnic groups. Nor was the post–Cold War landscape notably *new*. The collapse of the Soviet empire led in many respects to a reversion to the world that existed in Eastern Europe before 1939. Similarly, instability returned to the Caucasus and to Central Asia—within the boundaries of the former Soviet Union. National ambitions, ethnic rivalries, and simple thuggery that had long been held in check erupted once again.

No one should have been surprised. As long as the human race is around, turbulence is to be expected. Yet, many—most notably, the idealists—were surprised indeed!

Among the many reasons that the vision turned out to be misplaced, two in particular stand out. First, the task of deterring the Soviet Union was inherently a far simpler task for the United States that that of imposing order on an unruly world. The Soviet Union provided a single, massive, seemingly permanent threat, against which the United States *alone* had the resources to serve as counterweight.

Second, the American people are simply not up to *multiple* crusades. Many of the numerous irruptions that occur (not backed up by the Soviet superpower) can now be handled by others. But in any event, the American public is not likely to accept involvement in numerous engagements. It lacks the inclination. It lacks the necessary ruthlessness (which may in itself be another aspect of the lack of ambition). Unlike some of our allies, we have scant experience in bearing an imperial burden. Especially in their present mood, the American people have little desire to do so.

All this has led to a notable gap between what the American nation was really prepared to do and what many of the elites were eager to do. Though the stakes have shrunk with the collapse of the Soviet threat, our political elites (including the journalistic fraternity) have sought occasions to exercise the expertise built up over many years. For government officials, foreign policy experts, defense intellectuals, and so on, the Cold War was a lot of fun. While the end of the danger may be welcome, the end of the challenge in some ways is not. Also, the political Left, which had been fearful of and inhibited by Soviet military strength—and also had become disgusted with the uses of military power after Vietnam—was once again liberated. Its Wilsonian juices flowed with renewed force and it was eager to right injustices around the world. (This did not preclude an eagerness to continue to shrink America's forces.)

Thus, we find an explanation for many of the events of recent years: bold rhetoric that turns out to be too bold; an eagerness to lead that is unsustained by the American public. Despite the frustration for many of our foreign policy gurus, this outcome is understandable. The departure of the Soviet threat has substantially reduced the stakes for this country. The post–Cold War world, after all, is richer in ironies that it is in serious problems.

Whatever may be true for other societies, in the American democracy policies that are unsupported by the public are simply unsustainable. This imposes upon our policy makers, if they are to be effective, a requirement for rigorous selectivity, especially if the United States is to continue, as the world's leading power, to play a constructive international role. It is also desirable, if not essential, for the United States to reacquire a certain reticence in expressing its views and not engage in bold rhetoric regarding international events that it is unprepared to back up.

It is these realities and these requirements that make this unusual book so valuable. Jonathan Clarke and James Clad understand the character of this post–Cold War world and the tempo of American society far better than many of our other foreign policy authorities. In the place of the several visions of a post–Cold War utopia they recognize that, as they put it, "the *primal* temperament of international politics has reasserted itself." This implies that the world inevitably will remain a messy place, far beyond the limited capacity of American society to cure. They therefore urge not only that we exercise rigorous selectivity but also that we adjust our attitudes. They do urge the continuation of America's critical involvement in the world. But they are not put off in their strictures by the repeated and ill-focused "warnings against neo-isolationism" parroted by the authorities that they decry. They wisely urge that most engagements by this country be within the framework that they call "the 'historical memory' of our Republic." Departures from the constraints of such historical memory should be few in number and well justified to the public.

In my judgment, the authors are quite trenchant in their criticism of what is the fashionable, indeed prevailing, view of the ambitions of America's foreign policy. While the experts may differ among themselves regarding where the United States should become involved, there is a clear bias among the commentators, as we emerge from the Cold War, towards international activism. It is right that this reflexive activism be criticized and curtailed.

The authors may have gone a bit too far for my taste in treating "the establishment" as a monolith. There is widespread recognition that, while the world is rather messy at the end of the Cold War, it is far less dangerous from an American perspective. Clarke and Clad may have overstated the cohesion and dominance of the views they criticize, and regard themselves as lonely voices crying in the wilderness. Yet, they are right about the prevalence of the fashionable view and its risks. In a sense, Clarke and Clad are themselves embarked on a crusade, against misplaced idealism, reflexive activism, and just plain silliness. Their advice is clear and cogent and (for most readers) will be compelling. Read on. Listen to, and largely heed, their wise counsel.

— James R. Schlesinger

Preface

Lies and lethargies police the world
In its periods of peace. What pain taught
Is soon forgotten; we celebrate
What ought to happen as if it were done,
Are blinded by our boasts. Then back they come,
The fears that we fear.
— W. H. Auden
The Age of Anxiety

At various junctures during the writing of this book, we asked ourselves whether we were wasting our time. The foreign policy debate seemed polarized into two broad camps: The old foreign policy elite seemed intent on defending the habits of international intervention built up over three generations, while the country beyond turned its back on foreign policy, dismissing it as boring and irrelevant to daily life, as just another symptom of government failure.

The trouble was that these two great bodies of opinion were sailing past each other like ships in the night. No one evinced any interest in reconciliation.

Instinctively, we sided with the skepticism of popular opinion. In insisting on protecting its traditional privileges, the foreign policy establishment seemed to have cut itself off from wider sentiment. At the same time, the experts were right to insist that foreign policy was important. Just because we no longer risked blowing the planet into oblivion didn't mean that foreign policy mistakes would not exact costs. In one way or another, the outside world still mattered a great deal to the United States. It was still worth making the effort to get foreign policy right. And, given that foreign policy cannot be easily privatized, getting it right meant trying to reform the foreign policy bit of government—however low in popular esteem this had fallen.

We came to regard the fact that the nation was at loggerheads with itself as representing the real waste of time. Over the long term, neglect of foreign policy would severely diminish the national welfare. Moreover, a great opportunity was being lost to recreate the sense of judicious American stewardship of global affairs from which Americans and the rest of the world had so enormously benefitted over the past fifty years.

After careers abroad in the diplomatic services of countries closely allied to the United States, and as believers in the importance of keeping America ascendant, we wanted to do something about these shortcomings. So we began to look at ways to help bridge the gap between the experts, to whom falls the task of foreign policy leadership, and the vastly larger number of nonspecialist citizens, without whose consent any leadership, in any field, is an empty vessel. Our aim was to strike the right balance between an instinctively cautious public opinion and the effective execution of vital foreign policy business. As we began to write, four major themes emerged:

First, the era starting with Pearl Harbor in 1941 and continuing through the Cold War until 1989 represents a remarkable period in American history. Civilized people everywhere owe an immense debt of gratitude for the

American contribution to human liberty during this period. But, in the longer perspective of the Republic, the Cold War represents a very abnormal period, almost an aberration. This period, immensely successful though it was, bequeathed an awkward legacy—a set of habits of thought and action of dubious value for today's foreign policy purposes. We look at these habits—criticizing many of them bluntly—with the aim of retaining the useful while discarding the outdated.

Second, if this approach is right, it appears likely that an acute awareness of *limits* rather than the "pay any price, bear any burden"[1] mentality of the Cold War will determine future American foreign policy. Effective defense of the nation's foreign interests will demand a focus on what really matters rather than spreading ourselves thinly and ineffectually across the globe. To this end, we question some of the lengthy agendas and new causes championed by the foreign policy establishment and by the many single-issue lobby groups clustered in Washington.

Third, whenever foreign policy choices are made, they will also need to be consistent with what we describe as the historical memory of the Republic. In one way or another, the tried and true instincts of the American people have to play a larger part in the policy-making process. We look, therefore, at ways in which popular sentiment and expert knowledge might converge more closely.

Fourth, in reminding ourselves of these older instincts of forbearance, we found ourselves delving into earlier ages of American diplomatic activity to a time when there was far less disjunction between Washington and the citizenry beyond. The more we wrote, the less the much trumpeted new post–Cold War era appeared new at all. To be sure, factors such the globalization of the world economy and the telecommunications revolution have created an image of an entirely new world, but we found that the instincts of earlier generations retained vivid lessons for today. We draw on these throughout the book.

The overall implication of these themes is that the present system in the United States for conducting foreign policy is ill-adapted to the challenges we face in the modern world. The system lacks focus and is overlarge. American strength cannot be built on such a weak foundation. This book is not about budgets. But the suggestions we make for greater selectivity, more realistic military planning, and bureaucratic reform would all yield substantial savings without in any way sacrificing American vital interests. If implemented, these ideas for a reformed foreign policy can play their part in the most pressing substantive and political issue of the day: putting America's financial house in order.

When we hesitantly ran these ideas past our colleagues in Washington's foreign policy elite, many gave generously of their time to police our thinking. A good number of cheerfully critical comments found their mark. In their particular criticisms, our Beltway Brethren helped us a lot. We received especially valuable encouragement and editorial support from Eric Peterson and Brad Roberts at the Center for Strategic and International Studies in Washington, D.C. From them came the initial prompt for this book.

Easily our greatest surprise, however, came in the denial of our central thesis—which not only challenges most foreign policy directions emerging since the end of the Cold War, but also points to the root of the deficiency. For in this book we throw down a challenge to the foreign policy elite itself, a group of highly driven men and women who, though divided by various persuasions, still act as if the custodianship of the ship of state should pass to them—and to them alone—whenever this vessel lifts anchor and steams toward foreign climes.

As the book took shape, our best interlocutors turned out to be the people facing us during question time after our speeches at meetings convened by America's small galaxy of World Affairs Councils, or to service clubs in places like Anchorage, Palm Springs, Milwaukee, and Grand Rapids. There we found a mixture of care, concern, and caution about this republic's place in the world. These people want to maintain the best traditions of American leadership, but they worry that this supremacy is being frittered away by misguided, unsustainable policies that really reflect Washington's preoccupations rather than the nation's wider interests.

These anxieties caused us to reverse the normal line of approach for a book like this. In the manner of other foreign affairs books, we could have identified successive issues, threats, geographic trouble spots, and so on. But this would have required starting on the outside—in Russia, China, or wherever—and then sketching in issues like strategic waterways, economic challenges, and resource choke points. But we sensed that this omitted something vital. And so we decided to take as our starting point this gut instinct of priority and caution.

For the message from Americans up and down the country is unmistakable. They are proud that twice in the past century they have helped rid the world of a pervasive tyrannical creed. They want the country to remain strong so that they can do so again should the need arise. But until it does, Americans want to mind their own business, to keep themselves in reserve for a true emergency, but otherwise to live and let live. If anyone suggests a different course of action, then there had better be a good reason.

In Washington, the notion of standing down after the Cold War is a profoundly disturbing idea that threatens status, relevance, and careers. It runs counter to instincts and training compounded for more than fifty years, challenging what the late diplomat George Ball called the "satisfactions of power." Former Defense Secretary James Schlesinger has also noted that "it is going to be less fun."[2]

Inevitably, much of the establishment has counterattacked those questioning a policy of incessant proactivity. Warning against neo–isolationism and putting our heads in the sand, a range of personal and institutional voices has developed new reasons for American action abroad: Proliferation, narcotics, ethnic conflict, terrorism, human rights, the environment, family planning, biological diver-

sity, collapsing states, AIDS[3]—all these and many other
agendas provide the raw material for Congressional committees, op–ed pages, talk shows, and seminars. We will
return to them several times through the course of this
book.

Is there a master key to all these stratagems? Yes, we
think there may be. Each amounts to an assertion—
whether conscious or implicit—that the United States
should retain its posture of sweeping global engagement
and that the abundant resources budgeted in bygone decades to combat the Soviet Union should remain available
to new causes and crusades.

It is on this point that debate should be joined. Where
does the popular instinct for caution meet the elite predis-
position toward activism? To resolve this question sensibly, the foreign policy debate needs to be as accessible as
any other and as welcoming of all strands of opinion. Why
does America's role in the world need to be discussed in
obscurantist jargon or impenetrable terminology? Americans of any background can and should bring the same
confidence to foreign affairs as they do to health care, education, welfare, or the economy.

To this end, we have tried to be both concise and read-
able. At the same time, we have not cut intellectual corners nor have we scrambled to reduce our thinking to
quotable sound bites. We don't claim that our prescriptions
or vision are superior to other alternatives. Nor do we ex-
empt ourselves from the criticism that the foreign policy
mainstream has so deservedly attracted. After all, we have
been part of this mainstream as diplomats, foreign correspondents, and residents of think tanks. Where we apportion criticism we hope we do so on the merits and not in
order to discredit a particular political party, viewpoint, or
person. The gestation of this book survived through three
different dispensations of power in Washington. It was
conceived under a Republican president, written when the
Democrats controlled both the White House and the Congress, and is being published as the Republicans assume
power on Capitol Hill. We hope that its themes remain

valid through all these changes—and indeed for the other transitions that inevitably lie ahead. Thus, when we advocate specific courses of action, we do not do so on behalf of a partisan political manifesto. We are neither globalists nor isolationists; neither liberals nor conservatives. We are all groping toward answers in this area. We will do better at the job if we unload the excess intellectual and emotional Cold War baggage accumulated, like Jacob Marley's chains in Charles Dickens's *A Christmas Carol*, bit by bit over the past fifty years.

Unlike most blueprints now in circulation, we do not lay down what "America must do" in Japan, Europe, or elsewhere. Our chief currency is common sense—we aim to leave our readers with a type of conceptual tool kit to help them grapple with those most intractably difficult questions: When should the United States do something and when should it back off?

For all the finger wagging about neo–isolationism from the foreign policy establishment, the popular mood aims not at abandoning the world, but at forcing some tough questions about the long-term fundamentals of foreign policy. What are the real reasons behind the proposals for action? Do these accord with Americans' intuition of what is doable, at reasonable cost, and with a tolerable chance of success? How do these insistent calls for action square with all the other claims on America's time and money?

Difficult questions. And we do not have answers for each specific problem. But we find a type of bedrock historical wisdom in the cautious instincts of Americans who have no trouble recognizing hideously complicated problems when they see them. Intuitively they discern the vainglory that comes from the let's-do-something siren calls issuing so often from lobbyists, academics, think tanks, journalists, columnists, and talk show hosts who, together with the government itself, comprise the foreign policy establishment.

Introduction

"The Rest of the World Ah! there is the rub."
— Franklin Delano Roosevelt,
1936

In his foreword to the published dispatches of George Ernest Morrison, the finest Far Eastern correspondent alive in 1900, Australian historian C. F. Fitzgerald stressed[1] an enduring facet of world affairs that we in America have neglected for half a century.

For Morrison and others of his generation, "in the years before the [First World] War, the forthcoming contest was seen as a fight between the great powers and their allies, and *not* as the confrontation of Good and Evil which wartime propaganda was soon to make it." The famous journalist knew only too well, Fitzgerald continued, "that Britain would have to fight for her place, as all empires had to fight. But, *the challenger was not a moral outcast*; he might be foolish, arrogant, and insufferable but he was only doing what others had done before, and he would meet the same fate."[2]

What does a long dead foreign journalist have to do with modern American foreign policy? Simply this: One of the central themes around which we build our proposals for foreign policy reform is that, far from being deposited directionless and clueless into a *terra incognita*, we are returning to a world not unlike that in which Morrison lived.

Do we mean that the 1990s and beyond are just a repeat of the pre–1914 world? Not at all. What we *do* mean is that the thoroughly abnormal situation in which two powers with global reach dominated international relations for half a century has given way to a more normal disposition. The primal, underlying temperament of international politics has reasserted itself. The post–Cold War world is coming to look like the world of contending states that the stewards of American foreign policy from the eighteenth century until 1945 would easily have recognized.[3] They would see, at once, a world of recognizable gradations of threat and danger despite the arrival of new actors on the world's stage.

This notion of a world regained rather than a blank slate remains rather rare today, five years after the demise of the Soviet Union. Ever since George Bush proclaimed his vision of a "new world order,"[4] most foreign policy thinking has worked on the premise that we have moved into a new era for which we must invent new rationales for action. But America's need today is, in Warren Harding's much maligned words, not for "heroics, but healing; not nostrums but normalcy."[5]

Effective diplomacy requires Americans to realize that the world since 1988-90 has *not* yielded to some new and disturbing order of power relations. We are neither happily encompassed by a brave new world of peace dividends and universal democracy nor, taking the pessimistic tack, are we rent asunder by horrifying new passions. No new malevolent era of atavistic hatreds has abruptly emerged, even if the world's cacophony seems amplified by Cable News Network's (CNN's) real-time coverage and by the ubiquity of black-market weapons easily bought in any number of depots brimming with surplus equipment from east and west.[6]

Many Americans outside the foreign policy profession appear to grasp in a broad sense this concept of historical continuity. For the most part, expert opinion does not. In his 1993 book, *Out of Control*, for example, former National Security Adviser Zbigniew Brzezinski wrote that "discontinuity is the central reality of our contemporary history."[7] For this reason, we take issue with some of the positions that comprise the foreign policy mainstream. In chapter 1, we review and assess the contributions of the many distinguished foreign affairs experts. We examine their sincere and often cogently argued agendas for continued global engagement.

In doing so, we try to avoid treating the foreign policy community as a monolith. It is not.[8] We do, however, detect a prevailing ethos among officials, analysts, and commentators—whether they describe themselves as "idealists," "realists," or some other title—in favor of a foreign policy posture described by Yale professor Eugene Rostow as "at least as active and probably no less expensive than the policy . . . pursued since the Second World War."[9] The members of this elite group harbor many mutual disagreements about America's foreign policy agenda, but in one crucial respect they are united: They regard the *level* of activism undertaken during the Cold War as the *norm*. Even in books such as the one published by the Council on Foreign Relations, *Rethinking America's Security*, which purportedly sets out a less ambitious overseas program, or Henry Kissinger's magisterial *Diplomacy*, which seeks to establish "criteria for selectivity," this activist theme is restated in such assertions as "the need for American leadership on the international stage has not ended" and in Kissinger's advocacy of extended American security commitments in eastern Europe.[10] In setting out its foreign policy prescriptions, the Heritage Foundation acknowledges that the United States does not have "endless resources to squander," but still manages to fill forty-five pages with locations and reasons for American intervention overseas.[11]

Why do these experts' arguments tend to be more fertile in finding new causes to pursue than in defining criteria for a more selective approach? Why does it seem so easy to succumb to transitory distractions and so difficult to concentrate on the enduring bedrock problems of real importance to the United States. In chapter 2, we probe into why so many visions of today's world appear to draw their inspiration from Dante's *Inferno* as depicted by Brueghel. Does this correspond to the world as it really is? Or, are other mechanisms at work?

Against these apocalyptic views we offer a different image. Let us explain it by drawing on an historical parallel from another country—Britain—with which we have some familiarity. At the height of the British Empire last century, two brothers administered an area of the Indian subcontinent called the Punjab. The Imperial Office in London wondered why "no action" had been taken in respect to an obscure colonial dispute with Russia and prodded the brothers with messages. The brothers sent back a note insisting they *were* watching the situation very closely. We are fully aware of the situation, the Lawrence brothers replied. They recommended a policy of masterly inactivity.[12]

Later, masterly inactivity would come to characterize one side of the debate a century and a half ago in Britain between advocates of waiting to see what moves czarist Russia would actually make to threaten India and those who wanted to set out in every direction from India to be the first to establish lines. What in today's jargon would be called preventive diplomacy or preemptive strikes, was then called forward policy. Masterly inactivity was, in fact, the best approach—least costly in lives and treasure, and most supported by public opinion.

No era or time has an exact equivalence to another. Nor does masterly inactivity mesh exactly with the restless dynamism of the American spirit. To most Americans, this attitude means doing nothing and thus smacks of passivity and neglect, benign or otherwise. They overlook the implication of inner strength and subtle maneuvering betokened by masterly inactivity. In any case, although the

Lawrence brothers' credo can never serve as a model for the United States, its inherent qualities of guarded watchfulness and prudent aversion to impulsive expeditions abroad remain as useful today as they were a century ago.

In charting this thesis—and in accepting the risk of opprobrium from our colleagues—we have sought advice and wisdom from unlikely sources, from names now found only in diplomatic history textbooks. We have looked anew at men like Charles Evans Hughes, a secretary of state during the 1920s, and at William Henry Seward, Lincoln's secretary of state.

They and their peers knew their geography; they knew when to stay *out* of conflict beyond our shores (which was most of the time). They also knew how to husband power, to use it sparingly. They appreciated how vast was the task of mobilizing Americans to risk lives and treasure abroad. In short, they knew when to fight and, much more important, when not to fight. In chapter 3, we show how today this natural connection between resources and aspirations has been lost. And we suggest how to put this right.

With the landscape of the post–Cold War world depicted in this way, we then move on in the next four chapters to look at how such present-day activities as foreign intervention, military deployment, and the rhetorical selling of foreign policy fit the picture we have painted.

In doing so, we draw on other founts that have nourished earlier visions of American independence and prosperity. The insistence upon having the same advantages in trade and navigation as other countries guided the young republic. So did an insistence that the United States would never accept one country, or coalition of countries, seeking to deny it entry to commercial advantage or foreclosing the choice of projecting what power America had at any given time. A steady opposition to strategic denial, whether practiced by Barbary pirates, the Royal Navy, or Japan, always provoked American intransigence. And rightly so. These are the same imperatives that demand American engagement today.

Yet having these imperatives is a very different matter from assuming to ourselves the tendency to identify disorder *per se* as somehow inimical to the future of the American achievement. The truth is that large stretches of the inhabited world can go to blazes without Americans suffering a challenge to their security or a threat to their subsistence.

Force-fed on a diet of tragic images from Sarajevo, Americans see the persistence of suffering as evidence of U.S. failure, yet the sad truth is something else, found in the weary observation of the journalist David Marash, who wrote that "the Bosnian government, embittered and abandoned by the West, would say the reporting [by Western journalists] has not been good enough—that it has failed to communicate the full moral horror being committed in the ex-Yugoslavia. But the truth is sadder than that. The truth is that journalists did tell the tale; the world does know, but it knows this too: It's their war, not ours, and theirs are the consequences."[13]

Marash has a point. There has been much talk about the revolution in telecommunications, about pictures driving policy—as if Americans, with their especially fine-tuned morality, are aroused, like Pavlov's dog, each time CNN rings the bell of outrage.[14] Instantaneous communications and rapid air travel make our forays abroad as much metaphorical as spatial. One day we see hard pictures showing an American soldier's body dragged about the streets of a dusty African capital. The very next day, this prompts the U.S. administration to order a ship landing UN-sponsored military trainers in Haiti to apply reverse thrust and back away from a wharf when street toughs come too close and brandish sticks and knives.

Yet these mood swings do not carry any especial post–Cold War label. One day in the early 1980s more than two hundred marines lost their lives in a Lebanon suicide explosion. The next week, Americans invaded Grenada to overthrow an unruly leftward-leaning regime. Is it the pictures? Without resolve, the merest reversal spells doom. With resolve, which comes from basic agreement about the ends of foreign policy, reversals stiffen determination.

Thus, whether we speak of literal or metaphorical voyages in the projection of America's power and influence abroad, each raising of the anchor raises troublingly similar questions. Voyages for what purpose? To what ends? At whose cost? At the root of this critique lies a central idea: The experience of half a century's Cold War soldiering and global alliance management has put America's foreign policy leadership under a collective trance.

Choose any simile you want. U.S. foreign policy is like an airplane on auto pilot, or a ship with an empty bridge steering to pre-coded navigation coordinates while the heavens above have lost their timeless constellations. The military establishment resembles a Robo-cop, bristling with advanced spectrum electro-magnetic weaponry yet vulnerable to the lowest grade virus. Members of the foreign affairs elite in Washington—yearning to be everywhere at once and still close in spirit to what Theodore White in 1967 called a "priesthood of action-intellectuals"[15]—offer "road maps" or "blueprints" for incessant activity.

We examine in chapter 4 how this yearning manifests itself in that uniquely American phenomenon in foreign affairs—the moral crusade. We show how the moral crusaders, willing to take us toward hazardous shores in service of their ideals, happily conjure new doctrines to justify the latest extension of American diplomacy. Yet too often the apostles of a "feel-good diplomacy" are pounding the lectern, hammering home points that the audience long ago accepted or modified to taste.[16]

"Democracy?" "Yes, thank you, heard of it already."

"Free markets?" "Been using them for the last 40 years, thanks."

"Justice?" "No lectures, please, until you pacify your own streets."

"The environment?" "We started cleaning up when we got richer."

These are the responses that American hectoring elicits. It's not that specific feel-good aims are derisory or pointless; nor do we question the sincerity with which these aims are pursued. It is rather that they do not equate to the comprehensive nature of the anti-Soviet struggle just ended, which rested on rejecting a system, an army, a rocket force, and an ideology profoundly inimical to America's survival.

As we outline in the pages ahead the best ways to remain diplomatically effective, we draw liberally on historical analogy. Looking back through American diplomatic history in chapter 5, we discover that—contrary to the images favored by policymakers at home and abroad of foreign policy as a journey into "uncharted waters"[17]—the old charts for voyaging abroad in a world of unclear dangers still exist. Crafted for a world of gradation overshadowed by no demonic creed, these maps remain legible, still clear enough to reveal the shoals and whirlpools. The compass bearings have never really been lost; they lie in the memory of the Republic, in the American experience of a world just as fathomless and unpredictable today as it was two centuries ago.

Maybe more so. America's old notions about the limits of force, the dangers of involvement, and the necessity to protect the national interest retain their relevance. We take a detailed look at the limits of military force in chapter 6, and then in chapter 7 we examine the implications of these limits for the American diplomatic posture. The hardest thing in the world for Americans to do is to appear to do nothing. We must always be up and doing even if, as Sylvia Earle, chief scientist at the National Oceanic and Atmospheric Administration, has commented about environmental emergencies, "sometimes the best, and ironically most difficult, thing to do in the face of an ecological disaster is to do nothing."[18] Perhaps more than any other reason this workaholic compulsion explains the outpouring of post–Cold War paradigms and organizing principles.

We fully expect this book to draw criticism from those who, misinterpreting our views, believe that we are advocating passivity or neo-isolationism. Far from it. We set no value on activity for its own sake, but we do treasure *effective* policy. Getting it right. Getting real. Thus, in chapter 8, we discuss the concept of national interest as the proper basis for effective diplomacy. In this discussion, we agree with the majority of analysts in advocating national interest as the central determinant of foreign policy success, but take issue with the conventional view that popular sentiment should not play a part in defining national interests. We continue in chapter 9 to examine some of the implications of such a policy on international structures.

The point about an effective foreign policy, demonstrated in the Clinton administration's controversial decision to raise the trade dispute stakes with Japan in February 1994, is that it must have strong connections with the domestic mood. Rightly or wrongly, Americans have become convinced that Japan plays by different rules than other mature industrial economies. If capitalized upon properly—and we make no comment about the tactical success of Clinton's trade diplomacy with Japan—a conviction like this can give any American administration enough maneuverability to play, convincingly, the high-stakes poker with Tokyo that improved market access may require. We look at U.S.–Japan relations and other recurring issues in chapter 10—where we also analyze the all-important place of public opinion and discuss the means by which public opinions can be better marshalled. We also discuss the vital role played by presidential leadership.

As the book developed, two questions recurrently surfaced. Why the need for such a fat agenda? Why must we brace ourselves for new swarms of enemies, and roll up our sleeves to remake the world? In part, the answer lies in part in missionary zeal, in the so-called Wilsonian temperament,[19] but also in old-fashioned bureaucratic politics—the struggle for self-preservation which forms such a staple in Washington's political diet. In October 1994, for example, the *Washington Post*'s banner headline announced "Air Force Chief on Attack." Had the general concerned launched a lightning strike to dispose of one of America's designated enemies? No. His attack was directed against the other arms of the U.S. military services![20] In chapter 11, therefore, we take a brief look at two modest proposals for bureaucratic reform. We could have devised many more but these two would, if implemented, bring greater focus and impact back into foreign policy.

After assembling in this way the components of our foreign policy tool kit, in our final two chapters we look ahead toward new policy directions. In chapter 12, we draw together the book's major themes into a sort of behavioral etiquette of better foreign policy management. We try to dispel here the idea that foreign affairs is a kind of international football game where the objective is to "put points on the board."[21] In chapter 13, we look at the implications for practical policy. The coming years may see fewer expeditions abroad and more quiet nudging of countries afflicted by intraregional problems to solve them intraregionally. We examine the areas where the United States should concentrate its purpose, and those from which it should hold back in committing its power and prestige. Call it doing nothing if you like. We prefer to call it the regaining of a purposeful, effective diplomacy— husbanding resources for the moment they will really be needed.

Chapter 1

Looking for that Hole in the Doughnut: Foreign Policy Thinking after the Cold War

Who will trade old lamps for new?
— *The Arabian Nights*

"We Americans today face a challenging opportunity, perhaps the greatest ever offered to a single nation. It is nothing less than the chance to use our full strength for the peace and freedom of the world."

If these words have a familiar ring, the reader can be excused for imagining that he or she has heard them in a recent speech, or read them in any number of books appearing since 1989, the year in which the Cold War can be said to have ended. Uplifting phrases like these have pumped many prognostications from the foreign policy establishment since the demise of the Soviet Empire. Indeed, when it comes to charting What's Ahead, there may have been more Heads-Ups in Washington than heads to read them! Learned position papers fill the major foreign policy journals: Op-ed pieces crowd the newspapers. Earnest remarks hang in the broadcast ether.

Yet the words cited above appeared nearly fifty years

1

ago, in a 1947 *Foreign Affairs* article written by Henry Stimson, secretary of state in the Coolidge administration and secretary of war during World War II.[1]

Stimson's generation found their challenge in the Cold War. As another generation coming to maturity in the wake of a successful but herculean effort, we seem to want to rediscover the same mobilizing motivation. In the manner of Victorian hymnists marching as to war, we seem to need a struggle, a cause, or an epic to replace the half century just passed, those fifty years of ultimately victorious confrontation.[2] Modestly getting on with the job of ensuring that the United States receives the best possible foreign policy that limited resources can buy seems not to satisfy this millennial urge.

Thus, the search is on for a Post–Cold War Paradigm, or even for the Post Cold–War Reality. Books on New World Orders and Old World Disorders vie for our attention in campus bookstores. General audience magazines have also rushed to put their imprimatur on the globe, *sans* the Soviets. Contributors to the *Atlantic Monthly* describe a nightmare world of Malthusian distress, terrorist zeal, and porous borders, a world that has invented destructive nationalism yet again. Other journals profess optimism, seeing a planet yielding to irresistible waves of democracy.

Many country-specific or issue-specific matters continue to receive attention, but *the* vexed issue for every foreign policy thinker worth his or her salt remains the quest for what professor Michael Mandelbaum of Johns Hopkins University calls the "hole in the doughnut."[4] It's a useful phrase. For the United States, the ring of important, yet somehow secondary, issues remains clear, according to Mandelbaum. Economic competitiveness, counterterrorism, regional instability, nuclear proliferation, ecological redress, democratization—yet all these issues only circle the gaping space vacated by the vanished Soviet Threat.

Where can we find the big, unifying, all-pervasive, organizing principle large enough to fit that hole? The explanations vary from assumptions resting on optimistic, global trends (the equalizing reach of CNN, the sweep of democracy to the world's furthest corners, or the triumph of liberal capitalism) to the more somber expectations of Islamic threats dubbed a "hand grenade in mid flight"[5] and new "arcs of crisis" straddling Southwest Asia and the Near East.[6] Implacable, substitute foes for the vanished Soviets can be found—take the Chinese or North Koreans, still conveniently Communist, or the aggregate effects of plotting by various Middle Eastern tyrants, or unrepentant old Communists in the former Soviet Union scheming to reestablish domination over the plucky new nations on Russia's periphery. If war between nation states fails to curdle the blood, other observers offer the prospect of clashes between entire, albeit ill-defined, civilizations.[7]

In the remainder of this chapter, we argue that much of this intellectual energy is misplaced. It is not that the facts are wrong or the analysis slipshod. Instead, the fault is in the fact that much of this thinking reflects the false premise that we must now devise new reasons for Cold War-style global engagement and that this must be our starting point. As the authors of the American Assembly's *U.S. Intervention Policy for the Post-Cold War World* put it, "intervention is a fact of life."[8] Against this, we posit our central thesis that the Cold War posture of all-purpose activism—a posture with which we agreed and in which we were active participants during our diplomatic careers—represents a deviation from the nation's traditions of much more limited intervention. The Cold War has disappeared. But this does not mean that there is a gap to fill. We do not need to seek a one-for-one substitute.

To attempt a full compendium of the New Agenda literature would have exhausted us—and our readers. The list of precepts and admonitions is formidably long; let all bean counters in the foreign policy establishment know that we have opted here for a selective approach only, picking and choosing among post-1989 writing for illustrative purposes.[9]

To make an arbitrary beginning, we might examine the

agenda of Morton H. Halperin, formerly of the Council on Foreign Relations and now with the National Security Council. In an influential 1993 *Foreign Policy* article, he urged the United States to "take the lead in promoting the trend toward democracy." He also thinks that "when a people attempts to hold free elections and establish a constitutional democracy, the United States and the international community should not only assist but should guarantee the result." He continues, "We are now at a historical crossroads. The opportunity to take a giant step toward universal constitutional democracy is here and should be seized."[10]

Halperin's voice only adds to a cacophonous chorus; talk shows, radio interviews, editorials, op-ed pieces, new book titles, and policy seminars all ask, in effect, "what's next now that the Reds are gone?" The strategic thinker Edward Luttwak thinks he has an answer, sketching an awful specter of American decline, a descent into third-world status aided by the ease with which global capital markets enable manufacturers to shift production out of the United States.[11]

Other savants hazard their hand in the quest for, you name it, a new Organizing Principle, Global Paradigm, Transcendent Vision, Lodestar, Weltanschauung, or Leitmotif for our New World Order, New World Disorder, Unipolar, post-industrial, post-hegemonic, globalized economic world. In short, the Hole in the Doughnut. Few of the aspiring grand theorists are as honest as James Schlesinger, who says, at the end of a January 1993 *Foreign Affairs* article, that precious few answers lie between the choice of "persevering with a fixed design" or "awaiting consequences with patience."[12]

As Schlesinger notes, various fault lines run through the body of the What's-Next literature. The world is varyingly described as either less, more, or just about as dangerous as it was before. The analysts say that it has fewer, more, or about the same number of problems. It seems to be less, more, or about as susceptible to American influence as before. Another divide distinguishes devotees of the History-Is-Back school from those who believe that the pretty much unqualified triumph of liberal capitalism has kicked off an entirely new, global, and (in the absence of contending dogmas) history-less era.[13]

The What's-Next literature also encompasses a fair sprinkling of tinkerers—analysts who dream up new tasks for U.S. engagement abroad. We find stirring calls for American leadership in many of the arenas we have mentioned, whether in global environmental control, population growth abatement, democratic expansion, global climate change, and the decline in biological diversity.[14] Halperin's writing was the precursor to National Security Adviser Anthony Lake's 1993 speeches urging "democratic enlargement"[15] as the nation's principal foreign task and his 1994 speeches outlining a global contest between the United States and all "extreme nationalists and tribalists, terrorists, organized criminals, coup plotters, rogue states, and all those who would return newly free societies to the intolerant ways of the past."[16]

Schlesinger's list sets out the reach. At one and the same time, the United States is being urged, he says, to "advance democracy and all its procedures, human rights, civil liberties, equality before the law, protection of minorities, self-determination, an orderly world, international law, economic growth, free markets, privatization, free trade, limits on environmental degradation, curtailment of the arms trade, prevention of the spread of advanced weapons, etc., etc."[17]

As an example of a new and over-ambitious agenda, examine a proposal by Steven Ratner and Gerald Helman, who are interested in rebuilding, from the basement up, non-Western countries no longer capable of managing their affairs, i.e., "failed states." In an article in *Foreign Policy* in 1992 and again in the Council on Foreign Relations publication, *Enforcing Restraint*, Ratner argued that the United States should work to revive the United Nations Trusteeship Council, long moribund after overseeing the decolonization process three decades ago.[18] Others have joined him in this proposal—even to the extent of suggesting that the United States should set up a "world steering committee" to bring order to the regions of chaos.[19]

But what does he want this bit of UN machinery to do? To become a repair facility for the mounting roster of failed states, whenever agreed boundaries, flags, and the other paraphernalia of sovereignty do nothing to slow their disintegration. Is this a laudable aim? Yes. Is it a practicable one? The answer is less clear now after the initial Clinton administration doctrine of "assertive multilateralism" has collided with complicated realities abroad and casualty aversion at home.[20]

Ratner's piece and others like it came ahead of the odd fiasco in Somalia. At the zenith of American high purpose, also in mid-1993, an attempt was made to refashion in its entirety a Somali administration, police force, courts, and civil administration. The ignominious departure of American troops—and by all U.S. personnel on September 15, 1994—left a small and resentful UN force behind to carry on as best as it could. This denouement put an end to breathless, multilateral illusions; it also ruined for some time to come new efforts to enlist American forces in UN plans for civil administration and reconstruction.

Behind these notions of ambitious outreach is a belief that the deterioration of the international system marks another byproduct of the Cold War's end. In this deterioration, we are "confronted by countries without leadership, without order, without governance itself," in the words of Agency for International Development Director J. Brian Atwood.[21] But the internal rot in these fragile sovereignties began much earlier, often from the moment of independence thirty or forty years ago or—in Haiti's case—in the first years of the nineteenth century. It is only the abrupt ending of forty-five years of confrontation that has thrown these secondary but obvious enough features of world politics into very sharp relief. We now see the deterioration better, but it has been there all along.

To discover these problems now—as the New Agenda school has done—and to put them forward as though they were new undermines the authenticity of their claim that these new causes represent vital interests of the United States. If we have been able not to become involved in many Third World basket cases for fifty years, why should we do so now?

These failed states mark, as it were, the downside of globalization—itself another apparent facet of world politics since 1989 attracting considerable attention from many eminent scholars. By globalization, we mean changes in communications, the emergence of various layers of common world culture, and a widely accepted belief in market economies and in the legitimacy of political power achieved by periodic, fairly counted elections.[22]

This vision of the future, its believers say, is benign. It rests on commerce, not war. It determines success by economic performance. It relies on norms emerging from thousands of international conventions and treaties, the cumulative effect of which is to tie even the most unruly of nations into a gentle web of mutual obligation and reward. Political scientists interested in the rule-making effect of literally thousands of treaties and conventions call this process international regime formation. By this they meant that the bestial habits of nation-states can be tamed, and *are* being tamed, by a web of special-purpose, multilateral networks, bureaucracies, and adjudicative procedures.

It is a quintessentially American vision. Thomas Jefferson's insistence upon popular sovereignty has coalesced with David Ricardo (Comparative Advantage), Adam Smith (the Market's Hidden Hand), and Hugo Grotius (the universal acceptance of sovereignty sustained by law). Bit by bit, sovereignty itself becomes willingly subsumed into larger entities where social power is pooled to increase the size of the market place—as in the European Union or in the North American Free Trade Agreement. Meanwhile, the universal marketplace—the ultimate vision of GATT (General Agreement on Tariffs and Trade) and (since 1994) of its successor agency, the World Trade Organization—retains its impetus from the conclusion, half-hearted though it was, of the Uruguay Round in 1994.

As far as economic globalization is concerned, the message is more mixed. We can accept without question the profound shifts in trading patterns away from the Atlantic and toward the Asia-Pacific. We acknowledge the extraordinary growth in international remittances, telephone calls, faxed messages, and satellite transmission reception. More people travel than ever before, more invest in foreign countries than ever before, and more are employed in trade-based enterprises than ever before.

The question is, what does this imply for traditional definitions of security? Does it lessen or remove the threat of force? Amid the bustling metropolises of East Asia, a region riven by wars and distress just decades ago, or the Central Asian steppes can the evil genie reappear?

Yes, it can. Without a genuine surrender of sovereign choice to supranational authority—and we are still light years from taking that step—the prospect of armed hostilities remains. This prospect engenders its own process, in which the sovereign prerogative of force requires an exclusive chain of command and the accoutrements of force—armies, navies, and the like. And the security horizon in areas most transformed by economic globalization does not look unblemished: much-ignored issues of political legitimacy and transition may again rear their heads in the newly rich countries of East and Southeast Asia.

Commercial globalization does not, therefore, of itself provide the golden key unlocking the post–Cold War dilemma.

To sum up: The What's-Next literature since the end of the Cold War reveals an abundance of prescriptions, diminutive and grand, for the foreign policy of the United States. If even a tenth of them were to become adopted policy, America would soon become an overworked global handyman, with the domestic politics behind our foreign relations rapidly degenerating into a scramble for resources to enable the attainment of this or that objective—robbing Peter to pay Paul.

As we argue further, even the most compendious attempts to rationalize the post–Cold War world fall victim to several extremely important conceits that, unconsciously, have grown in their seductive power ever since 1945. What we call the impulse toward proactivity—the notion that America, whatever the ill (and whatever the bill), must take charge and set things right—still rules supreme in Washington. Thus:

> The United States must formulate a post–Cold War agenda that will keep it fully engaged abroad even as it attends to its problems at home.[23]

Deputy Secretary of State Strobe Talbott wrote this in September 1991 when he was still a columnist for *Time* magazine. Examine the words closely: "Fully engaged abroad." But why *fully engaged*? What about being *fully attentive* instead, to potential but direct dangers to the nation's security and vital interests? The Carnegie Endowment's Dimitri Simes has identified in U.S. foreign policy what he calls a "well-meaning but arrogant temptation to fix other people's problems."[24] He sees this tendency in the calls for democratic enlargement, and in the policing rationale following the feel-good motives involved in the 1992 Christmastime impulse to feed starving people in Somalia. From these, it is but a short step to full-blown but fanciful doctrines of humanitarian intervention or nation-building. Sometimes, as in the expensive UN operation in Cambodia from 1991–93 or in the 1994 intervention in Haiti, an effort can achieve some success but mostly, as in Angola, it is simply too hard.

We stress again: It is *not* that these objectives are harmful or insidiously bad. They are not. Rather, the desired change comes best when those experiencing it initiate it themselves. As we argue in chapter 3 and elsewhere, the resources, the will, the commitment to do this work can no longer be taken for granted in the United States.

This is why the enthusiasts for new efforts, new challenges, new orders, or new crusades find few takers outside the Beltway. William Pfaff's 1993 book, *The Wrath of*

Nations: Civilization and the Fury of Nationalism is an example of a book that charts new directions for American involvement:

> The immediate future of Africa, including that of a majority ruled South Africa, is bleak, and it would be better if the international community would reimpose a form of paternalist neocolonialism in most of Africa, unpalatable as it may seem. The mechanism of the international mandate . . . might be revived. However, the mandated power today would have to be the UN itself, rather than one or several outside powers, as in the past.[25]

Reviewing Pfaff's book in *Foreign Affairs*, the Irish statesman, Conor Cruise O'Brien, describes its tone as not dissimilar to the 1960s-era Cold War crusade—keen to "bear any burden, meet any hardship," as in President John Kennedy's inaugural address—an approach that yielded the long United States phase of the even longer Vietnam War.[26] Kennedy's rhetoric remains alive today in, for example, the words of former Joint Chiefs of Staff Chairman Colin Powell: "The vital interests of mankind are the vital interests of America, no matter how far from our shores."[27]

As for using the UN to tidy up Africa, O'Brien tartly notes that "an experiment on similar lines to what [Pfaff] advocates for Africa generally is currently being conducted in the Horn of Africa, with results not conducive to emulation on a continental scale." O'Brien describes the strength of nationalism as a credo for which people are prepared to kill and die in large numbers. "On the other hand," notes O'Brien (referring to recurrent calls to intervene in the Balkans), "very few people are prepared to die for an altruistic project where no national interests are clearly involved."[28]

We close this chapter with a recitation of one of this country's most respected—not to say, hoary—homilies about statecraft. Even now, two centuries later, it retains an almost mystical significance for Americans. In the modern era, George Washington's Farewell to the Nation usually kicks off an essay excoriating head-in-the-sand isolationism, but Washington's *prudence* is what we admire and wish to stress.

On September 17, 1796, Washington urged his listeners (and the posterity of which he was acutely aware) to make the most of their "detached and distant situation." "Enjoy," he told us, "the benign influence of good laws under a free government" well away from Europe's "set of primary interests which to us have no, or a very remote, relation."[29]

He added that the world beyond inevitably would be "engaged in frequent controversies, the causes of which are essentially foreign to our concerns." And while he was speaking of the only area of the planet (Europe) then possessing enough projectable power to harm America, if we substitute the words "the world" for "Europe" in the text, the flavor remains the same.

"Why, by interweaving our destiny with that of any part of Europe, should we entangle our peace and prosperity in the toils of European ambition, rivalship, interest, humor or caprice?" he asked. Why indeed? Unless checked, the Cold War tendency to behave proactively in the wider world has no limit. It results from an aberrant era of global containment, an era in which chessboard moves, feints, preemptive aggression, and the rest of the Great Game seduced us into believing that this was the natural, ordinary state of affairs—that this, in short, *was* foreign policy.

Yet an older tradition still exists, a tradition that sees merit in despatching a few warships to impress—directly—upon Arab privateers that kidnapping Americans for ransom would not be tolerated and to impress the indirect point upon the European powers that the United States was, already, capable of protecting U.S. interests offshore. That was the objective of the expedition to the shores of Tripoli, not the containment of backlash or rogue states nor the enlargement of democracy.[30]

As American power increased, affronts to it have been identified more readily and tolerated less easily. This is so true that the maintenance of our existing position—the Cold War *status quo*, that owed its existence to circumstances now dead—becomes the real, if not the acknowledged, end of U.S. diplomacy.[31]

But this is far from where the earlier stewards of American foreign policy wanted us to go. Unthinkingly to retain our posture of global proactivity invites us today to reach beyond our means, for purposes few understand and for which still fewer will risk their lives or those of their sons and daughters.

When the temperament of American assertiveness abroad was first forged over a century ago, when America augmented its ideology of Westward expansion to reach across the Pacific and into the Caribbean, even then the nation's leaders seldom fell prey to propagandistic, global or overarching distractions. We wanted, we *deserved*, to become a global player. And we refused, rightly, to be left out of Asia or outmaneuvered in the Western Hemisphere. But we did not equate disorder and failure anywhere and everywhere on the planet with challenges to American interests.

Unfortunately, so many post–Cold War analysts now want to lead us in the opposite direction. If we follow them, we risk imaginary dangers and pointless crises that consume our republic's resources for no good purpose, either for the citizens of this country or for the general good of the rest of the world.

Shortly after he ceased to be American ambassador to the United Nations in 1976, Daniel Patrick Moynihan critiqued American foreign policy under President Lyndon Johnson with the words that "American Liberalism had in those days lost a sense of limits. We would transform the Mekong delta, resurrect Detroit, enlighten South Asia, and defend it too for that matter. It was all too much and invited ruin, which readily enough comes even uninvited."[32]

Wise words then, as now.

Chapter 2

What Kind of World?

Present Fears
Are less than horrible imaginings.
— Shakespeare,
Macbeth

As we have just seen, the end of the Cold War has opened up a bazaar of visions of the new world. Policymakers and commentators have hawked their ideas, competing like rug merchants to praise the unique artistry of their stitchery. The intellectual efforts of many commentators to fashion new agendas for the post–Cold War world have depicted this world as facing the same level of physical threat as during the existence of the Soviet Union. Not only do we detect the workings here of an unreconstructed Cold War set of habits, but also we are uneasy that some of the post–1989 analysis may be at least partially self-serving.

Threat assessment lies at the center of foreign policy decision making. We need to spend a little time establishing common ground. At present, no one can agree on what sort of world we live in. Is it dangerous? safe? complex? straightforward? To add further confusion, the answers depend on the laws of relativity: experts see a series of looming disasters; lay people seem generally more relaxed.

Are they right to be? The answers to the questions about the nature of the new world are not so straightforward. Is China a military threat or a commercial opportunity? Is Russia tamed or revanchist? Ambiguities abound, but the verdict from many foreign policy prognosticators is already to hand.

Leslie Gelb, the president of the Council on Foreign Relations, thinks he sees a "world drifting toward perpetual violence."[1] James Woolsey, CIA director from 1992–94, describes a kind of Jurassic Park-like "jungle filled with a bewildering variety of poisonous snakes."[2] Spy chiefs tend to be gloomy fellows. Another former CIA director, Robert Gates, used to say that his job was to "look into the sewer."[3]

To be sure, our daily newspapers feed us a steady diet of global horror and, beyond the headlines, CIA directors preside over an unrivalled wealth of information. But can we treat them as entirely disinterested observers of the world's flora and fauna? What of their policy conclusions? Might not their professional interest in protecting an intelligence budget at its Cold War level of approximately $30 billion per year make it more likely that they will see vipers where others only see grass snakes? Do Gelb, Woolsey—and, indeed all of us in the foreign policy community—need a relentlessly pathological world to safeguard what Gelb calls the "excitement and primacy of foreign policy?"[4] Does not a conflict of interest arise when or if we overstate the dangers and understate the good signs?

Unfortunately, we may need to ask some of these questions of the foreign affairs establishment. What is verifiable fact? And what is the self-interested or institutional agenda? If, as happened on either side of the 1994 midterm elections, the two top Pentagon officials take wholly contradictory positions on American military readiness, can we be sure that political calculations are not contaminating national security assessments?[5] For these reasons, that jungle, those snakes, and that perpetual violence all merit a closer look. Do they really exist or have they been conjured onto the stage like stock figures in a medieval morality play?

The purpose of these questions is not to impugn the integrity of public officials or well-respected analysts but to arrive at a candid assessment of the world in which we live. We make the general argument that, in a democratic society, effective foreign policy depends in large part on trust between leaders and governed. Specifically, we believe that, during the Cold War, this trust forged a strong bond between policymakers and the mass of Americans about the nature of the threat to the nation. That trust is now in doubt, and people today find it very difficult to support policies that are not discernibly grounded in current realities.

Since 1989, the establishment orthodoxy has been that the end of the Cold War did not lessen the dangers to the United States; it may even have increased them. Secretary of State Warren Christopher describes his job as "navigating between submerged rocks and whirlpools on every continent."[6] On Capitol Hill, we find Senator Daniel Patrick Moynihan reviving the theme of his 1975 book *A Dangerous Place*. He has written of an "age of chaos."[7] Meanwhile, Senator Robert Dole, while the Senate minority leader, invoked the memory of Pearl Harbor to chastise the administration for its (as yet modest) defense reductions.[8]

In the midst of these dire prognoses, the blunt statement of William Hyland, the former editor of *Foreign Affairs*, that "the foreign policy agenda of the United States is easy," and consists mainly in *staying out* of no-win conflicts like Bosnia, stands out as a rare exception to this way of thinking.[9] Nonetheless, this insight may be better in tune with popular instincts.

A short anecdote may illustrate the point. A class given to a graduate seminar at the Georgetown University's

School of Foreign Service afforded one of the authors an opportunity to test out reactions from young Americans to a truly apocalyptic version of the trend of global events set out by the *Economist*.[10] In this vision from hell, everything that might go wrong in the world had done so: an authoritarian leader once again held Russia in his thrall; China was throwing its weight around in Asia; radical Islam was rampaging in the Middle East and beyond; and the military had again seized power throughout Latin America. It was a dream scenario for war correspondents, arms merchants, and national security bureaucracies.

The class did not bat an eyelid. Their reaction was "Yes, the world is headed for hell in a handcart, but how does this affect us? Perhaps the best policy for us is to hunker down, see how things go. Let's stay out of other people's quarrels."

In speaking engagements around the country—even in the suburbs of Washington, D.C.—we have heard sentiments so invariably similar that they cannot be dismissed as wholly unrepresentative. Their message is simple. People are perfectly willing to listen to experts' opinions but, in the foreign policy sphere, they are increasingly inclined to weigh them against their gut instincts. They do not function as passive recipients of wisdom from on high.

The laws of relativity apply: Threats are not absolute quantities but depend on assessments measured against a spectrum of calls on a citizen's time and attention. To one observer, Bosnia means genocide; to another, quagmire. Whereas in 1991 George Bush warned Ukraine against playing with the fire of "suicidal nationalism" by seeking to secede from the then-Soviet Union, in 1994 Warren Christopher sees a plucky young nation struggling for self-determination. He specifically supports the territorial integrity of Ukraine against Russian claims on Crimea.[11]

Professionals bridle at amateur participation in what they like to regard as an intimidatingly difficult task. Policymakers prefer an image of themselves with rolled-up sleeves, barely coping with a world where, in the words of British journalist Henry Brandon, "problems are unprecedented, and of a magnitude never encountered before."[12] Foreign policy, they assert, is by its nature an immensely complex undertaking. Traps and dangers abound for the unwary and the unsophisticated.

We do not dispute this. On a daily basis, the experts have to deal with the myriad daily explosions that make the world seem a mad house rather similar to the Cold War era when the President's daily briefing from the CIA could be—and often was—filled with news of fresh Soviet probes against the United States and its friends.

But, we argue, this view offers only one perspective. As the Georgetown class demonstrated, another view is also in circulation. Can these be reconciled? Let us take a moment to look back at the world from which we have so recently emerged. Let us remind ourselves why it was that a consensus that spanned the divisions of American society was able to endure throughout almost the entirety of the Cold War period.

The ultimate threat of that time—total national annihilation through mutually assured destruction—concentrated minds wonderfully. It united the nation; everyone from city dwellers in the East to defense workers on the West Coast knew they would share the same fate. Now that this threat has fallen to "an all time low," in the words of Senators Sam Nunn and Richard Lugar, it requires a major effort to recall that a few short years ago nuclear submarines roamed the ocean depths on high alert status, strategic bombers waited on around-the-clock alert, hardened silos remained on active maintenance.[13] All this had the sole purpose of preventing the destruction of the United States in a thermonuclear holocaust.

Below the level of nuclear Armageddon, the Soviet Union mounted a second, global challenge to American interests and values. This challenge took the form of regional oppression in its East European backyard, armed aggression in Afghanistan, and clandestine subversion through the First Chief Directorate of the Soviet secret police, the KGB. Commentators might disagree about the ebbs and flows in the historical pattern of Soviet aggression but, when all was said and done, no one could gainsay the fact that the Soviet system represented a repudiation of nearly everything that America valued. As Nikita Khrushchev said in 1961, the victory of communism would be obtained by a series of "national liberation wars" in Africa, Asia, and Latin America that would act as "centers of revolutionary struggle against imperialism."[14]

In other words, there was no letup. The challenge came as easily in Angola or Afghanistan as across the north German plain. Americans recognized this challenge for what it was—an across-the-board threat to the security, even to the continued existence, of their society.

As noted in chapter 1, much of the establishment orthodoxy today holds that the new threats in aggregate equal this former Soviet double threat. The implicit corollary is that a similar strategic approach, based around resources as equivalent as possible to those garnered by the Cold War, remains appropriate. In fact, Federal Bureau of Investigation Director Louis Freeh has explicitly argued that the "vast resources" devoted to fighting the Cold War be diverted to the fight against organized crime and energetically protested the slightest suggestion of a reduction.[15]

All this begins to look a shade too convenient. In bureaucratic terms, this analysis produces the gratifying result that most of the familiar Cold War structures and attitudes, perhaps with a nip here and a tuck there, remain serviceable. Foreign policy can continue to do business as before. At the margin some adjusting and downsizing may take place, but real change remains taboo.

Bureaucratic self-interest existing within a policy of instinctive proactivity does not by itself disqualify that policy. But it does strengthen the need for public vigilance. In this context, the central question voters should be asking is how can it be that these new problems, which even administration officials agree do not even remotely threaten the immediate physical annihilation of the United States, add up to something as dangerous as the Soviet threat, which did so threaten? If this is so, what does National Security Adviser Anthony Lake mean when he said in a major policy speech 1993 that, in approaching today's international security problems, "we can pick and choose?"[16]

Lake was certainly not trying to diminish the reality of any of the new threats. But his words do reveal an important insight into the nature of the new world: Unlike the threat from the Soviet Union (which, in Eisenhower's words, represented a "battle to extinction between the two systems") today's threats do not present a *systemic* challenge to American interests.[17] They are discretionary.

In 1947, Dean Acheson saw the world's problems as a whole, like "apples in a barrel infected by one rotten one."[18] Today, only sensationalist novels claim to detect a cross-infection between the remnants of the Medellin cartel, Iranian mullahs, and the defiance of aging and isolated dictators. Their posturing seems comical next to the ballistic missiles, massed armor, and industrial base of the Warsaw Pact.

This is where establishment self-interest and public intuition parts company. Those of us who care about foreign affairs, and worry about world trends, complain that Americans prefer reading about the latest sexual abuse trial than worrying about Ukraine's missiles. But, we have only ourselves to blame. To argue that today's discretionary problems carry the same weight of threat as yesterday's life-threatening dangers strains anyone's credulity. Constantly to sound the alarm when there is no fire causes attention to stray. Not every two-bit dictator can be the latest incarnation of a new Hitler, even if he also has a moustache.

Public reaction to the perfervid prose of syndicated columnists, who claim that the Bosnia tragedy contains the seeds of a general European war, illustrates the point. When members of Congress return to their districts at the weekend, they discover that their constituents remain unmoved. Seasoned perhaps by Vietnam, the American people demonstrate that they have intuitively moved beyond the Cold War mindset. They refuse to see a generalized threat in each and every local incident.

In essence, popular judgement follows that of our
Georgetown students. Christopher's assertion that America's foreign policy agenda is "overflowing with crises and
potential disasters" seems out of synch with popular instincts.[19] In the twentieth century, the threat that has moti-
vated massive American intervention—be it twice in
Europe, in Korea, or in Kuwait—has been that of the
potential rise of an expansionist hegemonic power, what
Jefferson called the "force wielded by a single hand."[20]
Americans are saying that they do not see such an ap-
parition today.

This change in popular perceptions makes a huge difference from the Cold War, perhaps the most consequen-
tial one of all. It brings with it important policy
implications. Whereas before, policymakers could count on
robust domestic support for American intervention in most
regional crises, especially where the United States provided the only credible counterweight to Soviet ambitions
(with Vietnam being the obvious exception), today American forces are not heading off a global menace whenever
they intervene abroad. As Christopher has observed in a
more optimistic vein "no great power views another as an
immediate military threat."[21]

This judgment utterly undercuts the prevalent insistence on the need for undiminished international engagement. If the foreign policy establishment persists in
advocating this position, it will dissipate its energies and
the nation's resources on frivolous adventures. As we argue repeatedly in this book, effective stewardship of the
nation's interests only occurs when citizens trust the foreign policy leadership. The leadership risks diminishing
trust if it too often invokes a crisis atmosphere that, when
measured against the broad popular historical memory,
appears exaggerated.

Some foreign policy analysts seek a way out by
misrepresenting the nature of the Cold War. They assert
that, in contradistinction to the unprecedented free-for-all
of the contemporary world, the Cold War was a period of
"unique disciplines," as former Defense Secretary James

Schlesinger describes it.[22] British journalist Martin Walker extols the geostrategic stability of the Cold War, writing that "the Cold War became, in the end, a resilient and predictable system for the preservation of human civilization."[23] In wistful nostalgia for this alleged predictability, President Clinton has even commented—albeit ironically— "Gosh, I miss the Cold War."[24] During that period, the argument goes, both sides recognized the constraints on their own actions implicit in the other's ability to retaliate massively.

Thus, the superpowers mostly contented themselves with playing through surrogates a painless version of the Great Game. Both used a mutually agreed upon set of Marquis of Queensberry rules that imposed limits on conflict. The theorists of mutually assured destruction now argue that the removal of the fear of nuclear holocaust has substantially increased the risk and incidence of conventional war. And they claim that small wars, as in the Balkans or the Caucasus, can more easily ignite continental warfare. Once again, the conclusion is that today's world is equally as dangerous as the Cold War. Does the record bear out this idea?

Carried to extremes, this assertion suggests that much of the past fifty years passed during an almost cordial Soviet-American condominium. Luckily, witnesses from that time such as Willy Brandt, the former German chancellor and Nobel peace laureate, remind us that it did not. Shortly before his death he wrote evocatively of the many "frosty seasons" he endured as mayor of Berlin, when Soviet pressure squeezed out light and warmth.[25]

Some condominium! Do we need reminding already that the Soviet Union really did try to blockade Berlin and draw Greece behind the iron curtain? That children really did hide under their desks during the Cuban missile crisis? That Soviet tanks really did roll into Prague, Budapest, and Kabul? Remember: On Soviet orders, refugees really were shot and allowed to bleed to death under the Berlin Wall. Dictatorships in Cuba, Ethiopia, Angola, and Mozambique really did rise on the back of Soviet

equipped and trained security services, while state spon-
sors of anti-American terrorism really were feted in Moscow. Have we forgotten that the Soviet Union really did
bankroll the communist parties of Western Europe and
Latin America? None of this had anything to do with a
joint enterprise with the Soviets to nurture civilization and
the future of humankind. We really did live on the nuclear
high wire, and we really had to marshall our energies to
deflect intrusions and deny advantage to this mercifully
departed adversary.

During the period of this falsely lamented unique discipline in global affairs, many conventional wars erupted.
The history books bulge with the record of these conflagrations—Vietnam, Biafra, Chad, the Iran-Iraq war, successive Arab-Israeli wars, the India-Pakistan war, Nicaragua,
El Salvador, the Indonesian confrontation with Malaysia,
the annexation of Tibet, the ethnic massacres in Sri Lanka,
the Turkish invasion of Cyprus, the Indonesian takeover
of East Timor. A rough tally of the numbers killed during
1945-1992 runs to twenty million, with a further twenty
million refugees.[26]

The hard reality is that the Cold War was a "bitter,
dangerous, and costly" period of sustained global *instability.*[27] Whatever one may think about the brutishness of the
world after 1989, the United States surely can breathe a lot
easier today. This is not to downplay today's threats. Quite
to the contrary, we need to meet them with an appropriate
response. But we will not be able to do that if we persist
in imagining, even unconsciously, that each problem presents the same level of threat as an intercontinental nuclear
exchange.

To be sure, at the subglobal, or local, level the world
gives the appearance of being a more unstable place. This
is why the Heritage Foundation's description of the world
as a "bewildering international landscape of wars and crises" seems to make sense.[28] Across the map, more red
lights are blinking in such hitherto unfamiliar places as
Abkhazia, Armenia, Bosnia, Georgia, South Ossetia,
Tajikistan, and the Trans-Dniester Republic. Elsewhere,

Rwanda, Somalia, and Yemen disintegrate. North Korea plays nuclear poker—and, as demonstrated by the 1994 agreement with the United States that brought it diplomatic recognition, money, and two new nuclear reactors— plays it very well, too.[29] Introducing the Pentagon's Bottom Up Force Review in September 1993, former Defense Secretary Les Aspin (now chairman of the president's Foreign Intelligence Advisory Board) highlighted these regional hot spots as a reason why the United States needs to keep its guard up.[30]

The presence of TV and film crews at the scene of these conflicts paints them in the lurid colors of "Apocalypse Now." Partisans of each and every conflict are periodically afforded the courtesy of 750 words on the *New York Times* op-ed page to argue why their struggle should be seen *sub specie aeternitatis*, and why their struggle should become the defining paradigm of American identity in the post– Cold War world.

Yet, most Americans show a consistent ability to avoid these overheated interpretations. Their judgment is that these conflicts remain significantly different from the Cold War's small wars. Rightly or wrongly, they saw the latter as a manifestation of the Soviet Union's ambitions of global takeover—in Richard Nixon's words, as part of a "third world war" and therefore worthy of their attention if not, as Vietnam and Nicaragua show, always of their enthusiasm.[31]

But no agreement exists that today's conflicts—not in Yugoslavia nor even in a nuclearized Hindu-Muslim confrontation in South Asia—threaten a global crisis of the sort that would necessarily embroil the United States. Strategic rocket forces will not move to a higher state of readiness as a result of any of these current disputes. Opinion polls show that most Americans feel that Europe should take primary responsibility for Bosnia. And they (properly) don't care about ethnic conflict and national dissolution in most places if the cost of putting matters right translates into body bags filled with *our* dead.

Resentful at suggestions that the American foreign

policy agenda is quite straightforward, many commentators from within the foreign policy establishment counter
that the world is really a more complex place. Let us at
once make an easy concession: Foreign affairs *analysis* has
certainly become more complex since 1989. We no longer
have the luxury of a single prism through which the
world's problems can be dissected. Rather than forcing
facts into an anti-Communist matrix, problems have become multifaceted and individual.

Bosnia is a perfect example. Had the Serbs been seen
as Kremlin surrogates, they would have been bombed back
to Belgrade without further ado.[32] Just like the CIA's
Khyber Pass donkey delivery system to the Afghan resistance, fast patrol boats from the Sixth Fleet would have
delivered Stinger missiles to Muslim and Croat *mujahidin*.
But now, absent the anti-Communist theme, the Yugoslav
problem resembles Churchill's intimidating description of
Russia as "a riddle wrapped in a mystery inside an
enigma."

In this respect, expert knowledge is all the more
needed today. The country really does need foreign policy
specialists who understand the Japanese, Chinese, Russians, Europeans, and Arabs. (In chapter 11 we make an
explicit appeal for area expertise and knowledge to receive
a more prominent place in foreign policy decision making.)
The difficulty comes, however, when the issue of complexity serves as yet another reason for continuing business-
as-usual in Washington or for excluding popular input
from participation in the debate.

The question is, has the demise of the superpower rivalry simplified American diplomacy? We say it has.
Whereas once such problems as the Middle East peace negotiations, Bosnia, or Iraq would have had to be approached through an infinitely complex mine field of
Soviet-American competitiveness, now a broad international collegiality exists. This does not mean that differences of view will not arise—they manifestly have done so
over Bosnia, Iraq, or the expansion of NATO—but the
search for solutions is no longer subordinate to super-

power rivalries. The United States is at ease to involve Russia as a partner over Bosnia whereas once it would have labored mightily to prevent Soviet meddling.

This means that problems can be approached much more *on their merits*. Russian concerns over developments in neighboring states together with Western worries about Russian revanchism can be addressed in a collaborative manner—as the British and Russian foreign ministers demonstrated in a joint declaration in December 1993. The Middle East is another beneficiary. It is difficult to imagine that a meeting between the presidents of Syria and the United States would have taken place had the Communists still been masters of the Kremlin. "For the first time in modern history," Zbigniew Brzezinski noted in 1992, "the Middle East is free from great power competition."[33] This is a boon, not a problem.

True enough, the problems themselves remain complex—the Institute of Geography at the Russian Academy of Sciences, for example, has identified 160 border disputes within the territory of the former Soviet Union.[34] But the passing of the Cold War has stripped away the superpower rivalry aspect that, while there, was all-embracing. The United States has, for example, no geopolitical stake in Chechnya. As affects national security, the world is certainly complex. Complex yes, but not *more* so. To say that the diagnosis is more complex does not of itself mean that the illness is also more complex, or as serious, or as life-threatening.

In 1948, the Soviet blockade of Berlin presented General George C. Marshall, then secretary of state, with his gravest post–World War II challenge. The story is told that, at a staff meeting in Washington the panic level among the younger participants was rising as they contemplated the imminent outbreak of World War III. Asked how he could stay calm in the face of such a crisis, Marshall replied briefly, "I've seen worse." Up and down the country, Americans are voicing much the same sentiment. They too have seen worse. And when they are told nothing much has changed, they begin to ask questions.

Chapter 3

The Gap between
Resources and Aspirations

We were kids, captains and majors, telling the
whole world what to do.
— Carl Kaysen,
Deputy National Security Adviser
to President John F. Kennedy

American taxpayers will have noted anxiously that few
proponents of the myriad new tasks for American foreign
policy have come up with any *costings* for their ideas. This
omission itself reflects Cold War thinking that assumed
that money would always be found to combat the Red
Menace. But implementing even a fraction of the programs
in today's bloated agenda would far outstrip popular or
congressional willingness to pay for them.

In his 1989 inaugural address, George Bush noted that
the country has more "will than wallet."[1] He was, as it
were, right on the money. But, since then, the rhetoric of
ambitious proactivity abroad has further outstripped the
means of support.

We already have been through this in our national debate. The publication in 1987 of the historian Paul Kennedy's *Rise and Fall of the Great Powers*[2] touched a raw nerve. As Kennedy himself admitted, his book was in many ways a conventional description of the historically verifiable fact that great powers have both risen and declined. But it appeared at an awkward time: The Reagan administration was drawing to a tired and messy end amid the Iran-contra hearings while, on the other side of the Atlantic, the apparently dynamic leadership of Mikhail Gorbachev presented an energetic image and the European Community was on the point of taking a great leap toward union through the Single European Act. Meanwhile, Japan was seen as about to destroy the American semiconductor industry. In this climate, Kennedy's book seemed like a gratuitous injury to a great athlete (us), a memento mori that our best playing days might be behind us. Other gloomy books soon followed—*Trading Places: How We Allowed Japan to Take the Lead* by economist Clyde Prestowitz comes to mind.[3]

Then a reaction set in. Before long a counterindustry was born to proclaim anew America's power and prestige. *Bound to Lead*, written by Harvard professor Joseph Nye (whose recent public career has included stints as the head of the National Intelligence Council and as a senior Pentagon official) led this genre.[4] Proponents of this school amassed statistics to prove that the United States remained easily the world's most powerful nation. In 1993 in France, Alfredo Valladão's best-selling book *Le XXIème Siècle sera Américain (The Twenty-First Century Will Be American)* prophesied that the United States will dominate the next century through its control of international corporate and media networks.[5]

Today, of course, the Soviet Union has disappeared into the dustbin of history originally designated for capitalism. A new bout of political sclerosis and financial scandal has stopped Europe in its tracks. Japan remains mired in recession, no matter how much its exporters sell.

The America-as-Champions school accordingly believes itself triumphantly vindicated. In an interview to survey his first one hundred days in office, President Bill Clinton repeated the now conventional view, "The United States" he said, "is the world's only superpower."[6] The Gulf War, the Haiti intervention, aid to Russia—about which then Secretary of State James Baker commented that "only America can do it"—seem just three of many examples to support this assertion.[7] We ourselves have argued earlier that, secure in its borders and with its democratic values in the ascendant around the world, the United States finds itself in an enviable position.

In the early days of the Clinton administration, however, it became clear that the superpower image was an unsatisfactory basis for practical policy formation.

In May 1993, Peter Tarnoff, the third most senior official at the State Department, gave an off-the-record briefing about some of the new administration's ideas on fresh directions for foreign policy.[8] Tarnoff presented what he undoubtedly thought was an uncontroversial account of the administration's wish to give primacy to domestic renewal while safeguarding the main American foreign interests. He mentioned the country's well-known budgetary problems and speculated that the United States would not wish to take the lead in each and every world crisis—a thought that American officials had voiced many times in discussions about burden sharing with allies and friends.

The reaction to Tarnoff's words was instructive. For uttering these conventional views, Tarnoff was immediately engulfed in an avalanche of criticism. The political and foreign policy community sought to occupy the high ground of undiminished American leadership. Articles with such titles as "Like It or Not, We Must Lead" filled the op-ed pages.[9] Meanwhile, Secretary of State Christopher repudiated Tarnoff's views in a ringing speech that proclaimed American leadership from the rooftops.[10] For this action he received plaudits from Democrat and Republican leaders alike. Bustling, feverish activity filled the rest of the year as the new administration tried to demonstrate America's continuing ability to take on all comers.

In taking this stance—perhaps the most decisive of his

tenure—Christopher missed what may have been his best opportunity to put his stamp on a truly new post–Cold War foreign policy. What held him back? Surely not fear that the American people would not have backed change. Having just voted out the Republicans, in large part because George Bush spent too much time on foreign affairs, they were clearly not keen on foreign hyperactivity.

Perhaps Christopher was guarding against possible Republican charges of weakness. After the Reagan era's massive military buildup, the triumph of the Cold War, and the smashing Gulf War success, the Republicans—with some justification—prided themselves as the architects of a strong and, to use the word of Theodore Roosevelt's adviser Henry Cabot Lodge, a "large" foreign policy.[11] They stood ready to exploit any indication that the Democrats might slip into the Carter era's "malaise."[12] The Republican heavy guns, led by Jeane Kirkpatrick as Captain of Artillery, soon started to take ranging shots at policies they criticized as underselling American interests.[13]

By 1994, the debate had, in this fashion, lost its original purpose of analyzing America's relative position in the world; the goal of adapting policy to build on American strengths and to avoid weaknesses had been forsaken. Instead, an emotion-laden mud slinging match emerged in which substance was missing as orators sought to wrap themselves in the flag. The cry of "who is the best patriot?" drowned out rational discussion.

Unfortunately, the reduction of this important debate to a sort of mano-a-mano prize fight between declinists and patriots has trivialized and obscured the central issue. This was, and remains, rather straightforward: How does the United States apportion its resources intelligently to achieve its foreign policy objectives? Where is the trade-off between foreign and domestic spending? These classic, totally nonmysterious questions of political economy should not divide the country into mutually antagonistic groups. Even today, as the aftershocks rumble on, the style of the discussion resembles the taunting of high school cheerleaders ("We're number one!") rather than a sober debate about the means and ends of American foreign policy.[14]

Patriotism in this debate is the reddest of red herrings. The more we raise it in discussion, the more obnoxious it becomes. None of the foreign policy reformers—least of all ourselves or Paul Kennedy, who ended his book quoting the French political scientist Pierre Hassner's comment that the United States remains the "decisive actor in every type of balance and issue"—wants to challenge the assertion of American interests, the propagation of American values, or the defense of human rights.[15] We do not subscribe to the pessimism found in such books as Arthur Schlesinger, Jr.'s *The Disuniting of America* and Seymour Itzkoff's *The Decline of Intelligence in America* to the effect that "dysgenic" trends are undermining America's ability to contribute to the world.[16]

What is overlooked in the seesaw of robust optimism and bleak pessimism is *how these objectives can best and most effectively be attained.* When in 1994, for example, the assistant secretary of state for International Organizations Affairs in 1994 calls a temporary halt to American involvement in Bosnian peacekeeping on the grounds that "we [the United States] have an acute resource problem that people have not been as attentive to as they should be," or when a Chicago research institute report shows that hunger is increasing in the United States, it becomes unambiguously clear that policy makers must now take much more account of resource scarcity than once was the case.[17]

In the same 1947 *Foreign Affairs* article we quoted earlier, Henry Stimson wrote that "we shall be wholly wrong if we attempt to set a maximum or margin to our activities as a member of the world."[18] Attitudes such as these— which the British historian Sir Denis Brogan in 1952 called the "illusion of omnipotence"—were born when the United States enjoyed a 40 percent share of the world's gross domestic product and a nuclear monopoly and when the citizens of Berlin and Tokyo were picking through rubble for firewood.[19] They do not necessarily serve the nation well now that the share of GDP stands at little over 20 percent.

This hardly comprises an insight of breathtaking novelty. In the 1970s, Henry Kissinger saw a need to tailor foreign policy aspirations to resource limitations.[20] To date, however, political fears (the patriotism canard) and politicians' natural inclination to talk a big game have stood in the way of translating these perceptions into operational changes. Every now and again, a crunch comes and the money runs out. But, as often as not, policy makers and commentators formulate proposals as if resources and willpower can be taken for granted. As we and others have pointed out, time and again this leads to aborted or half-completed operations.[21] The result is damaged American credibility. How can foreigners know when the United States is being serious and when it is merely playing to the gallery?

The British failure to bring ends and means into a coherent whole makes for cautionary reading. The British never accepted Dean Acheson's celebrated comment that "they had lost an empire, but failed to find a role." As far as they were concerned, they had never lost their leadership vocation. In 1957, *The Times* of London wrote that with President Eisenhower "a declining force, the German chancellor an old, unhappy man, and the French president fully preoccupied by other problems, the responsibility falling on the British prime minister to lead the [Western] alliance sensibly yet strongly . . . is paramount."[22] Talk like this provoked that very same Chancellor Konrad Adenauer to comment that Britain was "like a rich man who has lost all his property but does not realize it."[23]

Alas, this all proved to be a terrible illusion. Abba Eban, once foreign minister of Israel, commented that the Palestinians never missed an opportunity to miss an opportunity. The British have perfected this technique in their relationship with Europe. To this day, an insular *hubris* causes them to draw back from full association with their European partners. Some innate feeling of superiority—whether born of Empire or from the enforcement of unconditional surrender after World War II—constantly propels the British to overestimate their strength. They are paying a high price for their failure to adapt. As the Irish academic Desmond Dinan has noted, British high-handed tactics have "robbed Britain of a potential leadership role in Brussels."[24]

In a memorable rebuke to Jimmy Carter's habit of harping on about America's problems, Ronald Reagan once said, "there you go again." And Reagan would be half-right about the present debate over declinism. Americans need have no fear of replicating the British fate. The sheer differences in absolute size, power, and wealth between the two countries mean that the United States should be able to avoid the British fate—at least for the foreseeable future. For many years to come, foreign leaders will continue to beat a path to Washington, as did Yitztak Rabin and Yassir Arafat in October 1993 to sign the historic accord between Israel and the Palestine Liberation Organization.

But warning signs exist. No longer do overseas visitors hoping for American largesse present themselves, cap in hand, with their private secretaries hovering to transcribe American instructions. A notable vignette from the White House press room in February 1994 showed a grim-faced President Clinton announcing that he had broken off trade talks with Japan and would not reopen them until Japan accepted a comprehensive framework agreement—or, failing that, in the colorful phrase of then Deputy Treasury Secretary Roger Altman, "until hell froze over."[25] At Clinton's side, then Prime Minister Morihiro Hosokawa looked on in relaxed good humor before leaving the room to read the congratulatory press notices that his tough stand had won him at home. Far from folding his tent, he took his case to GATT where he was rewarded with forthright support. Three months later, the early summer dollar crisis forced the United States back to the table without having extracted any significant Japanese concessions, even though the country backed Clinton's tough stance to a very impressive extent. A further three months later in September 1994, an agreement was reached with Japan that relegated far into the distant future the hard-edged performance guarantees that the United States had once insisted on as indispensable.[26]

American policymakers need to remain alert to these signs if they want to retain American leadership. No longer do foreigners panic at the first sign of American censure. In 1993 and 1994, a motley crew of the world's petty dictators—Cedras of Haiti, Milosevic of Yugoslavia, Aideed of Somalia, Castro of Cuba, and others—came in for bouts of verbal tongue lashing from Washington. In one fifteen-minute speech, Clinton called Cedras a dictator fifteen times.[27] No noticeable improvement in their behavior occurred—in Cedras's case, seventy-hours later he was able to strike a highly satisfactory deal for himself, including persuading the American government to lease his three houses in Haiti after his departure (on a U.S aircraft) to Panama.

Neither did friends and allies escape unscathed. The Japanese prime minister was treated to open criticism of his country's bureaucracy by an American official.[28] The French were called every bad name under the sun for their intransigence in the Uruguay Round's end game. But, once again, behavior modification failed to take place.[29]

Episodes such as these are straws in the shifting wind. They suggest that the almost effortless leverage once enjoyed by American officials can no longer be taken for granted. When the need by foreigners for American protection from the Soviet peril disappeared and when American resources for overseas assistance declined, so also did the number of America's client states decline. This means that America needs to be smarter, not louder.

Unfortunately, too many officials and elected representatives have learned the opposite lesson. In the manner of British Victorians dealing with non-English speaking natives, they have convinced themselves that the best solution is to talk louder. American rhetoric has grown shriller, our gestures more extravagant.

For example, in April 1994, Nigeria was placed on a list of countries condemned for noncooperation on narcotics interdiction. Given the unassailable facts, this was a reasonable enough move, one might think. But a problem arose—finding a suitable punishment to match the crime.

As Congress had mandated when creating the narcotics cooperation list, all aid to Nigeria was suspended. A catastrophe for Nigeria? Hardly. In 1993 annual aid amounted to $32 million, an insignificant part of an economy a thousand times larger. In any case, however, aid had already been suspended a year earlier because of the Nigerian military's interference with elections of that time! We are reminded of how aid to Russia in 1992–93 was inflated by the double counting of governments competing to prove their generosity. Suspending aid that is already suspended represents a new act in the theater of the absurd.

Or consider the official American reaction to disturbances in Bangkok in May 1992. When Thai troops fired on demonstrators protesting against political machinations by a military politician, Washington suspended aid. The cost? Fifty-two million dollars, mostly in military training assistance projects. Thailand's economy, growing at seven times the speed of America's, managed to do without; the net effect furthered Thai military cooperation with China. The issue, therefore, went far deeper than a simplistic morality play pitting pro-democracy forces against ruthless military autocrats, and the Thais understandably dismissed America's gesture as naive and pointless. They could recognize another exercise in feel-good diplomacy, even if we could not.

These and many other examples show a troubling intersection of curves on a graph of American foreign policy. The first line, descending since the 1970s, represents the amount of resources available to influence the direction of foreign countries—aid, free visits to the United States, giveaway grain shipments, and the like. The second line, ever rising, represents the number of conditions that the United States has placed on its diminishing largesse. These include conditions promoting human rights, green sensitivity, trade union organizing freedom, endangered species, a reduction of female genital mutilation, a better balance in public accounts (!), reduced weapons procurement (!), and others. The threat to cut off aid heard so often on

Capitol Hill no longer sends shivers down Third World spines—the United States now ranks bottom in the Organization for Economic Cooperation and Development (OECD) league table showing aid as a percentage of Gross National Product (GNP) and well behind Japan in absolute terms.[30]

Theodore Roosevelt liked to quote the old maxim, "speak softly and carry a big stick."[31] His successors today have reversed this maxim; now the decibel count rises in inverse proportion to American leverage. As Christopher toured Asia in March 1994 and before visiting China, his words on Chinese human rights infringements scaled new heights of pugnacity, particularly from the distant safety of Sydney, Australia.[32] The result? The Chinese rounded up all their well-known dissidents and bundled them out of Beijing during Christopher's visit—which proceeded in the iciest of atmospheres. Two months later, the State Department issued a paper over Christopher's signature certifying that the Chinese had made sufficient progress on human rights to merit extension of most favored nation (MFN) status.[33] Less than six months after that Defense Secretary William Perry described China at a speech at Beijing's National Defense University as "one of the most important countries in the world, both from an economic and military point of view."[34]

The same story repeated itself when an American teenager received a sentence of corporal punishment in Singapore. The government there—which had hitherto enjoyed high esteem in Washington for its agreement to provide the U.S. Pacific Fleet with bunkering facilities to substitute for those being lost in the Philippines—found itself denounced as a throwback to the Spanish Inquisition. To little effect. We huffed and puffed but the sentence proceeded, albeit with a reduction of two lashes. What was the purpose of the highly public presidential intervention in Singapore? To prevent the punishment itself? No—because the very act of going public gave Singapore almost no wriggle room at all. Or, create a new doctrine of extraterritoriality—that is, that American citizens should not be subject to the same (if harsh) local laws? That, too, is pointless—extraterritoriality belongs to a vanished, imperial age. Perhaps the uproar resulted from a need to feel good? That seems to have been the only concrete result— apart from the teenager's sore behind.

The point of these illustrations is not to portray the United States as a Gulliver beset by a thousand unworthy Lilliputians (but able, with a mighty exertion, to spring free from its tormentors). No, we wish only to emphasize that the central issue in this debate is not character, or decline, or patriotism. Dividing lines do not run between those who would weaken the United States and those who would keep her strong. The key question—around which all should be able to rally—is *how to get the job done.* And this, in turn, depends on credibility. Fine words will not deliver credibility. Credibility comes only when resources and resolve are matched to well-thought-out intentions.

In a prediction about his successor's prospects in office, Harry Truman commented of Dwight Eisenhower, "He'll sit here, and he'll say, 'Do this! Do that!' *And nothing will happen.* Poor Ike."[35] In fact, Eisenhower always had much more savvy than suggested in this caricature, but sometimes today's American foreign policy seems caught in the trap of imagining that talk equals action. Stern orders are barked out to recalcitrant foreigners but no one is snapping to attention.

During the 1992 election campaign and in the early days of his administration, President Clinton and his policy advisers seemed ready to adjust attitudes to resources.[36] They should revisit this path—as should those who seek to replace them in office. As we see it, popular sentiments are not the problem. Our own encounters throughout the country, plus polling data, convince us that most Americans, while still devoted to traditional values, understand that it would be "quixotic and almost certainly obnoxious," in Walter Lippmann's words, to impose these overseas.[37]

The difficulty, as we said, lies in Washington where the disjunction between the governed and the governing has never been greater. In the country as a whole, the Cold War is long dead; inside the Beltway, the habits of the Cold War era live on.

Throughout this book, we maintain that American values need to remain a potent global force. We also wish to maximize American welfare. We part company with parts of the establishment only over *method* not *aims*. We believe that instruments of the Cold War pedigree have lost their cutting edge. Rather than trying to resharpen them, we need to fashion new ones—not because the country is in decline, but because we are rediscovering America's former, pre–Cold War ways of interacting with the world. The danger is in America's leaders choosing to ignore this need and opting instead for vainglorious moral crusading. As we discuss in the next chapter, we see such crusading as a surefire way to guarantee the weakness and decline we all wish to avoid.

Chapter 4

Moral Crusading:
No More Sabers to Rattle?

Twice before we earned the right to be an arbiter
of a postwar world. This is our third chance . . .
America once again faces a rare opportunity, an
open but fleeting moment in world history.
We must seize it now.

— The Carnegie Endowment
National Commission on America
and the New World
Changing Our Ways, 1992

In the previous chapters we showed how, in their efforts
to paint a new, post–Cold War canvas, the experts are for
the most part still using the same old brush strokes and
coloring techniques characteristic of that departed Era. The
essence of their message is that—after a ritual endorsement of the need for selectivity—they go on to endorse
restless interventionism, undiscriminating global responsibility, the perception of all-pervasive threats. They assume limitless resource availability—or at least sufficient
for their own favored projects.

In the next section of this book, we describe how these outdated ideas exercise a baleful influence over practical diplomatic activity. They have transformed the admirable American embrace of moral values into a hectoring crusade, while military force has lost its credibility by being threatened so often and in inappropriate contexts. In domestic debate, it has become very difficult to talk rationally about foreign policy because its language and discourse remain locked in a Cold War time warp.

Let us look first at overseas intervention based on morality. The epigraph heading this chapter comes from an ambitious report summarizing, in the view of the eminent panel that wrote it in 1992, the shape of the international landscape after the Cold War.[1] It seeks to identify this country's priorities in a changing world. It notes our stake in such global issues as environmental preservation and heading off a proliferation of weapons of mass destruction. It lists the challenges to America from burgeoning world trade. We quote it here as one of the more convincing articulations of the tasks facing the nation in the foreign policy arena, and there is little in the report with which one can seriously argue or dispute other than to ask an apparently simple question about means—that is, how do we get there with the least cost? But there is also, inevitably, a messianic sign off at the end of ninety pages, where the authors describe America's need to aim "toward a freer world." As one might expect, the promotion of democracy takes a commanding place.

All nations think they are special. The British, French, Russians, and Chinese yield to no one in their innate sense of their own superiority. But only the United States was founded on the explicit premise that, in a profoundly moral sense, it was better than, and certainly distinct from, all nations preceding it. Americans have therefore always believed that they had an obligation to let this virtue shine forth to the world.

In the first century of the Republic's existence, this peculiarly American sense of mission took the form of celebrating the democratic achievement within these

United States. Americans contented themselves with hoping that foreigners would observe the intrinsic excellence of the American way and would spontaneously seek to imitate it.

As we will see in the next chapter, however, beginning from about the Mexican War in the mid-1800s, it was no longer enough for Liberty simply to shine as an instructive example to the world. It became necessary—at least at the level of political oratory—to seize the sword and rout tyrannical opponents or jackbooted dictators.

The uniquely American contribution of a moral foreign policy, to which these sentiments gave birth, must steer a careful course. After all, deliberately to make one's foreign policy hostage to issues of this kind amounts to a very remarkable exception, both in history and by comparison to contemporary realities. None of the United States' international partners ties its policies so closely to moral objectives. As the British commander of the UN forces in Bosnia remarked in 1994, "If someone wants to fight a war here on moral grounds, fine, great, but count us out."[2]

Even in the Cold War, a values-oriented foreign policy did not figure as much, or at all, in motivating American allies to oppose Soviet hegemony. Most of them were simply scared to death by the prospect of Red Army tanks; when, in the 1980s, this threat receded, they showed themselves disconcertingly receptive to Soviet blandishments. Soviet President Leonid Brezhnev's proposals for a Common European Home, for example, attracted considerable interest among European intellectuals in the early 1980s.[3]

This does not mean that the United States should abandon morality as a foreign policy component. We show later that morality can readily be encompassed within the national interest. But a warning should be heeded: other nations are not playing by the same rules as the United States. China, for one, has been able to profit by exploiting American adherence to a one-dimensional focus on morality. While the Clinton administration remained fixated on the treatment of a few score prominent dissidents, a vast range of security, political, immigration, trade, nar-

cotics, and environmental issues went largely by the
board—until the brutal lesson in power politics administered by the Chinese to Secretary of State Warren Christopher in Beijing in March 1994 brought about a belated
change of course.

Today, American messianic zeal is often more subtly
presented. The Carnegie report, and other voices, have
ostensibly grounded a foreign policy of democratic enlargement in terms of solid self-interest. Elements of this
include (a) national security (i.e., democratic societies don't
attack one another), (b) economic self-interest (i.e., democracy leads to stability and, thus, to more confident trade
and investment prospects), (c) environmental goals (an
aroused and participating citizenry forces ecological policy
changes), and (d) human rights (because free societies are
vigilant in protecting them). The Carnegie report con-
cludes: "Americans have two powerful allies in building
democracy—the world media and the world democratic
community."[4]

But is this right? This seems to us another variant of a
peculiarly American habit that universalizes its own values and demands that other countries accept these, even
at the cost of abandoning their own value systems. As two
persons old enough to have watched, on occasion from
close proximity, the Carter administration's emphasis on
human rights and democracy during the Cold War, we
found ourselves admiring its motivations but cringing at
its unintended effects. Conducted in the teeth of bureaucratic obstruction—from the State Department and the Pentagon, but also from so-called functional departments like
Commerce and Agriculture—the policy also met a poor
reaction, to put it mildly, from countries adjudged deficient
in democratic values and civil liberties. So strong was the
negative reaction that the Carter policy often backfired,
leading to unintended and repressive consequences. We
concluded that a change of tactics was needed, if the values we admired in a moral foreign policy—primarily a
sense that something more than an amoral anarchy should
govern the world—were to become practical policy. The

Clinton administration's democratic enlargement policy, like Carter's human rights crusade sixteen years ago, seeks out the moral high ground. But the operational details of a foreign policy hostage to certain self-important pressure groups do not present a pretty sight. Nor are errant foreigners dissuaded from thinking that domestic politicking, rather than deeply held human values, represents the driving force behind these crusades.

The devil—as always—is in the details. The poor showing by the administration's Asia policy during 1994 demonstrates this in ample measure. Over human rights and democratic enlargement issues, the United States managed to antagonize Indonesia, China, India, Pakistan, Singapore, and Malaysia.[5] Partly this resulted from poor footwork, but a deeper problem exists: What appear to Americans to be the self-evident virtues of a freer world do not always coincide with observable realities.

Investment stability? Inconveniently, Singapore's authoritarian system has achieved impressive stability and, thus, a fine investment climate to a degree much better than in the often chaotic democracy of the Philippines. Environmental protection? Nepal's new parliamentary government, which emerged after bloody riots in April 1990, has proven considerably more rapacious of endangered forests than the system in neighboring Bhutan—where an absolute monarch is widely acknowledged as having added to his kingdom's forest cover. Economic well being? Human rights and democratic liberties of the most elementary type find no favor and few takers in Saudi Arabia, the world's richest oil supplier.

During the Cold War, a values-oriented foreign policy prompted the United States not simply to oppose Russian imperial designs but to lead an all-out fight against the Soviet system itself. The United States went *mano-a-mano* against the ideology *per se*, which helped achieve a victory that, with regard to the extent of the comprehensive Soviet collapse, probably has no equal in the history of nonviolent political change.

But this highlights one of our central points. The Cold

War was not a normal period in American history. The values-driven foreign policy worked well at that time because of the need to combat an all-out threat and because of the availability of massive resources. These tactics worked in the special circumstances of the Cold War, but they cannot function without adaptation today.

We learned our diplomatic trade in the European tradition of *Realpolitik* and rather admire the American addition of moral purpose to the usual diplomatic mix. The philosopher Cornel West has noted that "the distinctive appeal of American pragmatism in our post-modern moment is its unashamedly moral emphasis and its unequivocally ameliorative impulse."[6] We want to do what we can to further this tradition. What we question here is whether America's devotion to democratic crusading abroad might be better expressed, and gain more results, if it were applied in a fashion different from the almost daily reaffirmation of ideals before the microphones.

There may be those who applaud the hostility that American human rights campaigns provoke. This hostility, they say, shows that the policy has teeth, that it is working.

We question this—as do others with far more impressive credentials. On a visit to Washington in May 1994, Kim Dae Jung, the tireless campaigner for human rights in South Korea, cautioned against the abrasive style in which the American humanitarian agenda was pursued.[7] As someone who has suffered repeated assassination attempts, kidnapping, imprisonment, and exile for his human rights beliefs, Kim's warning commands respect. We remember similar, private comments in the last year of the Carter administration from the exiled Philippines opposition leader, Benigno Aquino, later murdered in Manila in 1983. The Carter human rights policy had helped to release him from years in a Manila prison, after strong pressure on Philippine President Ferdinand Marcos.

We wonder whether there might be a better way. What do we mean? Simply put, America should have the faith of its conviction. If, as we believe, America's achievements through its history confirm the wisdom of the model, then Americans might be happier to let their liberty, like the statue that carries the name, remain as a standing inspiration to the world.

Moreover, exactly because the global reach of broadcast and print media is now so extensive, the interplay of ideas is so ubiquitous (and the bruising effect of the media and the ideas on established dogma so profound) that few areas on the planet can escape its influence. Iran, China, and Singapore may seek to ban satellite dishes from the rooftops of their more affluent citizens, but the omnipresence of the signal prompts irresistible efforts to receive it. In case study after case study of the history of press and media liberalization around the world, the relentless impact of foreign, chiefly Western and American influence, is noted, applauded, or excoriated. It certainly cannot be ignored.

As diplomats in Asia and Africa, and as correspondents writing from a goodly number of places around the world, we have had a chance to peer close up at the much-touted Democratic Revolution over the past six years. Unhappily, democratic processes can accelerate turmoil as easily as retard it—as is happening in the former Soviet Union.[8] Unhappily also, too clamorous an electoral contest simply reinforces old habits of patronage or leads to violence. Witness some recent elections in the Philippines or Pakistan for some sobering second thoughts about the sanctity of the ballot box.

Indeed, the outcome of fairly counted electoral exercises can often co-exist with the messiest politics imaginable. The democratic achievement of Sri Lanka, for example, held fast in the 1980s during two concurrent and brutal wars against ethnic and ideological opponents. The Sri Lankans employed tactics that would make an old-style East German secret policeman squirm with embarrassment. Yet Sri Lanka's governments routinely change by the ballot, and not by the gun. Debate in that country remains surprisingly open.

We hope the point is made. Like a powder puff, democracy covers a multitude of sins. Was it not the last foreign minister of the former Yugoslavia who, when asked by a journalistic novice about the progress of democracy in the Balkans, replied in a voice heavy with irony, that "democracy has had, let us say, a somewhat mixed effect on my country"? The clash of electoral politics deeply divided the constituent parts of the Yugoslav federation along ethnic lines that Tito (despite his other, autocratic faults) had done much to blur. Democracy therefore has unintended consequences. Tens of millions of Russians now regard the very word itself as a pejorative.

Is this then an argument for benevolent dictators? No. But it is an argument for caution when, for example, it comes, as it has during the early 1990s, to urging the Chinese government to allow more openness in its society.

Is this an argument for discontinuing America's emphasis on democratic rule? No. But we would urge that policymakers avoid fixations that, like the Clinton administration's 1994 imbroglio with China, can land us in a no-win situation. Few would argue that China's habit of using prison labor to manufacture exports offends many sensibilities—although several Asian diplomats (not Chinese) have wondered to us about how well the United States would receive a demand from Beijing to allow foreign inspectors into U.S. state prisons whose license plates, made by inmates, are sold to European car enthusiasts.

The problems that occurred in U.S.-China relations go well beyond the bungled handling of Secretary of State Warren Christopher's Beijing visit in March 1994. By linking progress in human rights and democratization to the continuing applicability of Most Favored Nation (MFN) treatment to Chinese imports, United States diplomacy became hostage to daily reports of differential Chinese treatment of various, well known dissidents. The contrast to Cold War practice vis-à-vis the Soviet Union is striking. There the Jackson-Vannik amendment enjoyed some success, particularly as it was maintained in place for so long. In China, the same weapon backfired, frustrating American objectives. The Cold War model is not working.

The United States has legitimate complaints over China's behavior on a large range of issues—missile sales, official connivance in drug smuggling, official collusion in illegal alien smuggling, false country-of-origin labelling on Chinese export goods, nuclear weapons modernization, naval force expansion, territorial ambitions in Southeast Asia. Not only did the MFN/human rights episode distract us from these problems, but it is not clear that human rights in China have improved comprehensively—or at all—because of American pressure.

Experience in Asia, as in Europe, the Middle East, and Africa, shows that linkage between democratic freedoms and progress in important bilateral commercial and strategic interests can be made without the publicity that drives each side into hardened positions. In Sri Lanka, quiet pressure by the largest aid donors prior to an aid pledging conference led, in 1990, to the admission of Red Cross observers into the country. In Africa, quiet pressure has spared, on many occasions, the lives and livelihood of political opponents from vindictive governments.

Unfortunately, the American moral mission—wholly praiseworthy in its motivation—too often veers dangerously close to the damning description of feel-good diplomacy. Do we wish to feel good about our high-volume protests over the treatment of some poor wretch in prison somewhere, or do we care about getting results? Sometimes the microphone may be needed, but (in our experience) usually as a last resort. The American approach in December 1994 that secured the release of a captured American serviceman from the North Koreans exhibited the right blend of determined behind-the-scenes pressure and subdued public comment.

Seeking a *better* world, seeking a *freer* world—these aims still form almost an obligatory part of any foreign policy peroration in America today: A peroration is that closing part of a speech or essay where the rhetoric really flows thick and fast. It is the place where we are invited, to recall the famous malapropism of the late Chicago Mayor Richard Daley, "to climb to ever higher and higher platitudes." Does the United States still need a high-decibel peroration in its foreign affairs?

We tend to doubt it. Without—let us say again—in any way disparaging the need for democratic rule in today's world, we think the advancement of American self-interest may also include a *sotto voce* democratic enlargement policy. But this self-interest also embraces, in an explicitly meat-and-potatoes way, the maintenance of material livelihood, the enhancement of export prospects, the closer monitoring of ecologically harmful practices worldwide, and the preservation of sufficient armed force to head off or, if necessary, repel ill-disposed states that might meddle in places where a thoroughly serious U.S. security commitment exists.

This is not to say that ordinary Americans (ah, those patronizing words) do not care about the world, and do not grieve for its calamities, whether natural or man-made. We believe they do—but not in the simplistic way suggested by political rhetoric. Michael H. Schuman, a San Francisco lawyer who helped to set up that city's Center for Innovative Diplomacy, reminded us in a 1986 *Foreign Policy* article that local activism in American municipalities forms a strong tradition in this country. "The still declining confidence of Americans in their government's foreign-policy institutions, and their evident dissatisfaction with many specific US policies . . . have stimulated many impressive citizen efforts," he wrote. "Washington often denounces municipal activism yet effectively sanctions it through incoherence," he adds.[9]

That is the glory of U.S. pluralism, but Americans are entitled to expect coherence and priority at the national level. Only coherence can imbue our entire foreign policy with the right moral aims without losing sight of our strong cards. They are important cards, and they must be played with great skill. As the Carnegie report said, "today, foreign policy can raise or lower the cost of your home mortgage, create a new job or cause you to lose the one you've got."[10] It's that simple; it's that difficult.

Chapter 5

Prisoners of Our Own Rhetoric

You will get nothing out of Washington
but words, big words but only words.
— Stanley Baldwin,
British Prime Minister, 1932

Alongside a crusading temperament, the Cold War has bequeathed a crusading language to the foreign policy
establishment.[1] We need to keep a critical eye on this be-
quest. It may have been appropriate for the great battle
against fascism and communism. But it produces flawed
policy when applied to contemporary problems.

Like any other form of human interchange, foreign
policy has its own specialized language. Sir Harold
Nicolson devotes a whole chapter of his classic study, *Diplomacy*, to the nuances of diplomatic language. His preference ran in the direction of menacing understatement, but
today the trend lies in the direction of soaring cadences.[2]

In an address to the United Nations in September 1993,
an imaginative speech writer provided President Clinton
with the description of the United States as a "fulcrum for

49

change and a pivot point of peace."[3] It is not easy to know how these words apply to the real world. One might as well consult Humpty Dumpty, who summed up his masterful philosophy of epistemology as, "When I use a word, it means just what I choose it to mean."

No matter. Hyperbole and oratorical flourishes have their place in building democratic support for policy decisions. All politicians have sinned in this regard. Voters have become highly skilled in reading between the lines of political promises and in separating out the likely from the improbable. In the normal course of events, no problem arises, except, as today, when oratory becomes disengaged from the historical memory and from a real will to turn the rhetorical longings into practical reality. This causes rhetoric to become empty, to act as a substitute for clear thinking rather than as a means to articulate it.

The result is bad, unsustainable policy. The situation will not improve until policymakers can satisfy two important requirements:

- First, in their own minds they must be able to distinguish between reality and rhetoric and to keep clear the lines of demarcation between fact and fiction.

- Second, policy analysis must precede, and be separate from, the artifices used to articulate that policy once it is formulated. The means used to sell a policy must come after, and be subordinate to, the policy itself.

In the past, presidents behaved a little like secret agents. They had a cover story or legend for their foreign policy actions: No Foreign Entanglements to safeguard the early Republic, Manifest Destiny to justify the Mexican war, The Duties of Civilization (also known as the White Man's Burden) to launch the seizure of Cuba and the Philippines, Making the World Safe for Democracy to explain the entry into World War I, and The Evil Empire of Cold

War fame. Behind these slogans, however, lurked a robust calculation of what they wanted to achieve.

Today, only the cover stories or legends hold sway—their connection with the underlying 'real world' has been severed. The rhetorical symbols of American foreign policy come second-hand from a bygone era, the Cold War: "World Leadership," "Global Responsibility," "Superpower Credibility," a unique American "World Mission," "Moral Ascendancy," and so on. These notions infest the language of foreign policy formation. President Clinton and Republican Majority Leader Senator Robert Dole may rarely agree but, hands on hearts, they readily employ nearly identical language to invoke the obligations of American leadership.[4] These days, these and other cliches do service as substance. Instead of taking their place at the end of the foreign policy process, they stand at the head of the queue.

We now need to reverse this sequence—no easy task. The policy assumptions and habits of thought established during the Cold War have become second nature. They serve as a type of intellectual software for American foreign policy thinking. But, just as software needs frequent updating, so also do we need a new version of foreign policy symbols. The Cold War edition is obsolete—we badly need the latest WordPerfect upgrade and we must throw out the old start-up edition.

This fact becomes all too clear when we look at the symbolic terms in which today's basic foreign policy debate is conducted as an oratorical contest between engagement and isolationism. The former is regarded as the defining norm of good policy while the latter has been described by Bush as "folly" and by Clinton as "poison."[5] Isolationism has become an all-purpose code word to dismiss any effort to update and rationalize our diplomatic software. Those who suggest such ideas earn opprobrium, their efforts dismissed by National Security Adviser Anthony Lake as "the rhetoric of Neo-Know-Nothings."[6]

The older traditions of caution, of not moving without a good reason, have become objects of ridicule in Washington. They are cast as naive, even pathetic yearnings to turn our back on world problems that might contaminate the pristine quality of the Republic. Alongside its step-sisters Appeasement or, even worse, Munich, isolationism has become a routine insult, hurled at those who question whether Cold War habits of behavior remain the best way of conducting the nation's business in today's different circumstances.[7]

According to most of the received wisdom in Washington, America's pre-1945 foreign policy groped about in a sort of myopic lotus land. Sadly, so goes the story, earlier generations of Americans busied themselves only with their own affairs and failed to accept their international responsibilities. They stayed "above the fray."[8] There is just one problem with this isolationist theory—it makes for bad history. Simply repeating it time and again does not make it true. In point of fact, there has *never* been a time when the United States simply turned its back on the world. Even in the period between the world wars, the United States remained at the center of world financial activity. Despite the 1935 Neutrality Act, President Franklin Roosevelt came to the assistance of Britain on the outbreak of World War II. Today, both as the world's leading exporter and through its multifarious membership in international organizations, alliances, and agencies, the United States necessarily remains integrated with the rest of the world. The more one looks, the more the charge of isolationism takes on the aspect of a large and very overripe red herring.

From the very earliest days of the Republic, the Founders foresaw an intimate engagement in world affairs by the United States. Writing in 1787, John Jay advocated the advantages of a single government for the United States precisely on the ground that he fully expected extensive involvement with foreign countries: "America has already formed treaties with no less than six foreign nations and all of them, except Prussia, are maritime and therefore able to annoy and injure us."[9]

Actions by early Presidents do not provide evidence of

a wish to duck foreign responsibilities. President John Adams took the nation into an undeclared war with France to protect American commercial interests. President Thomas Jefferson sent an expeditionary force to Tripoli to counter pirate attacks on American shipping. President James Madison declared war on Britain over the issue of the impressment of American sailors. And the Monroe Doctrine, carrying another president's name, forestalled European ambitions in Latin America, and those of Russia on the Pacific coast.

The isolationism label simply does not fit. A much more satisfactory characterization for the strategic approach of all these statesmen is that they saw the national interest in maintaining, in the words of historian Foster Rhea Dulles, "unimpaired freedom in the pursuit of national aims and aspirations."[10] Therein lies the real meaning of Jefferson's warning against "entangling alliances." Jefferson did not see this as a call for the United States to bury its head in the sand; he was cautioning instead against formal, long-term commitments that might distort American policy choices. He wanted to keep options open.

To take a contemporary example, it is not isolationist or a fatal mark of introspection to call for a review of the American forward troop presence in Europe. The main purpose for which they were deployed—to ensure that the transatlantic defense guarantee would be activated in the face of an attack from the Soviet Union—no longer exists. All Soviet troops completed their withdrawal from Eastern Europe on the appointed day of August 31, 1994.[11] It may be that a new national interest, perhaps the need to maintain American influence in Europe, justifies the continued troop presence. If so, the case should be argued in those terms, and not by vilifying proponents of change.

This country's earlier diplomatic history contains many instructive parallels for the choices we face today between contending poles of moral theory and rational prudence. For example, in 1823 then-Congressman Daniel Webster, a future secretary of state, counseled against military intervention in the Ottoman empire, despite being a strong supporter of Greek independence from Turkey. He argued that the national interest was remote. Had it been more immediate, for example in Latin America, he would advocate a different course on the grounds that "our duty to ourselves, our policy, and wisdom might indicate very different courses as fit to be pursued by us in the two cases."[12]

Webster's words bring us back to reality: some issues exist in which American intervention can almost be taken for granted—massive challenges amounting to strategic denial, for example. But many more exist for which Webster's circumspect counsel makes a better fit.

It is apparent, therefore, that the dichotomy between isolationism and engagement serves no useful purpose. The United States has always been engaged in world affairs. The nineteenth century, for example, was particularly rich in international activity: the war with Mexico, the opening of Japan, complex maneuvering with Russia, Britain, and France, both sides in the Civil War were acutely aware of the foreign policy implications of their actions.[13] Yet, all this is somehow forgotten by many contemporary diplomatic analysts on the grounds that the United States did not directly participate in the European balance of power struggle or because—succumbing to the Manifest Destiny thesis—they regard the Western expansion of the United States as a purely domestic matter.

But even a century ago, a brief excursion into American history would soon expose the shallow nature of the isolationist charge. Three main factors—commercial opportunity, great-power competition, and the decline of British sea power—formed a tight nexus at the center of American strategic thinking 100 years ago. Then, as today, Asian trade exercised a compelling lure. Senator Thomas Hart Benton remarked "whatever power controls the Asiatic trade was destined to world dominance." [14]After the annexation of the Philippines, Senator Henry Cabot Lodge exclaimed enthusiastically, "we hold the other side of the Pacific and the value to this country is almost beyond imagination."[15] Sounds familiar? It is. Fulsome press sentiment reacted to a photo-op 1993 Asia Pacific Economic Cooperation (APEC) summit in Seattle by making heady comparisons between the Asia-Pacific's commercial evolution and the post–World War II settlement in Europe.[16]

At the turn of the century, burgeoning U.S. trade—exports tripled in the thirty years after 1870—reinforced arguments for a strong navy. William Henry Seward, Lincoln's and Andrew Johnson's secretary of state, had noted that "the nation must command the empire of the seas, which alone is the real empire."[17] Admiral Alfred Thayer Mahan now developed this argument further, in his advocacy of a naval building program "to affirm the importance of distant markets and the relation to them of our own immense powers of production."[18] The report of the Naval Policy Board in 1890 stressed the need for a fleet capable of protecting the "highways of commerce."[19] By the end of the century the American fleet was already the third most powerful in the world.

The same report also noted that the balance of power approach traditional in European geostrategy now had "world wide application." The United States was being drawn into the great power scramble for empire. In Mahan's words, "the American people were forced to look outward, whether they willed or not."[20] Henry Cabot Lodge noted "the great powers are rapidly absorbing for their future expansion and their present defense all the waste places on the earth. As one of the great nations of the world, the United States must not fall out of the line of march."[21] Typical disputes were those with Germany and Britain over Samoa in 1878 and with Britain over Venezuela in 1895.

At the same time, the increasing British preoccupation with the rising German naval threat in Europe began to weaken her activities in the Western Hemisphere, a fact manifested by the British concessions regarding Venezuela. This led some to reevaluate the traditional American distaste for international treaties. Mahan advocated an accord with Britain; one of President Theodore Roosevelt's advisers, Brooks Adams, wrote, "the continent which, when

Washington lived, gave a boundless field for the expansion of America, has been filled; and the risk of isolation promises to be more risky than the risk of alliances."[22] Later, the writer and historian Henry Adams wrote, "We have got to support France against Germany and fortify the Atlantic system beyond attack; for if Germany breaks down England or France, she becomes the center of the military world and we are lost."[23]

The rules of engagement for American involvement with the world that emerged from this period allowed for a broader interpretation of American interests than was the case in the early Republic. In Cabot Lodge's words, the American people "had begun to turn their eyes to those interests of the United States that lie beyond our borders."[24] In hard reality, national interest and freedom of action remained the key principles, much as they had in Washington's day.

At the rhetorical level, however, policy was increasingly assuming the vestment of a moral mission. Mahan said that the American people were taking on the "inevitable tasks and appointed lot in the work of upholding the common interests of civilization"[25] and Theodore Roosevelt wrote that it was "incumbent on all civilized and orderly powers to insist on the proper policing of the world."[26] The war against Cuba, long the object of ambition for American slaveholders, had been orchestrated in crudely moral terms thanks to a circulation war between the Hearst and Pulitzer newspaper empires. Victory against the Spanish led Senator Albert J. Beveridge to congratulate his countrymen on becoming the "master organizers of the world."[27] There was much talk redolent of the urging of the arch-imperialist Rudyard Kipling to "take up the white man's burden"—part of a poem he wrote to stiffen American resolve to retain the Philippines after defeating, in 1898, the Spanish in Manila Bay.

This trend brought about a decisive shift in the psychology of the American approach to foreign affairs. From earliest colonial times, Americans had asserted their special status. The classic statement remains Massachusetts

Governor John Winthrop's description of America as the "city on a hill." Jefferson proclaimed that the "last hope of human liberty rests on us." At the time, however, this notion did not kindle missionary zeal. Instead, Americans were nervous that an overclose connection with Europe would, in Benjamin Franklin's words, "corrupt and poison us," which led Jefferson to counsel that America should exert moral authority as a "standing monument and example for the aim and imitation of other countries." In 1841, John Quincy Adams said of America, "She is the well-wisher to the freedom and independence of all. She is the champion and vindicator only of her own."[28]

As the United States became more actively engaged in the world, this vision of America as passive role model began to metamorphize. In 1786, the Spanish Ambassador in London counseled John Adams, "Sir, I take it for granted that you will have sense enough to see us in Europe cut each other's throats with a philosophic tranquility."[29] By the end of the next century, this sentiment had diminished. The rhetoric with which political leaders now mobilized public opinion now portrayed the nation as an agent of divine regeneration. Beveridge proclaimed that God had "marked the American people as his chosen nation to finally lead in the redemption of the world."[30]

Today we are living with this psychological legacy. In a 1995 *Foreign Affairs* article, William Pfaff writes of a new neocolonialist policy toward Africa as "earning redemption."[31] Yet, as we have seen, this legacy has led to a mistaken reading of history. Rather than taking to heart the careful calculations that characterized the practical policy of this period, we remember Theodore Roosevelt's rhetorical flourishes that argued that "Chronic wrongdoing or impotence may force the United States, however reluctantly, in flagrant cases of such wrongdoing or impotence to the exercise of an international police power" or Woodrow Wilson's pronouncement about America that "she has a spiritual energy in her which no other nation can contribute to the liberation of mankind."[32]

Enter the (rhetorical) Global Policeman. The same president also laid the cornerstone of proactive world leadership by declaring "we have played a great part in the world and we are bent upon making our future even larger than our past." These words sound like an opening refrain for a yet-to-be-written symphony entitled *Sole Remaining Superpower.*

Despite the imperialist flourishes, deeper historical patterns continued into this century. Practical policy formation still placed pragmatic, close-to-home politics at the core. Wilson's decision to intervene in Haiti in 1915 had as much to do with a desire to protect American financial interests as to spread democratic ideals.[33] Later, Wilson did not take the United States into World War I until unrestricted submarine warfare posed an immediate threat to American security. In the interwar years, the United States remained reluctant to involve itself militarily in Europe as long as Britain and France were themselves reluctant to confront Germany militarily. Once they did, however, Roosevelt kept the British war effort afloat. After World War II, Truman understood the global threat posed by expansionist communism.

At the same time, the rhetorical superstructure of foreign policy grew ever more elaborate—for some good reasons. As the country has become more diverse, as communications have improved, as foreign policy interest groups have demanded an increasing role in the international sphere, presidents have seen that the easiest way to muster support for their policies is to present decisions as stark choices between good and evil.

Administrations of all persuasions have played this game.[34] Wilson said that "the force of America is the force of moral principle."[35] Reagan spoke of the "evil empire."[36] More recently, Bush portrayed Saddam Hussein as "worse than Hitler"—prompting the comment from former National Security Adviser Zbigniew Brzezinski that this was to "trivialize Hitler and exaggerate Saddam."[37] The Clinton Administration is continuing this approach as it applies demonizing labels to certain countries, such as Iraq, Libya, and Iran. These become backlash or outlaw nations beyond the pale of civilization.

This symbiosis between realism and redemptive idealism suited well the period of territorial expansion and the
fighting of two world wars. It reached its highest expression by underpinning the public conduct of the Cold War.
It is, however, much less well adapted to contemporary requirements. Practical politics, the credibility of the rhetoric, and the availability of resources have all changed. Not
that so many of today's policymakers and their academic
cheerleaders realize this: They commit a key mistake when
they fail to realize that incremental adjustments are not
enough. Nor is it enough simply to change the rhetoric.

A fundamental return to basics is required. The structural policy rationale provided by the Soviet Union for
fifty years has disappeared. As evidenced by the almost
invisible place accorded to foreign policy in Clinton's
presidential campaign statements and the Republican Contract with America document of November 1994, public
opinion displays minimal interest in foreign affairs. Eco-
nomically, too, the world is a different place. The American share of world production, which peaked at 40 percent
in 1950 when the assumptions of the Cold War were put
in place, has now returned to its 1870 level of 20 percent,
when the United States had a smaller navy than Venezuela.

As if these changes were not momentous enough,
policymakers are also having to cope with their own psychological disequilibrium. They have inherited attitudes
based on America's "monopoly on power,"[38] viz: George
Bush's comment about Somalia that "there is no one
else."[39] But the substance—whether of vital interest, public
consensus, or resource availability—is sending an entirely
more sober message. In their confusion, policymakers have
made a further mistake by misreading the last will and
testament of their Cold War predecessors. The latters' true
legacy was not their crusading language but the insight
that the Soviet Union represented a *systemic* challenge to
American interests—and did so on a *global* basis. From
this, an immensely complex set of actions followed: alliances, the Marshall Plan, the United Nations, GATT, the

IMF and so on. To put these structures into effect, the United States—in Walter Lippmann's words—had to sound "the tocsin of an ideological crusade."[40] The statement that became known as the Truman Doctrine is an excellent example. Truman said:

> At the present moment in world history nearly every nation must choose between alternative ways of life. The choice is too often not a free one. . . . I believe that it must be the policy of the United States to support free peoples who are resisting attempted subjugation by armed minorities or by outside pressures.[41]

Look at these words. This rhetoric has a manifestly sincere tone. It does not, in any way, diminish the sincerity to note that a clearheaded analysis of American self-interest (on the correct assumption that the challenge was systemic and global) *preceded* the rhetoric.

Today, this sequence of analysis is in danger of being lost. Florid words push national interest into second place. A *faux* Wilsonianism rules the roost—that is, a diplomatic culture that imagines that fine words matter more than rational calculation. By focusing on the public *words* of earlier generations of American diplomatists rather than on their more calculated *actions*, this culture traduces their legacy (most particularly that of Wilson himself). Today's officials, academics, and commentators—from both the Left and the Right—all share in this error. They still see the world in symbolic terms, in the words of one, as a "contest between an American master and a world donkey."[42]

In part, this approach has a trivial explanation. Like most other people, Americans feel squeamish about admitting that their overseas actions are self-interested rather than altruistic. In her book *Empire and the English Character*, Kathryn Tidrick describes a similar nineteenth century unease among the British middle classes, worried about the use of "armed compulsion" as their empire grew. They rationalized these concerns away by asserting that the empire provided superior administrative quality based on a disinterested motivation.[43]

Similarly, Americans have long preferred their leaders to express foreign policy goals in altruistic language. When building support for the Gulf War, President Bush recognized this by explicitly denying that the American goal was "simply to protect resources and real estate."[44] But this attitude does not mean that Americans are prepared to accept that foreign interventions may be justified on moral grounds alone. They grow leery if the connection with national interest appears thin or nonexistent. Ronald Reagan's faltering attempts to raise American enthusiasm for the Contra cause in Nicaragua illustrates the point—as does the cool public response to calls for engagement in Bosnia.

Foreign policy experts sometimes seem to act like manufacturers of the zanier brands of breakfast cereal; both think citizens unable to discern the difference between packaging and contents. President Nixon, for example, wrote that a weakness of American policy was that "we have never learned to act with the cold cynicism of Old World *Realpolitik*."[45] (That may be a little off the mark; we undoubtedly have acted in this fashion at many junctures in our history, including during the Nixon administrations, but in this century we find it hard to say so out loud.) In any event, Nixon's complaint appears frequently in the writings of America's major diplomatic actors.[46] We do not see a lack of cold cynicism as a weakness in the American armory but, even if we were to, the complaint would rest on a false reading of America history.

Self-interest has an excellent pedigree in American political thinking—take Patrick Henry, for example, who is certainly no one's idea of a hard-hearted cynic. Yet he wrote unambiguously that "the rock of political salvation is self-love."[47] The calculations of *Realpolitik* have a similarly prestigious lineage in American diplomacy. The hard headed (or cynical) decisions of President James Polk on dealings with Russia, Britain, and France—when he abandoned his election promises on the Oregon territory to clear the decks for the impending Mexican war—comprise just one of many cases in point.

The trouble is, politicians are forever confusing reality and rhetoric. As George Ball pointed out, "total-war rhetoric" bedeviled the American approach to Vietnam during three administrations.[48] This mistake threatens to repeat itself today. The means through which the United States pursued its Cold War goals—world leadership, global responsibility, strategic alliances—have become, by the mid-1990s, ends in themselves. Pragmatic analysis is taking second place.

Thus, when the president or other members of his administration speak about America's vital or fundamental interests, it remains unclear whether they are affirming something rhetorical, or substantive, or both. At various times in 1993, President Clinton described ethnic cleansing in Bosnia as touching on America's fundamental interests, whereas Secretary Christopher was saying that the Balkan situation "does not involve our vital interests."[49] Both reversed themselves many times on the issue. The residual impression, especially in the minds of foreigners, is that words from Washington are employed simply for rhetorical effect, and not to express an underlying reality. As the Bosnians discovered to their cost, however, a presidential articulation of U.S. interests holds no guarantee that the stakes will be sufficiently vital to justify substantive American involvement.

Rhetoric and oratorical poses will always form part of the foreign policy process. But—as America's historical experience demonstrates—rational calculations have up till now normally come first. This is a wise tradition. Until it is restored, a national consensus will prove elusive. Even that maritime imperialist, Admiral Mahan, would caution his devotees that "in our country, national policy, if it is to be steadfast and consistent, must be identified with public conviction."[50] To date, the Clinton administration, aided and abetted by too many foreign policy thinkers in and out of government, has tried to produce conviction through rhetoric, rather than through the fundamentals.

The result, as Mahan foresaw, is an erratic policy, lacking in credibility at home and in impact abroad. In his inaugural address, Clinton spoke in perfect Cold War cadence when he warned that the United States would use force "when the conscience of the international community is defied."[51] But few in his audience hurried out afterwards to update their Army Reserve status, and no one then rushed home to check the maps to find out where, exactly, are Banja Luka, Huambo, and Tblisi. Lastly, few strutting dictators quaked in their boots. Somehow, a general intuition emerged: These were mere words.

Over the years, Americans have responded to foreign policy challenges by echoing a question asked back in 1801 by Thomas Jefferson. While debating a proposed Mediterranean naval expedition to punish Arab pirates he asked, "what shall be the object?"[52] As we have seen, the answers too often come garbed in terms of allegorical righteousness, deliberately, to soften the hard edge of realism. This pattern will continue. But policymakers make a mistake when they assume that Americans up and down the country will support policies based on moral rhetoric alone. For a policy to carry conviction, reality must precede allegory.

In the foreign policy establishment, many do not know which is which. And those who think they do too often equate reality with armed compulsion. To persist in this view can lead to military miscalculation or worse, the topic of our next chapter.

Chapter 6

Military Force:
To Use or Not to Use?

To save your world, you asked this man to die.
Would this man, could he see you now, ask why?
— W. H. Auden
Epitaph for an Unknown Soldier

Foreign policy experts love to expound on plans to use force to put their policies into effect. Armchair strategists right down to their fingertips, nothing gives them more pleasure than sliding amphibious landing craft or fighter aircraft across the diplomatic chessboard to checkmate recalcitrant foreigners. Two hundred years ago Frederick the Great of Prussia observed that "diplomacy without force is like an orchestra without music."[1] In the United States, former Secretary of State Lawrence Eagleburger encapsulated conventional wisdom in a more prosaic way: "If you're not prepared to use force, then you're nowhere" he said.[2]

Force as an instrument of foreign policy enjoys a distinguished pedigree. With the exception of Vietnam, where many early warning signs of the looming obsolescence of high-intensity force (that is, heavily armored conventional forces) made their appearance, force has served the United States well over the past fifty years. Actual and potential opponents, most especially the Soviet Union, knew that the United States had drawn a rough line in the sand or tundra against any immoderate ambitions on their part. The territory of the United States and its allies remained inviolate.

On the back of this success, diplomats developed a kind of three-step approach to overseas problems: negotiations, sanctions, war—the last step normally disguised in the delicately refined language of UN resolutions as "all necessary means."[3] Richard Haass, a member of the National Security Council in the Bush administration, has codified this approach into a how-to book on military intervention, arguing that the opportunities for intervention today are greater than during the Cold War.[4]

"If it ain't broke, don't fix it," proclaimed Henry Ford. How tempting it would be simply to accept this maxim as an eternal verity in issues of armed compulsion. Certainly the world today seems no less violent a place, nor are calls on the U.S. military any less frequent. Victor Hugo's observation in 1870 that "in the twentieth century war will be dead" has fallen farcically short of fulfillment. So too has Norman Angell's 1910 treatise that sought to show that economic interdependence would make war between the great powers impossible.[5]

Similar hopes—that the Cold War's end would introduce an era of world peace guaranteed by a new world order—have also been cruelly disappointed. Instead of peace, mankind's predilection for slaughter continues to stoke scores of regional conflicts. Just since 1989, the United States alone has launched or threatened to launch military action against Haiti, Iraq, Libya, North Korea, Somalia, and the Serbian rump of Yugoslavia. In General Colin Powell's words, it has indeed been a "busy season" for U.S. forces.[6] And, in the technical aspects of the 1994 Haitian and Persian Gulf deployments, it has been a successful season.

Superficially, therefore, the traditional troika of diplomacy, negotiations, and war may look secure. A more searching observer would ask whether this tintinnabulation of American military might has in fact achieved its policy objectives. Has the United States emerged—as was the case with the Cold War victory—as a stronger, more secure nation as a result? Given the limited resources for foreign expenditure, does force deployment represent the most economic means of advancing the nation's interests. Or has an overeagerness to think in terms of forceful solutions to problems led the nation into expensive and time-consuming distractions? In short, do we need to look again at that neat equation between diplomacy and force to which so many have become so deeply attached?

We are entering dangerous political territory. Toughness stands high in the ranking of the American political lexicon. The grinding political process quickly consumes those who do not measure up to its demands. In the 1988 presidential campaign, the Democratic nominee, Michael Dukakis, committed a notable blunder when he refused to commit himself to vigorous and violent action in defense of a hypothetical attack on his wife. A similar trap awaits anyone who appears to question whether, for all its past effectiveness, the military option should continue to occupy its place of honor among the instruments of American foreign policy. It flies in the face of conventional wisdom to question whether we should regard war as the summit of successful policy making rather than as evidence of policy failure. To earn the reputation of being antimilitary is the surest kiss of political death in America today, as is evidenced by the fact that in the Republican Contract with America campaign document for the 1994 mid-term elections the sole reference to foreign policy was as an undertaking to increase defense spending. The Republican victory immediately prompted the Clinton administration to boost the defense budget.[7]

The hottest of hot potatoes though it may be, this debate about when to resort to force, and when not to, holds the key to how the country will present itself on the international stage in future. There is nothing unpatriotic nor antimilitary about wanting to ensure that this presentation remains the best it can be. Former Secretary of State George Shultz, himself no stranger to belligerent gestures, argues that force only has value when it is credible.[8] The Clinton Administration stressed the same factor before the 1994 intervention in Haiti.[9] As we examine the exercise of force against today's problems, we need to keep our eyes locked on that concept. Under what circumstances in a democratic polity can American force appear credible?

Today's debate about military force takes place on two fronts. In some instances, resort to force is uncontroversial and also likely to be effective. Examples might be a defensive response to any direct attack on the United States or on any vital American interest overseas by an identifiable enemy with conventional forces. (The contentious aspects of defining such vital interests are discussed in chapter 8.) These are the eventualities that fill military manuals and against which most planning takes place. These are also the eventualities that enjoy public support for the placement of American ground troops in harm's way (rather than relying on air power alone) and that win public acceptance of American casualties. We fully support such planning—although, for the reasons set out in chapter 2, we see these eventualities as relatively infrequent. Adequate military forces for such contingencies must be maintained and paid for.

The second aspect of this debate concerns the discretionary threats (also discussed in chapter 2) that do not constitute a direct attack on American property or lives or are more ambiguous in the involvement of American interests. This category of threat appears more likely to provide the stuff of future challenges to the United States. It also engenders much more dispute, because, in these cases, the use of force is less of a defensive reaction to imminent danger and more a deliberate act of will.

Eagleburger's embrace of force as a vital instrument of policy still rules the roost of conventional wisdom—as exemplified in Defense Secretary William Perry's threats of force against North Korea, for which he found support from George Bush's National Security Adviser, Brent Scowcroft, and from many foreign policy commentators.[10] The actual use of force in Haiti also gained wide support as evidence that military intervention works.[11] But other voices, such as the Brooking Institution's William Kaufmann and John Steinbruner, have raised doubts about whether the easy recourse to force practiced during the Cold War can continue today.[12]

Against this background, we must ask whether the *credibility* of force (as an expression of popular will that is ready to accept trade-offs in terms of loss of life and treasure) or its *utility* (i.e., its appropriateness to policy objectives) can be taken for granted much longer in those murkier cases that seem to characterize today's points of conflict. If they cannot, adherence to outmoded force doctrines could do us much harm.

In 1993, the United States spent $291 billion for defense, an amount almost twice as much as its North Atlantic Treaty Organization (NATO) partners *combined.* Potential or actual enemies, such as Russia, China, North Korea, Iran, Libya, or Iraq, are simply not in the same league, being outspent by factors of between seven and seventy. Every year the United States spends $200 billion more than *all of them put together.* In 1998, nearly a decade after the demolition of the Berlin Wall, real military spending on current projections will consume a similar proportion of national wealth as it did under Eisenhower—a time when the United States was living through the Soviet invasion of Hungary, confiscation of Western oil assets in the Middle East, and Chinese shelling of the offshore islands of Quemoy and Matsu.

Clearly the United States is not, as some have alleged, disestablishing its military nor is it letting down its guard.[13] But against what does it guard? What are American taxpayers getting for their money? If it is essential national security against those direct threats mentioned earlier, well and good. No one argues that the end of the Cold War means the end of any prospect of armed challenges to American interests. Nor do any, aside from fringe fanatics, urge the United States unilaterally to disarm. Far from it. As we file our taxes, we may grumble—but we pay up on the sensible ground that security represents a first charge on our resources, not an optional extra. As Adam Smith noted in 1776, "defense is more important than opulence."

However, a nagging suspicion remains that much of this money is going to support projects deriving *not* from direct threats to national security but from the crusading temperament of instinctive proactivity. As one American official remarked shortly after the intervention in Haiti, "It will bolster those who believe that we can intervene in places where our national interests are not vital, but where we can play a role in the building of democracy."[14]

This approach seems to harbor serious dangers for the country. Superficially it may project an image of strength. But it leads in the opposite direction—specifically, overreliance on force in inappropriate contexts can bleed a superpower dry.[15]

"High Force" as Popular Culture

The American attitude toward force has deep roots in popular culture. Americans have grown to expect their presidents to rattle sabers. In the words of the *Washington Post's* Jim Hoagland:

> Real Presidents lead, squeeze, intimidate or persuade. If none of these tactics works, real Presidents zap their enemies with the CIA or the 82nd Airborne. This constantly implied threat made American diplomacy far more brilliant and productive throughout the Cold War than would otherwise have been the case.[16]

Judged against this muscular scale, Jimmy Carter to this day remains derided for his hesitation to use force to meet the hostage crisis in Iran. His last-minute interventions to head off the aggressive use of force in North Korea and Haiti, his apparent endorsement of Serbian policies, together with the revelations that, before the Gulf War, he had written to leaders of the UN Security Council asking them not to authorize the use of force, confirmed this judgement.[17] He was not a real President. In the immediate aftermath of the Haiti intervention White House officials made haste to point out that Clinton was made of sterner stuff. "This president pulled the trigger," they commented. In response to the Iraqi provocation, he showed "splendid resolve."[18]

This tradition would have us believe that any diplomacy not backed by force is doomed to failure, in the manner of former British prime minister Neville Chamberlain at his Munich conference with Hitler. As we saw in chapter 5, the ghost of that ill-fated prime minister continues to stalk the subconscious mind of Western diplomats as one of the most potent (if most misapplied) symbols of weak statesmanship. Walter Lippmann wrote that the post–World War II generation of American statesmen "overlearned the lessons of Munich,"[19] while more recent writers have discerned a "Munich syndrome" in the psychology of American foreign policy.[20]

This thinking now finds expression in another figure of speech, what may be called the sole remaining superpower syndrome. This draws on the mundane fact that the demise of the Soviet Union has left the United States as by far the preeminent military power in the world. According to conventional wisdom, the implication is that the United States, if it chooses, has the ability to impose its will in any corner of the globe, to "harness history" in Brent Scowcroft's vivid phrase.[21]

It can readily be seen, therefore, that this tradition—let us call it one of high force—has pushed roots deep through the alluvial soil to burrow deeply into the sedimentary rock of American political culture. Let's see how it has performed in the new world circumstances.

At first sight, the high force tradition appears to have

little to do with the curiously unpredictable path that American military action overseas has followed in the years since the dissolution of the Warsaw Treaty Organization in 1989. Iraq, Somalia, Haiti, Panama, Macedonia, and the skies of Bosnia have all seen the deployment of the American military. Sometimes this has yielded short-term results—as in the capture of General Manuel Noriega, a brief lull in Somali clan fighting, a transitory Serbian pullback from a hill near Sarajevo, a change of tenant in the presidential palace in Port-au-Prince, an about-turn by Iraqi troop carriers.

Yet, over the longer term, the results have hardly been flattering for our own, self-styled Sole Superpower. In the same Iraq, in the same Libya ostracized for two decades, in the same miserably divided Bosnia, and in the same failed Somalia, momentary gratification has yielded to a realization that the root problems remain unresolved. In Panama drug traffickers still rule the roost and Haiti remains a fractured, poverty-stricken society. The same aging revolutionary runs his fiercely nationalist, anti-*Yanqui* regime 90 miles from Florida.

Why Isn't It Working?

Something is seriously wrong. The application or threat of American force has not led to a solution or even to an amelioration of the problems against which it was directed. Eagleburger's dictum is not delivering the goods. Why? Because of faults in the means of delivery? That is, has the military made mistakes in execution? Or have changes in the world robbed High Force of contemporary relevance? Have shifts in American democratic opinion overturned once well-established notions?

Military analysts admit that mistakes were made in recent deployments and that experience gained in them raises troubling issues for military planners. But, in fairness to the military, no amount of military reform or technological retooling can compensate for shortcomings in political management. Our focus, therefore, rests on whether a force doctrine that worked well during a time of direct threat to the United States from the Soviet Union and earlier enemies remains a useful instrument for asserting American interests in the new world circumstances.

Traditionally, American forces have been deployed either to counter or to deter a direct physical threat to American interests. Such threats usually came in the form of a recognized international state. The obvious examples in this century are Germany, Japan, China, North Korea, North Vietnam, and the Soviet Union and its emanations.

In speaking about the challenges that face the United States for the rest of the century, however, analysts now pay little heed to physical survival. Instead, in National Security Adviser Anthony Lake's words, the analysts may identify as a major threat the "sluggish economic growth which undermines the security of our people."[22] In doing so, they unconsciously echo Dwight Eisenhower's warning that "there is no defense for any country that busts its own economy."[23]

So much for the obvious change. A look at the problems identified by policy makers or in independent analyses, as in the Heritage Foundation's blueprint *A Safe and Prosperous America*, yields proliferation, terrorism, religious extremism, ethnic intolerance, or access to foreign trade as major issues.[24] Note the subtle change: these problems decreasingly express themselves as activities primarily between governments, let alone as between one government and the United States; more often, they are entirely "nonstate" or "transnational" in nature. They do not assemble themselves neatly or visibly for battle.

Potential adversaries of the United States have absorbed the main lesson of the Gulf War: never enter into a conventional, First World pitched battle with the United States. A senior American military official has commented that the North Korean "military appears to have studied the Gulf War. The lessons: don't let the Americans build up their forces; don't let them put in air power; don't let them take the initiative; don't let them fight a war with low United States casualties."[25]

The trouble is, too many analysts continue to think and write in terms of conventional state-on-state combat, deriving lessons from the Gulf War—such as of the advantages of a "reconnaissance strike force"[26]—which are much less applicable in today's much messier conflicts. We would do better to listen to the comments of a senior American commander about the lessons of the Somali campaign: his troops learned the hard way that "you cannot hunt individuals with a helicopter in the city. The tradeoff is not there when you use a $2 to $4 million airframe to hunt one guy with a $200 rocket-propelled grenade."[27] Another antidote to conventional thinking is to observe the appalling travails of the Russian army in Chechnya.[28]

An End to Clausewitz

In the conclusion to his *History of Warfare*, the military historian John Keegan throws down a daring intellectual challenge:

> Politics must continue; war cannot. That is not to say that the role of the warrior is over. The world community needs . . . skilful and disciplined warriors. Such warriors must properly be seen as the protectors of civilization, not its enemies. The style in which they fight for civilization—against ethnic bigots, regional warlords, ideological intransigents, common pillagers and organized international criminals—cannot derive from the Western model of war making alone. . . . There is a wisdom in the principles of intellectual restraint and even of symbolic ritual that needs to be rediscovered. There is an even greater wisdom in the denial that politics and war belong within the same continuum. Unless we insist on denying it, our future, like that of the last Easter Islanders, may belong to the men with bloodied hands.[29]

With these words Keegan is trying to banish the traditional concept of Western warfare inherited from the Prussian military thinker Karl von Clausewitz that "war is the
continuation of politics through other means." Keegan attacks this dictum on moral grounds, describing it as "poisonous intoxication." He says that "unless we unlearn the
habits we have taught ourselves, we will not survive."[30]
With these words Keegan takes direct aim at those who
argue that force is simply another implement in the tool
shed of international diplomacy, to be utilized as and
when circumstances suggest that it can be effective.

Keegan does not deny a place for force, but questions
our understanding of it in today's world. In doing so, he
raises the right issue but, in excoriating Clausewitz, he
may be taking aim at the wrong target. Clausewitz did not
intend to be determinative or approbative. He believed he
was expressing a cold, observable fact about human behavior: When peaceful means of conflict resolution fail, people
tend to resort to violence. Many would agree with this
conclusion. Moreover, Clausewitz's dictum has another
value: It focuses attention on *politics*. In doing so, he
causes us to reflect on the impact that changes in the politics of the post–Cold War world—both inside the United
States and elsewhere—will exercise on the acceptability, or
suitability, of war as an instrument of policy.

Lieutenant-General Rupert Smith, who commanded the
British armored division positioned within the U.S. 7th
Corps during Desert Storm and in 1995 commanded the
UN forces in Bosnia, draws a useful distinction between
war, an activity between states involving deployment in
open combat, and *conflict*, which covers other warlike activity but which stops short of formal war. He points out
that Western armies and Western governments understand
war well enough, but that they stand on much more uncertain ground when it comes to dealing with conflict.[31]
Herein lies the source of our confusion in America today.

While American military planners continue to place
their central emphasis on winning a conventional war,
Smith's conclusion that "war, at least in its western form,
to a large extent has lost its utility" may more accurately

describe the future. Instead, the United States is more
likely to face a series of conflicts in which its adversaries
conduct operations, in Smith's words, "below a threshold
in which the bulk of the West's technical superiority can
be brought to bear."[32] Again, the lessons of Somalia come
to mind, as does the bitter experience of Russian tank
crews at the hands of ill-equipped but highly-motivated
Chechens.[33]

Consider these words: "[they] fought like concealed villains who made cowardly disposition to murder us all."[34]
Do these scornful comments come from an American soldier speaking of the Somali irregulars or Haitian attachés?
No, they were uttered in 1775, by a British army officer
named William Sutherland, of the Thirty-Eighth Regiment.
Raised in the gentlemanly tradition of open-field combat
between formed units, Sutherland excoriated the Massachusetts Minutemen for having successfully neutralized
at the Battle of Lexington the British technological advantage (volley fire by lines of Redcoats). The Minutemen did
so by some very low-tech maneuvering—taking cover behind rocks, shrubs, and trees. Very ungentlemanly.

In this respect, the ending of the Cold War may have
returned us to conflicts not unlike those of 1775 and, this
time, the technologically superior Americans may fill the
Redcoats' role. War has not come to an end, but perhaps
our familiar notions about its nature no longer apply. Instead of representing the apotheosis of policy, it may more
closely resemble its bankruptcy.

Consider the following high-level provisos on the use
of American force abroad:

> First, the United States should not commit forces to
> combat overseas unless the particular engagement or
> occasion is deemed vital to our national interest or that
> of our allies.
> Second, if we decide it is necessary to put combat
> troops into a given situation we should do so whole-
> heartedly and with the clear intention of winning.
> Third, if we do decide to commit forces to combat
> overseas, we should have a clearly defined political
> and military objectives.

Fourth, the relationship between our objectives and the forces we have committed . . . must be continually reassessed and adjusted if necessary.

Fifth, before the United States commits combat forces abroad, there must be some reasonable assurance we will have the support of the American people and their elected representatives in Congress . . .

Finally, the commitment of United States forces to combat should be a last resort.[35]

This appeal for caution, democratic support, and emphasis on the last-resort nature of the deployment of force comes from Caspar Weinberger, President Reagan's secretary of defense, who presided over the massive defense buildup of that administration. His words echo sentiments from military thinkers throughout the ages. In AD 383, the Roman general Themistius wrote that the strength of Rome lay "not in breastplates and shields, not in countless masses of men, but in Reason."[36]

This thinking foreshadows the cautious tone adopted by Admiral William Crowe and General Colin Powell, the two immediate past chairmen of the Joint Chiefs of Staff, in their advice on various military undertakings carried out, or proposed, during their tenures. Yet this caution often causes exasperation among civilian national security staff, who believe they can out-general the generals. "What are we paying all this money for?" they demand. "What are all these guns, ships, and planes for?" Former Secretary of State George Shultz opposed Weinberger's conditions and wrote dismissively of them in his memoirs.[37] And in the first months of the Clinton administration, four State Department officials felt so strongly about the desirability of committing American troops to Bosnia that they resigned when they were overruled in the face of cautious objections from the Pentagon.[38]

Public Aversion to Casualties

The High Force tradition of American diplomacy will, we are sure, enjoy many more years as a staple of political stump speeches. We noted in chapter 5 that this sort of language has a compelling hold on the body politic. We regret this on the grounds that belligerent words rarely turn into effective policy. They tend to come to grief when policymakers find difficulty in answering one central question: Under what circumstances are they prepared to order American forces into combat and to defend the resulting loss of life to the American people? What answer do they have for parents like Larry Joyce who lamented the death of his son in Somalia by saying directly to President Clinton's face, "Mr. President, he *did* die in vain because the mission you sent him on was seriously flawed and you weren't even committed to it."[39]

For fifty years, the concept of national security was generally understood to mean opposition to Soviet communism, in whatever guise it took. Across a broad spectrum of political opinion, Americans recognized this as a genuine threat to their national welfare. Supported by this consensus, successive administrations had little trouble in persuading the "people to be in harmony with their leaders," one of the primary conditions of good generalship as identified by the Chinese strategic thinker Sun Tzu over thirty centuries ago.[40]

With the demise of the Soviet threat, public opinion can no longer be taken for granted. George Bush had to put in five months of unremitting effort to obtain a somewhat grudging approval from Congress of his actions against Iraq. The euphoria of the Gulf War victory did not translate into demands for fresh military glory. To the contrary, Bush is out of office while poll after poll puts foreign policy at the bottom of popular concerns. Even in surveys of specific foreign policy attitudes, such as the Gallup/ *USA Today* poll, economic security easily emerges as the top concern—a striking contrast to the 1950s and 1960s, when poll respondents regularly placed "keeping the peace" (that is, managing Russia) as the "most important issue" facing the nation.[41]

This ambivalence has already manifested itself as a constraint on policymakers' ability to deploy force or to sustain its deployment once casualties are incurred. From the earliest days of the Bosnian crisis, the Bush administration ruled out the use of American ground troops prior to a peace settlement, principally on the ground that neither congressional nor public opinion would tolerate such a move. The Clinton administration, despite its more activist approach to Bosnia, has retained this core limitation. Over a 100 years ago, the German chancellor Otto von Bismarck rejected Prussian involvement in the Balkans, saying that Serbia was not worth the bones of a single Pomeranian grenadier; instinctively, Americans endorse this view as applying (with different geographic locale) to the bones of their men and women, too. The available evidence, from opinion surveys and from reaction to actual armed encounters, suggests that an enormous gulf exists between those whose careers rest on a cold-eyed (and comfortably distant) application of force, and Americans at large, who strongly and consistently show no willingness to accept casualties in causes that appear remote from their traditional concerns and interests. The intervention in Haiti was chronically vulnerable to the loss of even one American life.[42]

In an article written before his nomination as defense secretary, William Perry tried to get over this problem.[43] He proposed creating a multinational force in which the United States would provide logistics, intelligence, and stealth capabilities while other nations, including Russia, Germany, China, and Canada, would provide troops. This and other ideas (see chapter 13) for multilateralizing military force now lie dormant after the poor results from U.S. humanitarian interventions abroad after 1991, usually with a tagalong UN presence.

In expressing cautious views, Americans are not collapsing into a new bout of isolationist exhaustion. Instead, they are picking up the threads of earlier instincts of caution, of staying out of conflicts where they discern little American interests or power to influence events. Americans, like Henry V's longbow archers at the battle of Agincourt, are of "unmatchable courage." In the right circumstances, they have no equals in their readiness to endure sacrifice. Witness Woodrow Wilson's 1917 speech that presaged the American declaration of war against Germany when he declared that "the day has come when America is *privileged* to spend her blood and her might for the principles that gave her birth."[44] Americans have no tradition of cowardice. But they are not fools. They naturally demand a persuasive reason to place their lives in harm's way. Such reasons do not materialize out of the ether.

Appropriate Technology
for Medieval Problems

In the search for means to make the application of force less costly in American lives (and, as a recent study suggests, to present warfare as almost an aesthetic activity fit for family viewing), Americans have become increasingly enamored with standoff weapons, that is, weapons delivered from a distance. The Tomahawk cruise missile is the perfect example of a weapon that reduces the risk to American lives to zero.[45]

This type of weaponry differs sharply from the force deployed by the United States in the past, when force meant American ground troops, whether in Europe, Korea, Vietnam, Grenada, Panama, Iraq, or wherever. Ground troops constituted the vital element in the 1994 deployments to Haiti and the Persian Gulf.

By contrast, today's standoff doctrine depends strictly on air delivery of high explosives. Aerial bombardment has enjoyed many extravagant claims from World War II onward, but the French General Philippe Morillon, the former UN commander in Bosnia, who knows the American military well, has put his finger on a new factor associated with today's preference for air power. He commented that "Desert Storm left one awful legacy: it imposed the idea that you must be able to fight the wars of the future without suffering losses. The idea of zero-kill

as an outcome has been imposed on American generals."
Morillon goes on to warn, "But there is no such thing as a
clean or risk-free war."[46]

Alas, just as military technology is advancing to allow
greater and greater precision from an ever more distant
remove (since 1990 the U.S. Army and U.S. Air Force have
doubled the number of attack aircraft capable of launching
laser-guided bombs), the nature of the problems facing the
United States increasingly demands hand-to-hand combat—as the pictures of heavily-armed American troops patrolling the provincial towns of Haiti graphically remind
us.[47] Technology may be racing ahead but the problems
compelling the application of force seem, if anything, ob-
stinately medieval. In this regard, Keegan makes an
interesting observation. One of the reasons for the series
of defeats suffered by Crusader knights at the hands of
Muslim forces in the twelfth century lay not, he says, "in
tactical accident, but in a structural defect in their method
of warmaking."[48] The knights were structured to fight and
prevail against an enemy who stood his ground in open
country, but this method came to grief against Saladin's
troops—who evaded open battle and relied on fighting
from behind obstacles. As we have seen, the British
Redcoats suffered a similar fate against the backwoods
American militia. American rangers in Mogadishu found
Somali irregulars shooting at them from behind women
and children.

A few years ago, the term *appropriate technology* became
a much-used buzzword in the foreign aid community. In
effect, the words meant that donors should avoid pressur-
ing developing countries to accept a grandiose hydroelec-
tric project if mechanically operated artesian wells would
do the job.

The concept also has application in the military sphere.
All the more so, when we think of the issues that the
United States has faced since 1989. Leaving aside the question of economic security (in which no one outside the lunatic fringe would consider a candidate for Tomahawk-
style intervention), the challenges have included sectarian

violence in Bosnia and the former Soviet Union, anti-democratic reaction, humanitarian intervention in Somalia, a wave of unwanted migrants from Cuba, nuclear proliferation in North Korea and Ukraine, religious extremism in the Middle East, human rights in China, democratic restoration (still in its first act) in Haiti. The Gulf War stands out as a stark exception to these examples.

These problems typify the issues that have already confronted, and may continue to confront, the United States for the foreseeable future. They share few obvious common properties, but we can agree that force—at least in the form of air-delivered munitions—does not appear to be a useful instrument for addressing them. Commenting on Russian tactics in Chechnya, National Security Adviser Anthony Lake made exactly that point when he said, "The issue for us is what their [Russian] tactics are."[49]

Defense Secretary William Perry also recognized this in a comment about Bosnia:

> The fighting still goes on in ways that are difficult to influence with the use of air power alone—in particular the small arms, close combat fighting around many cities and villages in Bosnia. Trying to use air power in such situations actually could increase rather than decrease the civilian casualties.[50]

In an interview during the Serb onslaught on Bihac in November 1994, he expressed the same sentiment more bluntly: "Airstrikes cannot determine the outcome of the ground combat."[51]

Douglas Hurd, the British foreign secretary, shares this view. He has repeatedly warned about "fostering illusions about what NATO air power can achieve" and has pointed to the futility of attempting to create fraternal love among the Serbs, Croats, and Muslims through aerial bombardment. Bombs cannot overcome social character.[52]

Military planners will often say that so long as there are no political constraints anything is possible. One senior UN officer, echoing a plaintive cry heard over and over again during the Vietnam tragedy, commented about the Somali operation that "this was a political war, not a military war. We could have ended this months ago but our hands were tied politically."[53]

Perhaps so, although one would like more information about what the officer meant by ending the war. Did he mean deploying superior firepower to eliminate any and all opposition to UN aims? We will never know. We *do* know, however, political sentiment in the West would never have accepted mass killing of Somalis in the furtherance of an ostensibly humanitarian mission.

Perhaps that wily old bird Clausewitz was right after all: Perhaps it's not possible to take politics out of war; there really is a continuum between the two. Lawrence Keeley, an anthropologist at the University of Chicago, has written "What prevents war is politics."[54] In democratic societies, this makes for extreme political complications but, as the Cold War demonstrated, the situation is far from hopeless. As long as the United States was threatened by the sort of unambiguous, existence-threatening challenge that the Soviet Union represented, consensus about the means and ends of force deployment coalesced easily. This consensus remains in place for a strong military capable of repelling any direct challenge to the United States.

The demise of the Soviet Union has, however, changed domestic attitudes to what are perceived as more indirect challenges. Other developments can cause the world to change again, perhaps to make it once again a hostile place for the U.S. Against that time of renewed hostility, adequate military appropriations must be made to guarantee national survival. But until that once again comes under threat, the application of American force looks less necessary, less credible, and less appropriate than at any time in fifty years. Politics has turned war into the bluntest of blunt instruments.

This fact complicates life for those responsible for protecting American interests. If gunboats no longer get the job done, what does? In the next chapter we explore the implications for force planning under these new conditions of constraint.

Chapter 7

Diplomacy beyond Force

Let us recognize that we owe it to ourselves
and to the world to explore every possible
means of settling differences before we even
think of such a thing as war. And the hard
way is to have the courage to be patient.

— Dwight D. Eisenhower, 1954

On April 5, 1986, a bomb exploded in a West Berlin night-club killing two people and injuring 155 others, including some sixty Americans. Intelligence derived from communications interceptions pointed the finger at Libya. Nine days later, American F-111 attack aircraft bombed the headquarters of Libyan leader Muammar el-Qaddafi. Asked by a journalist what message Qaddafi should read into the American action, Secretary of State George Shultz replied, "You've had it, pal."[1]

Following the raid, Libyan sponsorship of international terrorism declined substantially. The American action seemed well vindicated. But let's run the reel forward: In December 1988, a Pan American airliner was destroyed in mid-flight, almost certainly at Libyan instigation. As of 1995, Qaddafi remained as Libya's leader, still relishing his maverick role in the Middle East, while in the United States the democratic process of succession pushed Shultz's president aside and, four years later, pushed aside his party as well.

In the Libyan case, force performed the task it does well: to administer a short, sharp shock. But, as Libya also shows, many of the old problems remain after the smoke clears. American policymakers thus face a dilemma. First, the United States has an interest, along with many other countries, in a broadly peaceable world where international commerce can flourish and democratic values can take root. Against this, the average American voter manages to remain distinctly leery about getting entangled in the messy challenges to this interest.

If our thesis is correct—that is, that these popular attitudes reflect a return of historically conditioned and thus deep-seated sentiments of caution—then they will probably remain in the ascendant for many years. Policymakers will have to find new ways to solve violent foreign problems, of which, we all agree, there is likely to be a surfeit.

To date, attention has focused on reconfiguring existing mechanisms, with much effort going into how to better equip the large supranational organizations to face these issues. Brian Urquhart, a former senior UN official in charge of peacekeeping, has proposed the formation of a permanent UN volunteer force.[2] He wants this to be available to the secretary-general for use in early interventions in looming crises. In a parallel process, and after an agonizing reappraisal of its role, the NATO member states have agreed to consider requests for peacekeeping assistance outside treaty-defined NATO territory. Similarly, the West European Union has declared its readiness to act as the defense arm of the European Union (EU), if the EU itself becomes involved in conflict resolution.[3]

At a more technical level, a large volume of writing has appeared since 1989 to deal with such matters as the emergent legal issues surrounding outside intervention in the traditionally sacrosanct area of a sovereign state's domestic affairs.[4] Other questions include provision of equipment, and command-and-control mechanisms, especially within UN headquarters, where deficiencies of this kind have plagued blue-helmet operations of the past. The UN has compiled a database of equipment earmarked from national military inventories to be available for UN disposition. Improved intelligence-sharing with the UN is under discussion. The United States now regularly provides selected satellite photography to UN agencies.

These reforms attempt to place more and better policy options in the hands of what is somewhat grandly described as the international community. Grim-faced ambassadors glimpsed striding in and out of the security council, tight-lipped officials poring over satellite imagery, war planes standing fuelled on the runway, carrier battle groups patrolling offshore—all these images give a comforting sense to TV audiences at home that something is being done.

But what, if any, substance lies behind this busy exterior? Are there any real prospects that these actions will further the American interest in consolidating world peace?

We have our doubts—for one reason in particular. Those who have followed our logic so far will understand that we have a generic reservation about the use of traditional high intensity force against these non–state-on-state problems. If, as the Russian experience in Chechnya makes all too vividly clear, national governments experience enormous difficulty in making these tactics work in their own unilateral operations, there is no reason to suppose that re-badging and re-helmeting soldiers in the garb of global or supraregional organizations will do any better.

More specifically, new proposals for what is known as preventive or proactive diplomacy tend to perpetuate bad habits through which, defying the laws of political gravity, local quarrels devolve upwards and outward for solution. The Security Council has lost its aura as the ultimate international arbiter of war and peace and become instead, an "ongoing task force on global security."[5] To make a not-too-absurd analogy, it is as though all disputes between residential neighbors were immediately referred straight to the Supreme Court, rather than going through the lower court system. Dysfunctional overload would be the inevitable result.[6]

We rather like the opposite tack—to look for ways to enhance local responsibility and accountability. We think these will both work better and keep the United States out of the line of fire. Recent events show that those standing outside the immediate perimeter of a quarrel tend to respond inadequately, with insufficient local knowledge, and with far too short an attention span. As the belated formation of the Bosnia Contact Group between the United States, Russia, and the European Union demonstrates, outsiders have to consume precious energy and time in developing mechanisms to coordinate their policies. They may even take actions that make things worse and then, despairing of improving the situation—as happened in Somalia—abruptly abandon their enterprise, their mission half-finished. The result is that international intervention acquires a bad name. Through inappropriate action, the international measures become enfeebled and anarchy refills the vacuum.[7]

International intervention—as long as it is conducted at the *appropriate level*—has a valuable place in international relations. We want therefore to ensure that it does not become so discredited that it is abandoned altogether, leaving behind a huge hole in the world's ability to police itself. But, if international intervention is to work, we need to be aware of its inherent shortcomings. One of these is that, when wrongly applied, it tends to ignore what John Chipman, director of studies at the International Institute for Strategic Studies (IISS) in London, calls "parochialism."[8] He points out that international operations tend to develop their own internal logic that often may have little to do with the problem or operations they are intended to remedy. An indiscreet British officer argued as much when speaking in favor of NATO bombing in Bosnia: "Frankly, I don't care very much what happens in Yugoslavia. But I care a hell of a lot what happens to NATO."[9] In other words, much of the pressure for NATO involvement in that conflict derived as much from an institutional need to prove the alliance's "indispensability" as from a rational calculation of how NATO's capabilities might best apply to local conditions.[10]

The contrast between the internal logic of the international community and what best suits the particular crisis brings up an important point. In his 1992 paper, *Agenda for Peace*, UN Secretary General Boutros Boutros-Ghali advocated early international intervention to head off international or intranational conflicts.[11] On the American side, officials such as Jenonne Walker, senior director for Europe in the National Security Council from 1992–94, have echoed his call, as have others in the international community.[12] The usual analogy is to "fire fighting"—put out a brush fire before it turns into a conflagration and you save yourself a lot of trouble. This sounds like common sense—a stitch in time saves nine—but let us apply it to the real world.

In Yugoslavia, early intervention, let us say in late 1991 or early 1992—that is, at any time before the bestiality of ethnic cleansing became the dominant issue—would surely have been synonymous with an effort to maintain the integrity of the Yugoslav federation as it then was. This was reflected in the public statements of American officials of the day such as Secretary of State James Baker; it would also have accorded with the Helsinki accords of the Conference on Security and Cooperation in Europe and the UN Charter on the nonforceful changing of established state boundaries.[13] Most important of all, it would have been conceived as an essential complement to wider western attempts to slow down the looming disintegration of the Soviet Union. In short, the purpose of intervention might well have been conceived as a last play to preserve the Yugoslav federal government—perhaps exactly the opposite of what local circumstances then required, or permitted.

So, early intervention only assumes cogency in retro-

spect, when the returns of history are in. In a secret briefing given to journalists in 1940, Josef Goebbels, the future
Nazi propaganda chief, said that "they could have arrested
a couple of us in 1925 and that would have been that, the
end."[14] Knowing what we now know about Hitler's intentions, we wonder how we could have missed this trick.
But the point is that we didn't know. As late as 1931, the
German President Paul von Hindenberg dismissed Hitler
as "this Bohemian corporal" whose maximum career expectation, in his view, was postmaster-general.[15]

Let us submit ourselves to a simple real-life test. Bas-
ing ourselves on our present knowledge, can we identify
the latent crises about which our colleagues in the year
2000 will chide us for not taking action now—in the mid-
1990s? When we put this question to an experienced Western intelligence official, he conjectured that action today to
assuage the grievances of Hungarian minorities in Eastern
Europe would lie at the top of his list. To take other plau-
sible (if, at present, highly speculative) examples: Should
we have taken a closer interest in the unrest in Mexico's
Chiapas province before it spread north in 1996 and sent
millions of refugees across the Rio Grande? Should the
CIA have taken early action to frustrate the election of
Vladimir Zhirinovsky as Russian president, so that he
could never have ordered the reconquest of the Baltic republics, as he did in 1998? If we had fortified the Spratly
Islands in 1997, would this have deterred the Chinese invasion of 1999? And why didn't we sort out the tiresome
Ngorno Karabakh problem, which, as we all know, erupted
on New Year's Day 2000 into war between Turkey and
Iran, dragging in NATO as well?

Absurd scenarios? Perhaps—or at least when based on
what we know today. But you can be sure that, looking
back from the year 2000, we will kick ourselves for missing what will by then be obvious telltale signs that should
have enabled us to head off the problems that will plague
us at the century's turn—perhaps something akin to one
of the above possibilities, possibly something entirely unexpected.

Another difficulty exists for many enthusiasts of international intervention. Participants in local disputes possess a much longer attention span than outsiders. The horrific slaughter in Rwanda has roots much deeper than appreciated by those who glibly advocate Western armed intervention there.[16] As we see in Somalia, the warlords stay in business long after the reluctant outside warriors have departed. In Yugoslavia, historians had pointed to five centuries of (relative) ethnic harmony in Bosnia under successive centralized, authoritarian governments by the Austrians, Ottomans, or Tito. The eruption of civil war only eighteen months after the collapse of the centralized rule highlighted the skin-deep nature of this peace and illustrates another fallacy in the concept of early intervention. What does early mean in a conflict in which some of the basic divisions started with the tenth century split in Christianity? The resulting disaster since 1992 should teach us all a lesson about the long-term futility of seeking to defy parochial conditions.

It would be foolhardy to claim that we have a solution to this problem, but we would like to put forward an alternative perspective—an approach based not on the rickety *deus ex machina* of international intervention, but instead on a series of loose structures that might act as fire doors. As conflagrations erupted, these structures would function like the barriers of a chicane at a speed track, angled buffers that slow down an out-of-control car. Structures like these in a conceptual sense could increase the chances that local problems *stay local* as long as possible—in sharp contrast to the present system, in which local conflicts accelerate unstoppably up the international power escalator, reaching the UN Security Council's docket well before anyone has learned the correct spelling of towns like Srebrenica. In chapter 10, we look at some of the structural implications of localism. For the time being, however, we need to come to intellectual terms with this concept.

What, exactly, do we mean by fire doors or chicanes? In the heyday of mutually assured destruction, the strategic thinker Morton Kaplan devised a concept called the "unit veto system."[17] In plain English, this means the ability of each and every state to deter or neutralize an attack from any other state. Kaplan was thinking of a (theoretical) world where all states possessed nuclear weapons and thus would live, as he thought, in the same state of equilibrium to each other as the United States and Soviet Union. We have no wish to buy into arcane nuclear logic, but we do want to draw on his concept of unit deterrence because it implies a primary responsibility for conflict avoidance at the lowest level of the international system. By an arrangement of successive balances of power at the local and regional levels, the Security Council would become involved only as a last resort. The European Union has even coined an ugly new word—subsidiarity—for this concept of local responsibility.

If this seems improbable, let us remind ourselves that international security today too often rests on sets of promises that have lost their reliability. Even in the case of supposedly cast-iron treaties like NATO, doubt has arisen about the central premise—that an attack on one member counts as an attack on all. During the Gulf War, Germany openly questioned whether an Iraqi attack on Turkey would suffice to trigger an alliance reaction.[18] It is hardly surprising therefore that threats of coercive action by the major powers *outside* the primary arena of these structures lack credibility—Serb generals have been able to exploit this distance to their advantage, while the Haitian commanders discovered that the United States was a little too close for their comfort.

The problem is that both promises and threats lie too far away from the focus, and locus, of action. They are made by people with good intentions but little stake in carrying them out. Their local knowledge is often lamentably deficient; what expertise on local languages and clan systems did American and UN commanders have in Somalia? Virtually none. Asked about North Korean nuclear intentions in 1994, an American expert on Asian affairs replied, "the fact of the matter is that we don't really un-

derstand what they are doing."[19] Even the recent outpouring of books on the Yugoslav tragedy reveals diametrically contradictory accounts of Balkan history. If the
experts cannot agree, what hope is there for outside politicians?[20]

By contrast to the distant omnipotence of the formal
UN structure, our proposal directs attention toward a network of local arrangements, designed to put into the driving seat those who have a permanent interest in finding
(and living with) a solution. Many such collaborative organizations already exist. They range from continent-wide
bodies, such as the Organization of American States (OAS)
and the Conference on Security and Co-operation in Europe (CSCE—from 1995 reborn as the Organization for Security and Cooperation in Europe, OSCE), to regional
agencies such as the Economic Community of West African States (ECOWAS), the Gulf Cooperation Council
(GCC), the South Asian Association for Regional Cooperation (SAARC), and the Association of South East Asian
Nations (ASEAN). Other organizations, such as the Argen-
tina-Brazil Agency for Accounting and Control of Nuclear
Materials (ABACC) have come into being for specific regional purposes, in this case the verification of nuclear
programs.[21]

Some are more effective than others, but the present
tendency among American policymakers to attempt to order the world according to a single universalist standard
from the Security Council in New York, or from NATO
headquarters in Brussels, stunts their effectiveness and
devalues their potential utility. Rather than draining vitality from regional or local organizations, greater effort
should be made to strengthen them. With a greater sense
of purpose they can slowly turn into a type of primary
care network for local conflicts.

The ASEAN model may have wider application. It
replaced an organization, the South East Asia Treaty
Organization (SEATO), which had become moribund
because of uncertainties over France and Britain's
commitment to it. In its short existence since 1967, ASEAN

has defused (or at least deferred) some tensions among its six members; it has also entered into formal dialogue relationships with nonregional entities like the European Union or with powers such as China, Russia, and the United States. As such, ASEAN makes it more likely that local problems remain local, but has the potential to appeal for outside help, if—but only if—local resources prove inadequate. It required a UN transitional arrangement to end the Cambodian crisis in 1991, for example; to solve the dispute required American, Australian, French, and Japanese diplomatic pressure and collaboration.

The 1993–94 dispute over North Korea's nuclear program illustrates the point. The three countries most affected by the North Korean actions remain South Korea, China, and Japan, in descending order. All three countries oppose the program; all three can bring considerable pressure to bear. China, for example, remains North Korea's main supplier of oil; it has every reason to fear that a North Korean nuclear weapons program might trigger a copycat reaction from Japan. For its part, Japan has every interest in heading off a nuclear-capable and eventually reunified Korea.

Yet, despite the presence of these diplomatic opportunities, the United States insisted on grabbing the lead at the starting gun, relegating the countries most affected by the issue to the status of auxiliary players in an American scripted drama that at one point seemed headed for war. Only as the North Korean problem unfolded did American policymakers begin to see benefit in a more inclusionary approach, which did produce the October 1994 agreement.

No one would deny that the United States has legitimate concerns about the North Korean program. In terms of its potential leverage, however, its position at the height of the crisis in mid-1994 was objectively weaker than that of North Korea's regional neighbors. Unlike China, the United States had no common border over which trade and essential supplies flow; unlike Japan, it had no expatriate North Korean community remitting enormous sums of foreign currency to Pyongyang. Unlike South Korea, the

United States saw no advantage in investing large sums of money in the north against likely future reunification. The only real American advantage lay in an all-or-nothing use of military force, a sword blunt and so double-edged that it looked inherently implausible—despite periodic war-talk from, and posturing by, administration figures during 1994. In the North Korean dispute, locating the focus of policy in Washington actually robbed the United States of maneuverability. This was manifested in the agreement that was eventually struck in October 1994, in which the United States was forced to give ground on the important issue of securing a full account of North Korea's past history of plutonium extraction.

Islamic fundamentalism presents another case study. Here the United States has adopted a containment policy against Iran. Does this policy enjoy wide popular support among Iran's neighbors—analogous to the Cold War containment policy's popularity in Europe—or does the policy really have a lot more to do with protecting Israel and with shoring up pro-Western Gulf states? The latter motivations are in their own contexts eminently sensible, but if they are allowed to drive policy on exogenous matters, then, once again, American high-profile tactics look faulty. They result in giving another propaganda weapon to those who wish to exploit local grievances to excite popular resentment against the interfering Infidels. All across the Maghreb, for example, extremist parties are feeding on this passion to make advances into normally moderate groups.[22]

One of the more hackneyed, if accurate, sayings in American public life is that "all politics is local." Political Action Committees and interests groups have taken this adage to heart, striving to influence members of congress through grass-roots movements in their districts. Washington politicians have also learned this lesson and seek to work within the constraints imposed by their constituents. They know they commit political suicide by riding into town and announcing that they have a made-in-Washington solution for local grievances.

Yet this wisdom, somehow, stops at the water's edge. American leaders have few scruples about trying to have their own way abroad, and on their own terms, rather than making the most of local conditions to achieve their objectives. Forgetting their domestic experience, they baldly assert that global considerations (as defined in Washington) take precedence over parochial concerns.

American diplomacy will be better served if policymakers start to discard their telescope and pick up their magnifying glasses. The former instrument brings distant events much closer, to be sure, but it puts only a few salient features on the lens—a distortion that breeds errors of oversimplification. One example may be found in Bosnia where, as James Gow of King's College, London points out, much fighting occurs to settle purely local scores.[23] The situation there is far more complex than the simple tale of Serbian aggression against passive Bosnian victims.

What is needed, therefore, is a type of site inspection using a microscope to identify the microbes and germs. In the former Soviet Republic of Georgia, for example, a magnifying glass enables us to see that the contest is less straightforward than a simple struggle conveyed in CNN snapshots between plucky Georgian self-determination and bear-like Russian irredentism.

Overarching systems based on global or supraregional organizations cannot of themselves provide a panacea for America's diplomatic future. Global strategists or politicians may argue in the opposite direction. For the former, the potential for parachuting visiting firemen into a conflict has the virtues of neatness, simplicity, and order. When the latter look for an anonymous bureaucracy (on which they can dump unwanted or awkward problems), organizations like the UN can offer some attraction.

The trouble is, this approach works no better in the international arena than it does at home. People do not like being bossed around. Nor do they welcome the arrogance of outsiders who think they can run things a lot better than the locals can. So the locals do what locals have always done; in this era, they hunker down while the first and second waves of aircraft drop their bombs. Then they reemerge from their bunkers, with their will to resist much stiffened as a result.

In contrast to glamorous but ineffectual supra-nationalism, a strengthening of local and regional institutions offers more promise. This approach—what Brian Hocking has called "localizing foreign policy"—corresponds conceptually to the best of domestic political practice within the United States.[24] In the domestic arena, the thrust of American political empowerment devolves decision making to individuals, in the expectation that they know best how to calculate their own interests. (In response, for example, to the continuing decline in the performance of American schools, jurisdictions, such as Chicago, have devolved control away from citywide boards down to individual, locally elected school governing bodies. Welfare reform—specifically, the 1995 Personal Responsibility Act— is headed in the same direction. Vanderbilt University Professor Virginia Abernethy makes the same point about the supremacy of local factors in regard to population control. We don't want to stretch the analogies too far, but there is merit in them.)[25]

To be sure, a localized foreign policy will be messier than conventional diplomacy. It will take place in dreary town halls rather than in the international salons. Central governments, even in the crisis zones, will not always be in charge. Nor will Americans necessarily dominate the proceedings, or necessarily even be present.

For better or worse, this is the sort of politics that functioning decentralized states practice, whether they are the United States, Switzerland, or Germany.[26] It does not always work; occasionally in American history, massive interventions by the federal government have been necessary. We realize that decentralizing politics in the international arena does not guarantee a low-key result. The Gulf War provides an example of a strong regional bully utterly overwhelming the capacity of the relevant regional structure, the Gulf Cooperation Council. But this and other examples are exceptions, we believe; they are the crisis cases that make it up to the Supreme Court represented by the UN Security Council. Even so, this does not imply that all cases must make the same journey.

Even allowing for differences between federal systems and the far more lawless world of sovereign states, many of the same considerations apply. The IMF cannot dictate whether the Russian peasant should experience shock, or therapy, or both. Any number of White House ceremonies cannot compel Israeli West Bank settlers and Palestinian inhabitants of Jericho to come to peace with one another. But the job just might get done by initiatives like the Hebrew University of Jerusalem's Project on Prenegotiation, which brings together Arabs and Jews to discuss practical subjects such as health care and sanitation.[27] Many luminaries of the Western foreign policy firmament tried, and failed, to bring about a reconciliation between South Africa's Nelson Mandela and Chief Mangosuthu Buthelezi. But Washington Okumu, a Kenyan politician, achieved this feat—once Henry Kissinger and Lord Peter Carrington had departed South Africa after doing their best.[28] A reminder that so often the dynamics of peace remain primarily, obdurately local.

Our approach really comes down to a question of emphasis. We do not exclude United States intervention at the global level—indeed, in the right circumstances, we welcome it. But we argue that it should take place only after a succession of intermediary stages have been tried, a process that can proceed very rapidly indeed, as the Gulf crisis showed. The United States has a strong interest in international peace, but just as equally wants to avoid getting dragged into each and every threat to meet this goal. It also wishes to ensure that when American intervention takes place, it does so effectively, for the right reasons, and with full public support.

To return to the fire-fighting analogy, it's a bit like the reformed fire control policy operating in our National Parks. The federal government sets an overall policy of how fires should be fought, contained, or allowed to burn.

But the real work, and the decision making, takes place at the local depots.

The regional organizations of today's world of international politics have the potential to function in a similar way—groups like ASEAN, WEU, ECOWAS, SAARC, and others still on the drawing board such as an embryonic Northeast Asian Pact (if the Canadians and Koreans have their way) or an African peacekeeping force (as encouraged by the French).[29] The United States should place its energies *in these sorts of regional organizations*, rather than channelling all the ills of the world into an omnivorous Security Council, using instruments of force that have lost much, if not all, of their applicability.

To those who counter that this means we are abandoning wider American interests, we insist that we aim for exactly the opposite result. By bringing appropriate instruments to bear, we advance American interests. In the next chapter we take a closer look at defining these interests.

Chapter 8

Whose National
Interest Is It?

The business of Government is to organize
the common interest against the special interests.
— Woodrow Wilson, 1912

In a 1992 speech, former Secretary of State Henry Kissinger faulted George Bush for justifying the Gulf War in terms of international ideals rather than national self-interest.[1] He need entertain no such reservations about Bush's successor. When President Bill Clinton took to the radio on February 19, 1994 to explain the NATO decision to enforce the no-fly zone over Bosnia, references to interests peppered his talk like grapeshot:

> . . . in this crisis our nation has distinct interests. We have an *interest* in helping to prevent this from becoming a broader European conflict. . . . We have an *interest* in showing that NATO remains a credible force for peace in the post–Cold War era. We have an *interest* in helping to stem the destablizing flow of refugees. . . . And we clearly have a humanitarian *interest* in helping

101

to stop the strangulation of Sarajevo. . . . America's *interests* . . . demand our active involvement in the search for a solution.[2]

The president's speech writers in this instance clearly had studied in the school of diplomatic analysis typified by the late Philip Habib, councillor to the State Department in the 1970s. In a 1990 essay about the Middle East, he wrote,

> The United States has had important and long-standing *interests* in the Middle East . . . the United States has a vital *interest* in maintaining free access to the extensive oil reserves . . . the United States has a direct *interest* in nurturing cooperative relations with friendly moderate Arab states . . . in the widest sense the *interests* of the United States are linked directly to political, economic, and strategic developments in the area.[3]

Between just these two statements, we find ten mentions of the magic word *interests* in fewer than one hundred and fifty words. In fact, despite Kissinger's periodic assertion that American foreign policy has based itself more on idealist than on materialist considerations, we think we have shown, in chapter 5, that policy based on material national interest is far more typical of American experience—despite the ubiquitous moralistic gift wrappings of this century.

Going right back to the source, we find George Washington saying that "it is vain to expect governments to act continuously on any other ground than national interest."[4] And Charles Evans Hughes, secretary of state under Presidents Harding and Coolidge, also nailed down the point: "Foreign policies are not built upon abstractions," he said. "They are the result of practical conceptions of national interest."[5] Even Woodrow Wilson, hailed as the founding father of the humanitarian school of diplomacy, never strayed far from hard-headed calculation of national interest, or rights, as he called them. Whatever his rhetoric about making the world safe for democracy, the proximate cause that triggered Wilson's agreement to enter World War I came from German violation of American neutral rights on the high seas. Opposition to Germany's attempt at strategic denial became, once again, the classic cause for intervention.[6]

These statements achieve a rather high coincidence with European perceptions of diplomatic purpose. In 1848, British Foreign Secretary Lord Palmerston put it this way: "We have no eternal allies and we have no perpetual enemies. Our interests are eternal and perpetual, and these interests it is our duty to follow." A century later, Charles de Gaulle of France said that "nations have no feelings, only interests."[7]

These resonant invocations of national interest—both ancient and modern—have today come to form an almost obligatory voiceover for any serious American foreign policy pronouncement. Like the Fife and Drum Corps at receptions on the White House South Lawn, no one quite remembers why they are there but they sound important and, thus, they raise the general tone of the occasion. In the same way, national interest forms an indispensable, if often unclear, adornment of any statesman's rhetoric.

But what do interests mean? The trouble is, the Cold War made things too easy. The debate that settled the broad lines of the containment policy also preempted discussion of what is, and what is not, in the national interest. The famous 1948 National Security Council memorandum (NSC 68) defined the Cold War containment policy as follows:

> Our free society, confronted by a threat to its basic values naturally will take such action, including the use of military force, as may be required to protect these values. The integrity of this system will not be jeopardized by any measures, covert or overt, violent or nonviolent, which serves the purposes of frustrating the Kremlin's design.[8]

Under this all-embracing rubric, national interest became readily understandable as whatever it took to survive in the battle with an omnipresent Soviet enemy. In
pursuit of this goal, the American people showed themselves ready to rally to the banner of national interest in
support of practically any foreign activity—even in exotic
locations such as Angola or Grenada. The national interest
thus became an objective, self-evident truth. It didn't need
to be discussed or analyzed. It was just there. As the
threat to national survival has receded since the late 1980s,
so the national interest has lost its familiar, hard-edged
definition. In the run-up to the Gulf War, George Bush
found himself experimenting with a number of per-
mutations of the national interest—jobs, oil, resistance to
aggression, support for democracy, the sanctity of international law, American credibility as world leader—before
winning popular support for his actions.[9]

Today, a whole new industry has sprung up to retool
the national interest. Individuals and institutions of all persuasions assert the continuing primacy of national interest, whatever it might be. The Carnegie Endowment
intones that "America will vigorously pursue its self interest,"[10] while the more agenda-driven, conservative Heritage Foundation says the government must "above all else
defend the rights and interests of the American people."[11]
If only it were this easy! Unfortunately, exhaling the words
national interest does not, of itself, tell us what to do,
when, where, or why. As the historian Arthur Schlesinger,
Jr., has commented, national interest is not a "self-execut-
ing formula." The writer Barbara Tuchman has devoted a
whole book to showing how nations frequently act against
their interests.[12]

Let us look, for example, at the Heritage Foundation's
list of fundamental goals it sees as America's interests:

• to protect and defend the territorial integrity of
  the United States;

• to preserve and defend the liberty, democracy,

and economic system of the United States from foreign threats;

- to promote the long-term material prosperity of the American people.

Few people would quarrel with these. Yet the list is merely generic. Change the name of the mentioned country and a citizen of Costa Rica, Denmark, or Thailand just as comfortably could embrace these statements. In short, nothing specifically *American* is breathed by these and other guidelines. But whenever someone tries to add American beef to these bones, controversy immediately erupts.

The spread of putative national interests currently on offer in Washington really does stagger the imagination. Like a cruise ship's luncheon buffet, the selection overwhelms our palate. We hardly know where to begin. Those who prefer red meat can locate America's interests in guaranteeing access to Middle East oil fields or Atlantic sea lanes; those inclined to vegetarian taste find equally vital interests in threatened rain forests on the upper Orinoco River.

Does this mean that we overestimate national interest as a factor in foreign policy thinking? Not at all. In this book, we try to sound a warning bell whenever pundits or bureaucrats seem to be acting in cozy unanimity. But on this point—of the central importance of national interest—they are absolutely right. If we assume that government policy has—or at least *ought* to have—a purpose (rather than randomly reacting to unpredictable events), then this requires points of reference around which debate can cohere. In a democratic society, the public welfare—*salus populi*—normally represents this objective. As applied to foreign policy, welfare takes on a material expression and becomes the national interest, representing what the Brookings Institution way back in 1954 called the "general and continuing ends for which a nation acts."[13]

But the transition from theory to practical policy proves

devilishly hard. The Cold War approach rested on looking around the world, noting where Communist powers were interfering with the right to life, liberty, or the pursuit of happiness, and then unfurling the banner of national interest. Naturally enough, we all grew accustomed to this relatively uncomplicated approach; at least it set a stable course for the ship of state even if sometimes the sailing— as in Vietnam or Lebanon—occasionally became hellishly rough.

As officials, analysts, and commentators struggle to define national interest in today's world, one common denominator has emerged—that national interest exists as an objective thing discoverable by diligent searching, rather like a beachcomber with a metal detector moving along foreign shores. The venerable statesman George Kennan talks of national interest as something independent from "domestic-political realities."[14] This echoes views by the patriarch of national interest theoreticians, Hans Morgenthau. He described "the national interest of great powers and in good measure the methods by which it is to be secured" as "impervious to ideological and institutional change."[15]

As we noted about the Heritage Foundation's list of interests, we certainly accept that national interest rests on a core of fundamental verities. But we depart from most orthodoxy in how we derive specific guidance from the general principles. We have argued throughout this book that foreign policy cannot be effectively executed without reconnecting the leadership and the broader citizenry. Judged against this standard, many of these checklists of national interests produced by the administration and foreign policy institutions continue to seem disconnected from the broad constituency—in whose name they are invoked.

A surer way of establishing a sustainable definition for national interest may be in treating it less as a response to an external event and more as a sort of shorthand for a people's accumulated values, culture, and history. As Julien Benda cautioned in 1928, "how commonly men let themselves be killed on account of some wound to their pride, and how infrequently for some infraction of their interest."[16] In the case of the United States, we referred earlier to an 'historical memory' of foreign affairs from which a public consensus (or lack of it) for foreign engagements has emerged. "Home is where one starts from," wrote T. S. Eliot in *The Four Quartets*; if the national interest is really to reflect the welfare of the American people (in whose name this banner is raised), the best starting point lies here, in the United States.[17]

Seen in this light, the search for national interest ceases to be an insider's pedagogical performance (in which experts stride to the lectern and instruct the nation on what it must and must not do). In the place of dogma, the national interest emerges from a reflective process. This historical memory is based around broad instincts in a geographical place, and not on narrow knowledge. It coexists beside (but cannot be subsumed within) vital statistics of world resource locations, details of transpacific and transatlantic shipping tonnage, and variations in internationalist theory.

In the place of resource-driven conceptions of interest lie vaguer but less one-dimensional images of American interaction with the outside world. These images arise from a nation founded as a refuge from foreign turmoil, yet still capable of titanic intervention in conflicts abroad. They stem from a sense of high moral vocation, balanced by a cautious reluctance to incur costs in terms of American lives. One instinct, of generosity, opposes another—the feeling that foreigners have for too long had it too easy at American expense. Other images also compete—of a country capable of rapid and decisive action, yet intolerant of drawn-out engagements; of pride in economic success tempered by apprehension over rising foreign competitiveness.

Delving into these instincts, it becomes apparent that making laundry lists of interests that stretch from Abkhazia to Zaire do not correspond to popular sentiments. If Americans were able to stay out of World War I until 1917, and World War II until 1941, Americans can certainly resist the attraction of fresh commitments in the former Soviet republics of Georgia and Estonia. In fact, the whole approach of devising detailed lists, sub-paragraph by sub-paragraph, has little relevance. Top-down affirmation that this or that policy objective constitutes a national interest does not bring with it any guarantee of popular support.

It is not a mystic dodge to assert that the custody of national interest resides, ultimately, within popular sentiment. But foreign policy does not stand in some simplistic relationship with what, and *only what*, public opinion says it is. Nor is some romantic nineteenth-century folk consciousness a guide to getting the United States through to the next century. In chapter 11, we discuss the vital ingredients of leadership and education that indispensably can help Americans make up their minds. We are not talking here of moods and swings of popular opinion in response to media stimulation. Rational foreign policy cannot result from thumbs up or thumbs down gestures from crowds in Roman amphitheaters.

But public opinion matters. Mightily. As Oxford Professor Michael Howard has observed in a gentle refutation of Kissinger's power politics interpretation of national interest, what may have worked for the absolutist monarchies served by Cardinal Richelieu or Count von Metternich won't do the job in today's democracies.[18] However, when grounded in popular sentiments accumulated and adapted over the length of American history, our search for an effective foreign policy can truly begin.

By this, we do not mean usurpation of control of day-to-day policy processes by "The People" via electronic, town-hall-style popular referenda. We simply mean that policy that strays from the collective consciousness cannot be sustained over the long run. To deny this, as do—at least implicitly—so many partisans of the conventional objective interpretation of national interest, pushes the country into a series of perpetual false starts, of which Somalia amounts to one mild example.

The approach we are sketching in this book seeks to

avoid being prescriptive or didactic. In chapter 13, however, we presume to offer an overview of where, in practical terms, our concept of national interest is headed. This does *not* amount to a taxonomy of American interests in Asia, Europe, Latin America, or elsewhere. But it does explain American reluctance to become involved in Bosnia, hesitancy over financial aid to Russia, enthusiasm for a tough approach to Japan.

Chapter 9

Sovereignty and the Coming International Structures

The American people don't give a hoot
in a rain barrel who controls North China.
— *The Philadelphia Record*, 1938

On many occasions in this book, we have alluded to instances where policy actions have gone awry because of a
failure to update or, if necessary, to discard our Cold War
attitudes. A particular source of confusion at this juncture
of our history lies in the proliferation of separate nation-
states of vastly differing size, age, and legitimacy.

As Michael Mandelbaum points out in a *Foreign Policy*
article of June 1994, the Cold War and the decolonization
process have left behind a legal framework that treats all
these new sovereignties as equal, with border changes regarded as anathema.[1] And although we have no wish to
challenge formal structures, it strikes us as bad *politics* to
treat this concept seriously as a useable map of the world
out there. If we are now reverting to a world of contending states, then we must prepare ourselves for more frequent shifts in national sovereignty. We must become more

111

skillful in managing transitions and less dogmatically tied to the territorial *status quo*. In retrospect, the key Western mistake over Bosnia may appear to lie in an overrigid adherence to borders long after it became apparent that they no longer enjoyed local support.[2]

We need, in short, to see that modern states are not alike. At one level we know that Kiribati has not the faintest chance of being treated in the same way as China, but we need to develop a carefully differentiated approach as between fragile sovereignties and clusters of power and interests of true importance to the United States. As we noted, a bit smugly perhaps, the end of the Cold War spawned tremendous optimism in the United States. Many believed in a supposed clean sweep of democracy throughout the world. The triumphant victory of liberal market capitalism was trumpeted; so was an end to history itself—in the sense of epochal confrontations between ideologies or systems.

As for the international structures put in place after the 1944 Bretton Woods conference—the IMF, the World Bank system, and the GATT among others—victory also seemed complete. The former Eastern bloc nations clamored to join the IMF and to truly monetize their economies (in the sense of achieving real prices). A look at what World Bank lending had achieved in China led to illusions that democratization could not be far behind the de-communizing stampede.

As the years move on since 1989, however, the record is more mixed: the terrible reversal and renewed civil war in Angola after the UN supervised elections, the unraveling of the former Yugoslavia, and the impotence of small UN contingents there. Consider the paralyzed situations in Kashmir and Cyprus, or the helplessness of UN units in the 1994 Rwandan tribal war—these raise new doubts over existing or potential peace-keeping. The efficacy of Security Council resolutions has become more problematic: consider Libyan intransigence, still firm at the time of this writing, to defy UN sanctions rather than surrender people allegedly responsible for destroying Pan American flight 007 over Scotland in 1989.

Over-optimistic expectations for the UN have worsened the problem. Oxford International Relations Professor Adam Roberts notes that:

> in the post–Cold War world, the inherent limitations of the UN have been made cruelly evident by the collapse of various states into warring fiefdoms. In international relations, as in so many aspects of human affairs, people spend much energy trying to avert the last disaster. The disaster prompting the UN system was the Second World War.[3]

"The UN," Roberts adds, "was designed to cope with the problem of the excessively well-organized and aggressive state, exemplified by Nazi Germany. It was not designed to cope with the problem of communal conflict with which it is now confronted in so many countries, including Somalia and Yugoslavia. These cases present a form of anarchy, *within as much as between states*, which throws up special and difficult challenges."

As Roberts and others note, the international system is breaking down faster in areas *outside* Western Europe. To be sure, since 1989 the reordering of the political map from the Rhine to the Urals has been breathtaking. But much more redrawing of the map lies ahead in regions we still describe, for want of a better word, as the Third World. Scores of sovereignties were created during the time of hurried abandonment we now call the era of decolonization. By comparison to the tectonic fault lines beneath these flimsy creations, Europe's fissures look like simple hairline fractures.

Many ethnic wars wear the guise of nation-state rivalry, notably in the Balkans but also in Africa and the Caucasus. For example, does the sovereign state of Serbia now wage a covert war against the sovereign state of Bosnia-Herzegovina? Is this conflict even remotely analogous to the war between Argentina and Britain over the Falklands in 1982? It strains reality to describe this brutal, communal war in such a state-on-state way, yet support for Bosnia has been marshalled in the United States on that basis: that it is a recognized member of the UN entitled to the full panoply of protection implied by that status.

The European nation-state model still inspires Third World sovereignties, but the experiment rests on shaky ground. The raising at UN headquarters of more than 130 new flags since 1946 results from the uneasy interplay of two ideas. The first is the notion that separate peoples require a separate state. The second is the insistence, *by colonizer and colonized alike*, that frontiers positioned during the comparatively short era of direct administrative imperialism should remain fixed and unchanging (according to the doctrine of *uti possidetis*), to mark the boundaries of the new national identities. Even if these new boundaries were drawn (as was usually the case) with little heed to achieving much coincidence of ethnicity and territory, they have come to be seen as eternally fixed. This problem bedevils the once settled boundaries of eastern Europe and inside the former Soviet Union.

The Third World's malaise poses difficult challenges to American optimism. They will take many guises—migratory pressure, frustrated humanitarian impulses, or, increasingly, desperate efforts to find workable models of economic and political development. Already, scores of UN member states scarcely resemble functioning entities at all; denied their former transitory importance on the Cold War chessboard, the lack of even elementary governance in portions of Africa, Asia, the Caribbean, southeastern Europe, and the Caucasus dooms many of these so-called states to teeter perpetually on the brink of dismemberment.

John Chipman, director of studies at the International Institute for Strategic Studies (IISS) in London, noted in 1992 how "superpower participation in often arcane Third World disputes, (and the sometimes fanciful strategic calculations that accompanied justifications for intervention) lent international prestige to otherwise parochial quarrels. States in the developing world often lamented the participation of the superpowers in regional conflict, [but] they also appreciated that they could draw advantages from this competition."[4]

Without this external buttressing, these rickety states must rely on something they have never had: primal loyalty from those they govern and popular legitimacy. Sadly, the lack of political cohesion in the Third World has become glaring at a moment when, without the Great Game with the Soviets, Americans have scant reason to care. A sense of fatalism already pervades the Western world about the frequency of man-made calamities.

Let's bring these gloomy concepts down to some specific issues that carry a humanitarian or environmental guise. Floods from deforested Himalayan slopes slice too often through India and Bangladesh, where population pressures mount steadily but bilateral border squabbling impedes joint river and flood control management. In 1991, a single flash flood on the heavily logged Philippine island of Leyte took more lives in one night than the total toll of victims killed during that country's 20-year-old Communist insurgency. Government-induced famine in the Sudan (where the Khartoum regime wars incessantly against tribes in the south of the country) prompts no outrage in the West, partly because of a serve-them-right attitude after Sudan's support for Saddam Hussein and Islamic terrorism.

Certain regions of the world have become the preserve of bandits or gruesome insurgencies, such as in India's northeast, much of equatorial Africa, the gray zones of Croatia, Romania, and Russia's fringes, or the Andean Latin American countries. Is it any wonder that compassion fatigue, though hardly an attitude meriting praise, seems an inevitable response? In the years ahead, therefore, one trend seems to be the disintegration of what now seems an artificial building block fashioned in the salad days of decolonization. An immediate consequence for U.S. policy is that some sovereignties are already slipping out of sight, as in Azerbaijan, Liberia, Somalia, and Zaire.

Despite the initial optimism, the future may not belong

to an embryonic global identity—framed by holistic photographs of our planet from space and unified by the telecommunications revolution. Disruption aplenty may continue. The decay within, and partial collapse of, the international system results in entire regions slipping into a gray zone, which prompts the fix-it lobby in Washington to recommend putting resources and effort into rebuilding failed states. Judging by reactions to the Somalia debacle, Americans distrust these ideas.

Surveying these struggling countries, observers like Adam Roberts say that "in many such cases in the past, a traditional if flawed remedy was the intervention of external powers, even the imposition of colonial rule."[5] That option cuts little ice today. "When the United States, and the UN, intervened in Somalia in 1992-93," Roberts adds, "they were willing to use force but deeply reluctant to set up any administration, and they spoke of getting out even before they had got in." As more states fail in the years ahead, it is hard to see how Americans will accept burdening themselves with the Sisyphean labor needed to keep these territories, literally, on the map.

This is not to say that we should simply pull up the drawbridge and forget the Third World. We cannot, and it will not let us. But America must not almost casually meddle in these conflicts (as in Somalia) nor mistakenly intervene for reasons that apply in the First World but tend to cause counterproductive misery elsewhere. With national boundaries less firmly fixed, it makes no sense for the UN Security Council to pass resolutions condemning transgressions of these blurred lines as international aggression.

If this looks like a darkly lit world, it need not be. Even during the height of the Cold War, the major areas of importance to the United States remained at the center of things—Europe and Northeast Asia. Today, the United States and East Asia possess together over 60 percent of the world's GNP. Include Western Europe and the figure rises to 85 percent. In our view the appropriate place to find key national interests is in the interstices of economic and political influence in Europe, Northeast and East Asia, and in neighboring Mexico and Canada. The deeply intertwined security and economic reasons for this prioritization are not hard to find. Judging by their repeated highlighting of economic security as their first concern, most Americans feel the same way.

Turning first to Europe, here the omens for the United States shine bright—if only policy makers can avoid distractions of secondary importance. Western Europe represents one of the few areas with which the United States enjoys both excellent relations and a trade surplus. Such challenges as exist to this happy state of affairs lie partly in American reluctance to untie Europe's Cold War apron strings and to allow Europe to assume full responsibility for policing its own conflicts.

The primary task for the United States in Europe is to allow the European Union (EU) to mature into full independence. Most American politicians profess little conceptual problem with this, but execution sometimes has been patchy, particularly with regard to defense issues.[6] The EU is struggling to develop a defense identity that will be separate, but not separable from, the United States. On the premise that devolution of responsibility down to local structures is to be welcomed, the greater European willingness to assume responsibility for its own defense represents a pure gain for the United States.

As the post World War II American defense relationship with Western Europe wanes—a process that will take decades to complete—new possibilities of co-operation with Europe present themselves, primarily in the economic and commercial spheres. Here, both sides will need to watch that competitive juices do not fracture an essentially harmonious relationship. Institutional links across the Atlantic are less well developed on nondefense matters, an omission needing redress. Most of all, an integrated approach is needed to ensure that small but contentious disputes do not spill over beyond their natural borders.[7]

The EU will also play a major role as a global partner of the United States on such transnational issues as terrorism and nuclear proliferation. This is not to say that the two sides will always see eye to eye—the EU has less emotional commitment to Israel, for example—but overall it will be much in the American interest to encourage full EU participation in world affairs and also to listen to EU views in areas where the Europeans have valuable knowledge.

Eastern Europe stands with one foot in the EU camp and one foot uneasily emerging from a type of Third World vulnerability. The removal of the Soviet lid has allowed the ethnic cauldron to boil over into war in many locations, or to smolder suspiciously in others. The temptation for the United States will be to treat each and every outbreak of these tensions as a major crisis—or as evidence that Russia is auditioning for a reprise of its former predatory role.[8] If the Yugoslav tragedy has anything to teach us, it is surely that the soaring rhetoric of outrage may assuage consciences, but does nothing to prevent bloodshed or bring about reconciliation.

The way forward here is for the United States to encourage continent-wide integration, not necessarily with the EU but within some looser framework. The OSCE (formerly CSCE), to which all the countries of Eastern and Western Europe together with the United States and Canada belong, offers itself as a possible building block.

With its skills in mediation and conflict prevention, the OSCE also offers the best (or least bad) prospect for mediating the leftover disputes from the dissolution of the Soviet Union. The concept of fragile sovereignties applies with particular force to these disputes. Ukraine and Russia, for example, seem condemned to dance a complex and doleful routine with one another. Whatever the outcome, American reaction should pay careful heed to historical relationships; an overly legal approach may produce a bad political result. Not every dispute between Russia and its neighbors presages the return of the Soviet bear.[9]

In Asia, the likelihood for more formal intergovernmental machinery remains dim. The lack of clear divisions during the Cold War era, bolstered by overt military alliances, always made for more diplomatic fluidity in Asia than in Europe. The only regional grouping in Asia that has been able to promote real cohesiveness between its members remains the ASEAN. South Asia's consultative grouping known by its acronym SAARC remains hostage to quarreling between India and Pakistan.

ASEAN survives largely because of a happy coincidence of interest among the elites governing its six member countries—Brunei, Indonesia, Malaysia, the Philippines, Singapore and Thailand. It could do little, however, to avert destabilization flowing from badly handled political succession in, say, Indonesia, and it has yet to show it is capable of managing transition to a freer regional trading economy—as promised for the early years of the twenty-first century in an ASEAN free trade agreement signed in 1991.

Meanwhile, China's implacable sense of hegemonic superiority in the South, Southeast, and East Asian arenas portends a more difficult period, as it becomes richer, especially if Beijing continues to modernize its naval forces. The prospect of a nuclear-capable, unified Korea also gives Japan periodic heart failure, which is a major but often overlooked portion of the North Korean jigsaw puzzle. India's attempts to win acquiescence from Pakistan to Indian predominance in South Asia has many years to run, attendant with dangers arising from what has become one of the world's most intractable problems since the end of World War II—Kashmir.

In Asia, therefore, the looser and vulnerable structures of today, and the territorial shape of the countries participating haphazardly in them, looks set to stay in place. Despite occasional fears about the possible disintegration of some multiethnic states in the region—India, Indonesia, and even China—this will probably not occur. On the other hand, political transitions in some countries, notably Thailand, may not be smooth, but our sense is that national boundaries for many years to come will continue to look pretty much as they do now.

Despite the progress of the Asia Pacific Economic Cooperation (APEC) initiative since 1989, the chances do not favor APEC's rapid transformation from a loose trade and finance talking shop to a place where difficult regional political problems are brokered multilaterally. For the foreseeable future, therefore, the United States will gain most leverage in its Asian agenda via the bilateral approach, but will also need to work with a shifting coalition of regional forces. To take two examples: Southeast Asia shares many of the American concerns about market access to Japan. And Japan and China harbor as much if not more detestation for North Korea's nuclear program as does the United States. The moral is that we should be willing to work with regional partners whenever appropriate.

Perhaps it is America's globalism, perhaps it is her continental size; whatever the reason, U.S. leadership must come to grips with the complicated political processes occurring in Canada and Mexico. In each, the old ways of doing business are simply not up to the mark.

In Mexico, the abrupt and politically clever disruption by southern Mexican insurgents of the North American Free Trade Agreement's (NAFTA's) commencement day on January 1, 1994, caught Mexico's leaders by surprise. The assassination two months later of the ruling party's presidential candidate also damaged (despite the smoothly run and fairly counted August 1994 presidential election) Mexico's self-image and caused misgivings about ever achieving a true North American polity. The demographics, political and financial volatility, and migratory pressure from Mexico all impact on American politics—often in parochial ways as with California's passage of Proposition 187 to clamp down on illegal immigrants, but sometimes in dramatic ways such as the collapse of the *peso* at the end of 1994 that necessitated an immediate U.S. assistance program for Mexico far in excess of anything contemplated (or politically sustainable) for Russia. Yet many U.S. corporations plan on resuscitating their profitability through future exploitation of the Mexican consumer and labor markets.[10]

In Canada, the minuet between the federal authority in

Ottawa and the separatist momentum in Quebec has about played itself out. Rather as a tap dancer who too often comes too close to the stage's edge, the chances for one disastrous misstep grow ever stronger. Some day (and it might be sooner than we think following the Parti Québecois' electoral victory in September 1994), a break-up of the Canadian federation may occur—in the relaxed manner, we all hope, of the 1992 divorce between the Czechs and Slovaks. The readjustment of the English-speaking provinces within a North American economy and (increasingly) a common polity could place enormous new strains on our own, already highly stressed constitutional political arrangements.[11] Heretical though it sounds, the United States could itself be heading next century toward rewriting its own constitution, prompted by a need to fashion a North American polity to absorb a rump or bi-furcated Canada and an errant Québec. Many reasons ac-count for the singular inability of the federal government in Washington to devise solutions to the problems that preoccupy Americans. Among them, the continuing viabil-ity of our own eighteenth century arrangements may in-creasing come into question. Pressures within Canada and Mexico could be a catalyst for a fundamental reordering of our continent.

These are truly momentous foreign policy issues. Or are they domestic? The truth is, our ties with Canada and Mexico fit both categories. Both countries figure, impor-tantly, in helping bolster the U.S. economic strength and bargaining position in power games with East Asia and Europe. They also reach deep into American domestic con-cerns, such as agriculture, immigration, trade, or health care systems. Throughout most of this century, the United States has fixed its foreign policy eyes on distant horizons. The Cold War made intrinsically unimportant countries temporarily important. During this time, Canada and, to a lesser extent, Mexico were taken for granted as foreign policy actors.

In the wake of shifting public opinion, which we will be examining in the next chapter, foreign policy is coming

home—quite literally in some areas. The mayor of Baltimore, for example, has offered his city as a possible loca-
tion for research into AIDS by the United States Agency
for International Development, an agency within the State
Department that traditionally has worked exclusively in
the Third World. Because of this homecoming trend,
Mexico and Canada rise steadily up the scale of importance. No foreign country has Mexico's power to alter
American demographics, nor Canada's to affect employment levels in the border states.

This North American work will be unglamorous, much
less exciting than pushing geopolitical chessmen across the
global board. Yet, just as the relationship between France
and Germany determines the fate of Europe, so the North
American triangular axis will control the fate of the Western Hemisphere and the people who live in it.

Chapter 10

Toward a New
Public Consensus

To hell with public opinion.
— anonymous State Department
official, 1994

When opening this book, we made a declaration of faith
in what we called an American historical memory of foreign affairs. The end of the Cold War exposed a troubling
disjunction between much of the foreign policy leadership
and the wider citizenry in which this memory is deposited. In its turn, this disjunction significantly impairs the
nation's attempts to fashion a coherent foreign policy for
the post–Cold War era. The solution to this problem lies
in paying more attention to popular sentiments in favor of
caution, prudence, and husbanding resources.

This appeal for a tighter connection between the citizenry and the stewards of state runs directly counter to
classic foreign policy prescriptions. A century and a half
ago, Alexis de Tocqueville observed that,

It is in foreign relations that the executive power of a
nation finds occasion to exert its skill and its strength.

If the existence of the American Union were perpetually threatened, if its chief interests were in daily connection with those of other powerful nations, the
executive would assume an increased importance.[1]

De Tocqueville also posed an indirect challenge to our
notion of historical memory. Echoing Jefferson's assertion
that "we must consider each generation as a distinct nation," he wrote that "In America, society seems to live
from hand to mouth."[2] That is, he thought that democratic
societies would recreate themselves with each generation,
with the result that there might be even less likelihood of
the emergence of the enduring instincts that play a crucial
role in the formulation of effective foreign policy.

Our thesis looks even more vulnerable when we reflect
that, on the whole, Americans pay little day-to-day attention to foreign policy. In January 1994, a mortar shell landing in the Sarajevo market place galvanized NATO into its
first ever offensive action. But, even then, the opinion polls
showed fewer than 1 percent of respondents were following events in Bosnia closely, whereas nearly 50 percent
were following the soap-opera ructions then occurring inside the American Olympic women's figure skating squad.[3]

Apart from invidious comparisons like these, foreign
policy knowledge remains low. We are not talking about
detailed descriptions of the Transcaucasus region's ethnic
composition (which even baffles experts) but about basic
information. For example, how many Americans can name
three, or even two, presidents in Latin America? How
many readers of this book can do this? Yet this region is
habitually described as America's backyard.[4]

All in all, therefore, Americans seem to confirm Hans
Morgenthau's observation that "the rational requirements
of good foreign policy cannot from the outset count upon
the support of a public opinion whose preferences are
emotional rather than rational."[5] They seem neither especially interested in nor well prepared for the interlocutor's
role we describe for them. So why do want to drag them
into matters they seem willing enough to leave to others?
Why not leave things to the professionals?

At one level, we agree with these rejoinders but, taken as a whole, they seem to miss a crucial political fact. Since 1989, Americans have delivered at least two devastating reminders of their central place in both strategic and tactical aspects of foreign policy. In 1992, conventional wisdom sees George Bush losing the presidency because of his perceived indifference to the economy. But his defeat can also be seen as a decision to evict him because he offered voters *more* foreign policy than they wanted.

This represents an important judgment on the strategic value Americans attached then—and continue to attach— to foreign policy. To be frank, that value is not very high. Hence the reason why so many well-researched proposals for the post–Cold War agenda languish unread, and unfunded, in the archives.

The second reminder came in 1993. The same voters prompted a rushed withdrawal from Mogadishu because policy there demanded higher costs than they were prepared to pay. The tactical reverberations of this judgment continue to impair the administration's ability to deploy force overseas—whether in Bosnia or in preparation for a war against North Korea—or to go beyond a minimalist mission in Haiti.[6]

The mundane point is that, in any democratic society, but particularly in the United States, much more goes into the making of effective policy than executive power and professional expertise. At the end of the day, popular judgments count for more than either, which is why Duke University professor Ole Holsti has concluded that in the post–Cold War circumstances public opinion may acquire "added rather than diminished significance."[7] At some juncture, he notes, the foreign policy leadership has to do business with the wider population, ill-informed and inattentive though it may be. In the remainder of this chapter, we seek to discover where the points of intersection may lie.

The relationship between public opinion and the foreign policy leadership is complex. In their illuminating book, *Beyond the Beltway: Engaging the Public in United*

States Foreign Policy, Daniel Yankelovich and I. M. Destler produce a wealth of survey detail demonstrating beyond challenge that, compared to domestic policy, average Americans

> know less about foreign policy, care less, are more vola-
> tile in their views, and base their attitudes more on slo-
> gan-like generalizations (e.g. no more Vietnams) than
> on the specific merits of the case.[8]

This judgment agrees with other findings from the ear-liest days of public opinion polls, which discovered "dark areas of ignorance" in Americans' understanding of foreign affairs.[9] Yankelovich and Destler conclude that "the chal-lenge of engaging the public in foreign policy is formi-dable."

But even professional pollsters find public opinion maddeningly difficult to pin down. Also in *Beyond the Beltway*, Catherine Kelleher of the Brookings Institution produces data from the Chicago Council on Foreign Rela-tions showing that, in 1990, 62 percent of Americans de-clared themselves in favor of an "active foreign policy." This figure was less than ten points lower than the 1956 all-time high for that index and considerably higher than the 54 percent level at the beginning of the Reagan years.[10] She goes on to say that policymakers usually believe them-selves to be under considerable public pressure to do something on issues such as the Iraqi Kurds, starvation in Somalia, and ethnic cleansing in Bosnia. (Whether this pressure actually exits may be doubtful—a paper by a Brit-ish television journalist Nik Gowing presents evidence that people remain much less susceptible than conventional wisdom suggests to the proposition that doing something is the best way to react to TV pictures of outrage abroad).[11] Nonetheless, if this pressure is real, it betokens a more substantial public engagement in foreign affairs.

Herein lies a difficult paradox. In the foreign affairs world, American policy makers appear to be condemned to making decisions on behalf of people who—let's not mince words about the survey results—emerge as igno-rant, disinterested, impulsive, and, to cap things off, ut-terly unashamed to be those things. During the Cold War, foreign affairs experts tried to solve this dilemma by cre-ating a "foreign policy process [that] was relatively closed and substantially insulated from the hurly-burly of domes-tic politics," in the words of Arnold Kanter, under secre-tary of state for political affairs in the Bush administration. During this period Kanter adds that "the public's views were rarely solicited or offered."[12]

It is a central part of our argument that we do not agree either with this characterization of the average American or with this picture of the remoteness between policymakers and the electorate during the Cold War. Americans were pretty firmly engaged in Cold War policy and the foreign policy elite was more mindful of their views than Kanter is ready to admit.

Nonetheless, we take this dilemma very seriously. In earlier chapters, we looked at it under various guises—the gap between resources and aspirations and the disconnect-edness between rhetoric and reality. Unless these holes are plugged, we fear that foreign policy will continue as the faltering creature it has been since 1989.

We address it on three fronts: we want to encourage the public to treat foreign policy with the same familiarity as domestic issues; we want to get away from an opinion poll *du jour* approach to the interpretation of public senti-ment; and we want to see much more vigorous executive leadership.

With regard to the first notion, the familiar adage from the world of development aid says that if you give a man a fish, you feed him for a single meal; but it you teach him to fish, you enable him to provide for himself for a lifetime. The image of the tool kit that we introduced at the beginning of this book accords with this spirit.

Our objective throughout this book centers around this precise concept: to empower our readers in a modest way to come to *their* own conclusions about foreign policy in accordance with *their* priorities rather than as *imposed* by an establishment that has got out of the habit of *listening*. After reading our book, hopefully readers will feel more confident about throwing themselves into the foreign policy debate. Yankelovich describes this as "engaging the public."[13] We agree wholeheartedly. The more innate good sense brought to bear on today's overseas challenges, the better for all of us.

There may be those who cry halt here: how can 'innate good sense' emerge from what surveys show is a manifestly underinformed and undermotivated public? Get real, they say. If foreign policy really is a serious business that extracts serious penalties for mistakes, how can it take account of so flawed a source as public opinion? Should we not simply model our foreign policy arrangements on Plato's *Republic*, by awarding its stewardship to well-qualified guardians standing above the democratic process?

This tussle between elite and popular approaches has long marked foreign policy in this country. In the early nineteenth century, President Andrew Jackson rebuked a professional diplomat with the words that, for better or worse, "Our government, Sir, is founded on the intelligence of the people; it has no other basis; upon their capacity to arrive at right conclusions in regard to measures and in regard to men."[14] Or, as Abraham Lincoln put it more succinctly, "Public opinion in this country is everything."[15]

Part of the difficulty arises from the difficulty in measuring public opinion. The art of opinion polling is better developed in the United States than anywhere else in the world, yet the instances of where politicians misread the polling data occur no more rarely here than elsewhere. A notable recent example lies in George Bush's decision to send troops to Somalia in late 1992—allegedly in response to the public's urging him to do something about the starvation that it had witnessed on television. But when it became apparent after the October 1993 killings in Mogadishu that popular demands to do something did not include support for American combat fatalities, the response from many parts of the foreign policy establishment was not to censure themselves for squandering American lives and public confidence on an ill-considered foreign adventure. Instead, we heard moans about the volatility of public opinion. A Washington pollster even developed a quasi-academic counterattack against the electorate. "Look in the mirror, voters," he declared, "the trouble starts with you."[16] This ingenious argument soon found favor with the Washington establishment, thankful that someone other than itself could be blamed.[17]

The trouble is that those who live by opinion polls will also die by them. (That conclusion may, unnervingly, apply to the Clinton White House, which by mid-1994 had already spent the year's polling budget and was drawing upon the president's foreign travel budget to pay the number-crunchers!) We have quoted opinion survey evidence in this book, but only in relation to broad strategy. Opinion polls neither can nor should provide day-to-day models for effective foreign policy decision-making. Americans hold themselves at too great a distance from the tactical issues for opinion polls to predict reliably what they seek from, say, a renegotiated Non-Proliferation Treaty or the embryonic World Trade Organization.

Further, as everyone knows, the wording of a poll question can decisively affect the response. Whether choosing a desirable foreign policy outcome or indicating a preference for a particular toothpaste, Americans give a range of answers that depends, ultimately, on what they have been asked. Do you want creamy, alluring mint bedazzlement in a toothpaste? Or are you willing to settle for a salt-and-soda solution? No prizes for the most likely answer.

For four decades—a long time by any reckoning—the custodians of American foreign policy became accustomed to selling an easy question: "Do you, or do you not, want to keep a relentless adversary at bay?" With the Soviets obligingly providing irrefutable evidence once a decade for the premise behind this question with invasions in Hungary, Czechoslovakia, and Afghanistan, even the least trained of Pavlov's dogs would have had no trouble in pushing the correct lever.[18]

The questions today are more complex—as inevitably are the answers. In a discussion of public reaction to the United States acting as the world's policeman, Yankelovich demonstrates graphically how radically differing results are obtained depending on whether the question emphasized the going-it-alone (a strong majority against) or the standing-up-for-American interests (an equally strong majority for) aspects of this issue. When, in 1992, the question combined both dimensions ("should the United States share world power or ensure that no one can dominate it?"), opinion split down the middle.[19]

In other words, opinion polls do not provide unambiguous data leading in a straight line to policy decisions. If leaders launch hazardous foreign undertakings on the basis of fleeting poll soundings, they take their fate in their own hands. They cannot turn around and blame the messenger.

Andrew Jackson's remarks about the central importance of public opinion lies behind our concept of the American historical memory discussed in chapter 8. This concept may also have value in transcending a problem inherent in attempts to measure public opinion accurately.

The key point about historical memory is that it has staying power. It smooths out the ups and downs of ephemeral movements in public responses to transient events. The returns are already in. We know, for example, that the British are a martial people, forever celebrating glorious feats of arms at Agincourt, Trafalgar, Waterloo, or El Alamein. The British, therefore, welcome an opportunity to "respond to ancestral voices" summoning them to more glory, whether in the Falklands or Kuwait.[20] In contrast, the American relationship to war is less fond. Sad memories from the Civil War and Vietnam have just as much potency as those of famous victories at San Juan Hill, Iwo Jima, and Omaha Beach. This leads to what University of California Professor Bruce Jentleson has called a "pretty prudent public." Americans, he says, are ready to respond forcefully to direct attacks on the United States, but are much more cautious about accepting the Cold War thesis that American security interests are at risk throughout the world.[21] To relate this back to the American historical memory, ancestral voices here teach that war may sometimes be a doleful necessity when major issues are at stake, but it is not something to be reached for in the normal course of events.

Absent a clear and present danger, a military career has enjoyed little prestige in the United States, while appropriations have—over the long perspective—usually been less than generous. In the 1930s, the American army was smaller than those of Czechoslovakia, Poland, and Romania—let alone those of the major powers. The implication is clear: Leaders need an exceptionally convincing line of argument to take the nation into a drawn-out overseas engagement. The message to those who championed the invasion of Haiti or who advocate similar expeditions to other failed states should be *caveat emptor*.

Lessons in other fields also present themselves. Traditional American reluctance to convey sovereignty to foreign entities—especially those that smack of world government—may be seen in the successful 1920s congressional opposition to the League of Nations. This attitude will resurface in debate over the establishment of the World Trade Organization. On the other side, Japan should understand that the United States has wanted to open Japanese markets for nearly a century and a half. The pressure to do so will continue to be unrelenting.

For Americans as a whole, these deep-seated, long-term notions of what is reasonable and doable take the place of the foreign policy specialists' knowledge and expertise. Lay Americans may not know the difference between an Ustashi and a Chetnik, but they can recognize a no-win situation in Yugoslavia when they see it. Similarly, they do not carry in their heads the fathom depths of the submarine channels between the Pacific landmasses, but woe betide anyone who tries to bar the United States from access to these. Effective foreign policy results from uniting these

two dimensions—gut instincts and specialist expertise—
into a tight yoke. As recent exemplars, we would offer the
administrations of Harry Truman and Ronald Reagan. Going further back, we would make a similar argument for
the mid-nineteenth-century administration of James Polk
and the Continental Congress during the Revolutionary
War.

For the country's foreign policy actors—whether in the
White House, on Capitol Hill, on the op-ed pages, or in
the foundations and endowments—no surefire shortcut
exists to put them in touch with these long-term trends.
One way may lie in a serious study of American history,
another consists of an ability to look beyond the insistent
pressures of particular interest groups. Add to these a lot
of travel outside the Beltway—for more than a hurried
speech, an appearance at yet another local fundraiser, or
cocooned conference—in other words to reach beyond the
circles of the political activists with their telephone banks,
mass mailings, and machine-generated facsimile messages.[22]

Such efforts will lay the groundwork for establishing a
new consensus over foreign policy. In the absence of a
major external threat, it cannot be expected that any consensus will fall effortlessly into place. Major obstacles lie
in wait.

For those interested in reading or writing about foreign
affairs, it is a terribly difficult time. In newspapers as well
as on the TV screen, the foreign news hole is constantly
narrowing. For example, advertising managers in *USA Today*, as in most other newspapers, poach on the foreign
news page. Each foreign story put in place on the page
represents a hard-fought victory, with foreign editors often
going to enormous lengths to justify placement. Usually,
placement depends on the paper keeping up with a running story. It is even harder to offer something which,
from the editorial standpoint, comes out of nowhere.

So it is with the evening TV news, still a mainstay of
the overall declining network viewership and, thus, a vehicle that programmers, advertisers, and image-makers all

struggle to subvert to their own purposes. Soft features, violence, and human interest stories conspire to crowd out solid, workaday features that may come in from afar. There is no longer even the pretense of having an encyclopedic eye locked on the world. Honorable exceptions exist, but foreign news, as Mort Rosenblum's amusing *Who Stole the News?* makes clear, suffers even more from shortened attention spans and tight budgets.[23]

It's not that the airwaves and wire services lack for copy. Far from it. Editors are overwhelmed by material, from which they must pick and choose for an ever diminishing number of column inches, domestic or foreign. Another problem intersects with this trend. As the attention spans narrow, the audience for longer (in words or in air time) features that would give some texture to foreign events dwindles to those who really, in their work and in their material livelihoods, need it.

In sum, foreign news has become a niche or boutique market. For foreign affairs coverage, it has become a place in which—as one of us discovered—a journal with a circulation of just 75,000 subscribers can, because of those subscribers' institutional, corporate and private wealth, generate good advertising revenues. But—and this is the point—journals like this (we have in mind the Dow Jones Asia flagship, the *Far Eastern Economic Review*) remain a special vehicle.

Another aspect of the contemporary world needs elaboration. The simultaneous nature of reporting, so much a matter of awe during the 1991 Gulf War and the attempted Moscow coup later that year, have put reflective journalists into an impossible situation. On the one hand, operating budgets forbid much permanent stationing of correspondents abroad by the American networks, in even the major cities of Asia and Europe—for evidence of this listen or watch the foreign news for a week and note the proliferation of British and Australian accents. Few of those reporting foreign news have the local contextual feel therefore; even if they do, editors back home let precious little reportage of that nature into the final product.

On the other hand, there is no time to learn on the ground, even if a parachute journalist gets there: Once the bird (that is, the satellite on which some time is booked) has reached the necessary place in the sky, another on-the-ground story is beamed up, and then goes out via CNN or, condensed again, goes out via the networks' news programs.

This is a recipe for chronic, debilitating ignorance. Yet the forces of market competition, alternate entertainment options, and diminishing budgetary resources to keep people ready in the field all conspire gravely to inhibit our understanding of world events. What we lose most of all in America is the ability to triangulate overseas events—to have the sense that someone, other than the United States, is involved, concerned, and has a view. In Europe, in Asia, in the Middle East, triangulation of foreign news occurs almost without a thought. It is normal, it is essential to know variably what the British, French, Germans, Russians, or Japanese think about an issue or event. In the United States, it is not. How to rectify this deficiency belongs to another book, but the need is clear.[24]

The information base does not look good. The narrowing news hole, the diminishing attention span, the plethora of publications and TV cable channels, the instantaneous nature of reporting, the budget cuts, the inexperience of younger but usefully cheaper foreign news people, the triumph of images over written words—all these retard understanding. In Washington in April 1994 to introduce his book on diplomacy, Henry Kissinger said that most of the Cold War had been an era in which people still read rather than reacted to pictures. "A person who reads," Kissinger intoned, "works with concepts while one who watches pictures sees images, and therefore relies on impressions." [25]

So what, if anything, is to be done? How are we to counter these media trends which, unchecked, may do much to impede an effective foreign policy performance? Ultimately, little can happen until the notion that instinctive caution is not cowardice or wimpishness begins to receive a more informed press. We must regain the bigger backdrop or the urgent, pressing images of distress will

crowd out the leitmotif. To get there will take the forceful
impact of a hundred thousand essays like this one to make
even a hint of difference. The foreign policy establishment
and the forty years of Cold War result in tremendous pressure for presidents to be assertive. But a start can be made
to show, within resource limitations and the competitive
scramble, how it is still possible to see foreign affairs in
their irritating yet inevitable complexity.

Lest we sound too despondent about building *any* consensus, let us look further at that magic word—leadership.
There is no magic in the commodity itself; as Garry Wills
writes in the April 1994 *Atlantic Monthly*, leadership involves a deft balancing act between what the populace will
bear, plus adroit appeals and some fancy footwork to
make them feel good about themselves and accept the inevitable.[26]

"Americans like to lead," opines the *Economist*, "but
they also dislike paying the price. When it comes to seeing the need for foreign adventures, there is often a huge
gap between the professional foreign-policy makers and
the more reluctant American public."[27] The president's burden is "to close that gap," the same article says, quoting
Lee Hamilton, then chairman of the House Foreign Affairs
Committee. Effective foreign policy combines popular instincts and specialist expertise, the latter deriving from
classified information in a way that does not apply in the
domestic sphere. These two dimensions come together
uniquely in the office of the president.

For some years, observers have noted a decline in modern presidential authority. (Another way of putting is that
the modern presidency is reverting to the more modest
role envisioned for it by the framers of the constitution.)
Godfrey Hodgson's 1980 book *All Things to All Men: The
False Promise of the Modern American Presidency* and Charles
O. Jones' 1994 study *The Presidency in a Separated System*
both provide convincing evidence that the president's
power falls far short of public perceptions.[28] Many conservative thinkers regard this as a benevolent development in
tune with constitutional first principles.[29]

Nonetheless, in the foreign affairs field, no substitute is available for the primary task of, first, articulating, and, second, implementing policy. Additionally, the considerable communications resources available to any president allow the holder of that office to muster support for policies as no one else can. The president does not have to go all out on foreign policy—far from it, but if he does not treat it seriously, no one else will.

It won't be easy or part-time work, however. Foreign policy is a major subject in its own right; it can't be dealt with adequately if squeezed between forums on health care or welfare reform. Continuity of presidential attention must occur. If, for whatever reason, it does not, it is better to drop issues altogether rather than raise them in half-hearted fashion. For example, preparations for the Gulf War monopolized President Bush's attention, thus making it clear that he was deadly serious. In contrast, in mid-1994 when the media was earnestly discussing the potential for war in Korea, President Clinton continued to devote himself to the domestic agenda. There was nothing wrong with that, but it did signal that, with the commander in chief's attention turned to other matters, war was unlikely.

What follows is a modest how-to checklist for the foreign policy leadership when aiming to garner a new consensus about America's interests in the world. It is applicable to both speech writers and secretaries of state, to national security advisers and other executive branch freelancers.

- Don't think that discussion of national interests is out of place at a time when no foreign dispute, humanitarian disaster, or refugee crisis looms. Talk up your willingness to keep America (and Americans) out of foreign entanglements even when kissing babies, cutting shopping mall opening ceremony ribbons, or throwing out the opening pitch in a new baseball season.

• When you do this, speak about your restraint and describe America's readiness to help other regions to sort out *their* problems. Play down the expectation, at home and abroad, that America's good offices (or paratroopers) are perpetually on call to sort out other people's problems. Yet set out (it helps to do so from time to time) the areas and/ or issues for which America *will* fight, if necessary.

• Stress that a disposition to stand back is not inimical to a determination to get involved when necessary. The two go hand in hand. With less distraction in trivial foreign matters, the chances of moving (as we did in the 1990–91 Gulf crisis) for the right reasons are correspondingly improved. Tell your listeners that, Henry Kissinger and other diplomatic historians notwithstanding, such an approach does *not* mean involving America in some nineteenth century, balance-of-power role, with those disagreeable mechanistic connotations and amoral calculations.

• Keep to your story. If you make speeches purporting to set out the guidelines of your foreign policy, stick to them or explain, when necessary, the finer print and show how one instance fits into your road map while another does not. Voters like the appearance of continuity—that is, of sober continuity, not a continuity of fiascoes. Foreigners like continuity also, and will get the message if you stick by your words and involve America only when you *must*—that is, when the stakes have become directly imperilling *and* when intermediate steps have been tried and failed. When you do get involved, do so emphatically: no cutting and running as in Somalia, please. No huff and puff followed by long silences.

- Lastly, stay in the leadership mode. Foreign policy does not lend itself to public musing. Unlike domestic affairs, the executive holds the high cards in foreign policy, possessing much more information than Congress and the general public. Take advantage of this to lead your listeners through the options. Do not discuss each foreign policy problem as if it always involves basic fundamentals. This will make you seem out of your depth and erode your credibility.

These points seem easy. They are not. But nor are they facile snippets of advice. At the end of the day, after all the incessant uproar from Washington, the trillions of words gushing out prior, during, and after a major foreign affairs controversy—at the end of all this it comes down to a few men and women in positions of power asking themselves if it is better to do something, or do nothing.

The biggest problem for Americans now is that they don't really believe that doing something in so many of the post–Cold War flash points is either (a) necessary or (b) likely to change matters much. They do know, at the core of their memory as a people, that a middle course must be steered between telling the world to "go to hell," and telling themselves to "go anywhere" in support of some foreign crusade.

Safe navigation between these two courses will require reform of government structures—one of the key political issues for the coming years. Our proposals would both shrink the size of government and make it more effective.

Chapter 11

Changing the Bureaucracy

Tweedledum and Tweedledee
set out to have a battle,
Said Tweedledum to Tweedledee
You've spoilt my nice new rattle.

— Lewis Carroll,
Through the Looking Glass

Readers beware: This chapter makes depressing reading, not because of any lack of enthusiasm for the topic on our part, nor because a desperate need for reform of the foreign policy bureaucracy does not exist. No, the depression results instead from that familiar feeling that the path winds ever upwards when it comes to hacking away at government underbrush. Yet the task must be undertaken. Unlike other activities that have succumbed unnecessarily to government's gaping maw, foreign policy cannot be contracted out, cannot be privatized. As this book appears, confidence in government has reached an all-time low.[1] The hard fact remains, however, that government and foreign policy go hand in hand. To make foreign policy better, we must make government better.

The Clinton administration's slogan, Reinventing Government, appeared as a way to galvanize modern bureaucrats into a frenzy of rediscovery and renewed ardor to serve the public. Adopting the opposite approach, the Republicans achieved dramatic electoral gains in 1994 by promising to take a chain saw to government. Are we showing our age too much if we say, we've seen it all before? When we were both diplomats, various review committees sought alternately to reinvigorate or to cut back the British and New Zealand Diplomatic Services.[2] The publication of their massive tomes of cross-referenced recommendations encountered a reception not unlike that which the Chinese have been meting out to barbarian invaders for millennia: inscrutable smiling followed by relentless assimilation. In the bureaucratic world, nothing seems to change, or, if it does, it does so at an agonizingly slow pace.

So what's the point? Simply this: Foreign policy does not derive from ideas alone. It is made by people in bureaucratic structures. Within these systems lie opportunities for leadership. Because we argue for a greater influence in foreign policy for public sentiment, the structures that give direction and respond to these outside influences need to be as effective, as focused, and as tightly drawn as possible.

Many familiar reasons explain the slow pace of bureaucratic reform. Bureaucracies remain entrenched, while pressure for reform rises and ebbs like a tidal flow. The bureaucracy enjoys powerful patrons; even legislators who ostensibly criticize it will genuflect in front of it when tax dollars for their district are at stake. Witness the extreme difficulty all administrations encounter when trying to cut back spending on military infrastructure. Political appointees come and go too frequently to leave a mark. But, the permanent structures of government survive, enjoying the last laugh.

Or do they? John Maynard Keynes once remarked that "the power of vested interests is vastly exaggerated, compared to the gradual encroachment of ideas."[3] Bureaucracies can and do evolve; changes can occur. In this spirit we offer two ideas for change. They represent only the tip of an enormous iceberg of possible suggestions. Low-key in scope, they may possess the potential to effect over time a significant improvement in the way American foreign policy is conducted.

The conduct of foreign policy, as it is practiced almost universally throughout the world, clashes head-on with some basic premises of American government. The foreign policy of foreigners has an elitist and confidential air, intolerant of parliamentary oversight—in short, it reeks of qualities that run counter to the notions of good government that Americans imbibe with their mother's milk. This sets up a conflict between overseas practice (where the making of foreign policy in both advanced democracies and authoritarian backwaters is the pursuit of the privileged few) and American insistence on the observation of democratic processes.

Let us look briefly at British experience—not as a model for serious emulation but as an exemplar of foreign practice. In Britain, alumni of two universities, Oxford and Cambridge, fill the top echelons of the their diplomatic service; parliamentary oversight of the intelligence and security services encounters resistance at every turn; the foreign secretary hires and fires ambassadors without any need for time-consuming hearings before legislators; under the Intelligence Services Act of 1994 release of official papers dealing with foreign relations can be denied *indefinitely* if the government deems them to be sensitive—which it often does: British officials regularly visit Washington to ensure that documents relating to British interests are not released under the United States Freedom of Information Act. Most of all, the foreign secretary acts as lord of his domain. So long as he keeps the prime minister happy, his writ is absolute; he brooks no interference from cabinet colleagues, let alone from parliamentary backbenchers. The same pattern repeats itself in many other countries, sometimes, as in France, with an even more pronounced elitist ethos.

Practices on these lines would provoke a constitutional crisis in the United States, going as they do to the heart of the doctrine of separation of powers and the concentration of foreign policy influence in the hands of the president. Yet these practices remain absolutely typical of other foreign policy structures overseas, even in those not modeled on the Westminster models. In Britain's case, they bring the country regular accolades—whether deserved or not— as possessing the best diplomatic service in the world. They supposedly enable the United Kingdom, in the words of a British foreign minister to "punch above its weight,"[4] or to play a weak hand with such finesse that—even though Britain has long fallen below Italy in economic performance—it still universally ranks among the great powers.

American commentators occasionally feel the attractions of this and other foreign systems of foreign policy making. In 1955, former President Herbert Hoover recommended creating a second vice president's post to take charge of foreign affairs. In 1960, Nelson and David Rockefeller proposed the creation of a First Secretary to exercise preeminence over foreign policy.[5]

More recently, in his book, *Around the Cragged Hill*, George Kennan, perhaps the most distinguished American diplomat of his time, has endorsed the idea that the secretary of state be given a preeminent position behind the president.[6] He would like to see his new Super Secretary exercise "supervision over the [operations] of any and all other offices of the executive branch in the country's external relationships." To counter congressional pressure, which he dismisses as driven by lobbyists mindful only of the "parochial interests of minorities," Kennan recommends the creation of a European-style nonpolitical permanent under secretary of state post. The incumbent would hold "before the eyes of the president and secretary of state the interests of the country as a whole, as distinct from those of individual groups or bodies of its citizenry."[7]

Kennan further bemoans the influx of non-Foreign Service outsiders into American missions abroad. He describes

them as "the children of other and more influential departments of government" and sees them as "less able" than
Foreign Service regulars.[8] Other commentators, such as Jim
Hoagland of the *Washington Post*, join Kennan in hoping
that politics can be taken out of foreign policy. Echoing
Arthur Schlesinger, Jr's 1974 book *The Imperial Presidency*,
Hoagland advises the president to adopt an "imperial"
style and rule the foreign policy domain in the absolutist
manner of an imperial viceroy.[9]

Most foreigners will voice exactly these sentiments.
Both of us have endured litanies of complaint from foreign
officials visiting Washington. In their efforts to obtain a
reading on American foreign policy they traipsed through
the labyrinthine corridors of the State Department, the
National Security Council, the Pentagon, the CIA, and the
Senate and House office buildings. They waited in upscale
anterooms of lawyer lobbyists, think-tanks, CNN, and the
national networks. And the product of these labors? A cas-
cading cacophony of opinion as the competing branches of
government championed their own viewpoints. "In my
country," our visitors would say, "one call to one official
would tell me all I needed to know about government
policy."

While that might be stretching the truth a little, the
critics have their logic. But so what? Americans reject government by permanent civil servants. They do not believe
that a group of unelected officials enjoys a superior access
to wisdom in the manner of Presbyterian elders or Episco-
palian vestrymen. Americans want government to be conducted in the light of day—"open covenants, openly
arrived at," in the words of Woodrow Wilson.

Thus an American foreign policy Tower of Babel will
continue. The debate will continue to be noisy, ill-focused,
and competitive. Congress will eternally seek to clip the
president's wings; the president will complain that the
Congress is making his job impossible. The executive
branch departments will continue their turf wars, each acting out its ordained bureaucratic persona: The Pentagon
will garner resources for tomorrow's (theoretical) major

war while avoiding today's (actual) petty conflicts. The CIA will continue looking for storms ahead. The State Department forever will be sighting that old, elusive silver lining, light at the end of the tunnel, or some other optimistic cliché *du jour*.[10] As Yale Professor David Mayhew's book, *Divided We Govern*, makes clear, this is the way that the American government does business—and, according to Mayhew, does it reasonably well.[11]

Nevertheless, the voices of reform have a point. American foreign policy needs more focus on what is truly important. It needs more ability to bring American influence to bear and more sense that someone accountable is in charge. In chapter 4, we made the point that injection of moral principle into American foreign policy means that this country is not competing on a level diplomatic playing field with other countries. We are making a similar point here. Abroad, the foreign policy process has much more focus than it has in the United States. We need to recognize this, not necessarily as a handicap but certainly as a major difference. Only thus can American diplomacy do its job of protecting national welfare. So, how can we achieve this reform without interfering with American political mores?

It would be possible to run through a list of improvements to bring about these objectives—subparagraph this and subparagraph that, each with positive and negative points. The resultant discussion would bore any reader into a stupor. We will therefore confine ourselves to two suggestions—the abolition of the NSC and a reduction of political patronage for top foreign affairs posts. Both these proposals have their technical aspects but, if implemented, they would deliver two key results: more accountability and more impact.

The National Security Council
—Time To Say Adieu?

The American bureaucratic system operates for better or worse on duplication. In a huge country this is perhaps unsurprising. A vast number of interest groups and constituencies demand to be heard.

In foreign affairs, the president takes the lead but presides over many discontented and warring semi-kingdoms. The Pentagon will never entrust its foreign policy prognoses to the State Department. Nor will it allow the CIA to take care of its intelligence requirements. The Pentagon wants its own foreign policy and intelligence specialists, and it will continue to express its own independent views on these subjects.

Foreigners are thus often at a loss to know who speaks for the American government. Does the White House, the Pentagon, or the State Department have the last word on policy toward Bosnia?[12] The Russians have complained that Treasury economists advise them to reduce their budget deficit by keeping customs dues high; meanwhile, industry specialists from the Commerce Department urge them to lift tariffs to encourage imports of much needed foreign equipment. Other examples abound. The State Department even runs its own intelligence staff that regularly takes public issue with CIA assessments! Or consider the congressional habit of passing nonbinding resolutions (a difficult concept for foreigners brought up in parliamentary systems to comprehend) that conflict with the administration's foreign policy positions.[13]

Overseas visitors, who innocently believe that the United States as the arch exponent of private enterprise represents a haven of limited government and minimal regulation, are often amazed at the number of individual officials and departments they need to deal with. From personal experience, we know that, depending on minute differences in the nature of the enquiry, the appropriate antinarcotics authority in Miami, Florida, could be any one of twenty federal agencies and/or four state or county agencies.

In an interplanetary voyage across space where spare parts are difficult to come by, such redundancy would have its place. In terms of foreign policy structure, however, proliferation on this scale weakens American coherence and credibility. In the Somalia intervention, for example, no one seemed to be in charge in Washington. With regard to Bosnia, in one week in April 1994, three top officials—the secretaries of state and defense and the national security adviser—all made mutually conflicting statements about the bombing of a particular city.[14] In August 1994, the White House chief of staff spoke of a possible naval blockade of Cuba, only to be disavowed by the State Department an hour later. There was similar confusion in the run up to the intervention in Haiti.[15] Improving accountability and responsibility lies at the heart of our proposal.

Like most official bodies, the National Security Council (NSC) came into this world to meet a felt need. Recognizing the potential for bureaucratic civil war, President Truman created the NSC in 1947 so that he could receive advice with respect to the integration of domestic, foreign, and military policies. Given the character of the American government—*Pandamonium*, Daniel Patrick Moynihan's description of the global ethnic maelstrom, comes to mind[16] —the NSC seemed to answer a very specific need.

Reviews of the NSC's performance since then produce a mixed report card, however. In the early days of its existence, when the nation was mobilizing for what was to become the total commitment to the Cold War, the NSC functioned well as a loose coordinating body, putting the final imprimatur on the contours of the anti-Soviet containment policy and the establishment of the postwar alliance system.

If only it had stopped there. But during Henry Kissinger's tenure, the NSC began to assume the mystique of department in its own right. This was quite contrary to earlier practice; Truman and Acheson had treated it quite casually; Eisenhower sometimes disregarded it altogether; Kennedy and Johnson barely used the NSC machinery at all.

After Nixon's presidency, the NSC continued to grow under Carter, whose National Security Adviser Zbigniew Brzezinski further consolidated the NSC's policy-making functions, and under Reagan (when the 1987 Tower Commission report on the Iran-Contra affair actually increased its authority).[17] It also grew under Bush to a point where it now it represents a foreign policy entity in its own right. NSC personnel count as White House staff not subject to Senate confirmation, unlike officials in other departments of government. This staff acts as principals, rather than as adjunct staff, in the foreign policy debate—a development directly contrary to the spirit of the 1945 Eberstadt report that proposed the creation of the NSC as a nonexecutive body.[18]

During the period of post–World War II American economic dominance, this development may not have mattered much. But, in an age of reduced resources and a towering need for efficiency, American diplomacy needs to shift some way toward the more efficient, simpler foreign models. Even if, for constitutional reasons, the American system cannot aspire to these streamlined versions, this should not rule out all change.

In the contemporary foreign affairs of the United States, the State Department nominally enjoys sole authority under the president. But it is now always in danger of being second-guessed and not always by the NSC. Defense Secretary William Perry, for example, even obtained a full-page encomium in the *Economist* for his performance as *ersatz* secretary of state.[19]

In each new administration the secretary of state and the president's special adviser for national security affairs (to quote the full title of the senior NSC official below the president who is the NSC head) have to reinvent the foreign policy wheel. They waste much time in learning the steps of an ill-choreographed *pas de deux* called who is closest to the president?[20] People chuckle when Henry Kissinger relates that only during a brief period in 1973 (when he held both the NSC and State Department jobs simultaneously) have the White House and State Department been truly at one. But this is really no way to run a modern railroad.

Something has to give. Our suggestion therefore comes down to a modest proposal: either abolish the NSC or, more realistically, boil it down until it resembles the small office of a *chef du cabinet*, coordinating and summarizing incoming advice from the various departments that contribute to foreign policy questions.

Obviously, this change will not of itself solve all American foreign policy problems. But it may improve understanding of who carries the responsibility. In 1960 Robert Lovett, a deputy secretary of defense under Truman, testified before the Senate that, "the authority of the individual executive must be restored. . . . Committees cannot effectively replace the decision making powers of the individuals who take the oath of office nor can committees provide the essential tasks of leadership."[21] With the demise of the single unifying threat from abroad (the countering of which provided the reason for the NSC's creation), it may be more productive to let the machinery work as designed, without the NSC gatekeeping.

Reducing Patronage

Apart from some Central and South American countries and a few Asian countries like Indonesia, the American system of appointing a large number of non-Foreign Service officers to high-level diplomatic posts both at home and abroad finds few followers. By itself this pattern doesn't matter much. Foreign affairs is not a closed priesthood. Fresh minds with fresh ideas are much to be welcomed. Outstandingly able political appointees can often claim an inside track to the president or special knowledge of a region or dominant bilateral issue.

But there is a downside. It is no coincidence that the Foreign Service is so demoralized or that the fissures between the leadership and the permanent staff remain so wide. Both these features have characterized the mood of the State Department for some years, under administrations of both parties. Some Republicans convinced themselves long ago that Foreign Service officers are mostly Alger Hiss clones looking for an opportunity to betray the country; for their part, the Democrats, after their long years in the foreign policy outback, act as though the State Department was full of neanderthal rednecks out to sabotage any vestige of progressive innovation or any element of the nobler, values-driven foreign policy.

No single cure exists for this malady but we do submit that an urgent review should be made of the system of patronage under which the administration of the day appoints not only the top foreign policy officials but also those in the three or four levels below the top. This system extends political influence far too far down the ranks. Area expertise gets neglected, while foreign experience can be overlooked—an important omission. In the domestic private sector, it is possible to practice health-care, banking, or environmental protection on a more or less equal footing with government. It is harder to do this in foreign policy. No private sector counterpart to NATO, for example, can conceivably exist. Confidential exchanges with overseas governments form the central core of the job description.

Quick learning and cooperative teamwork within the State Department would overcome this deficit; but such cooperation happens infrequently. Political appointees bring with them staff assistants from outside the ranks of professional Foreign Service officers. All too quickly, the latter build walls between their bosses and the rest of the Foreign Service. The result is a choppy, stop-and-start foreign policy with top American officials perennially at a disadvantage to their foreign counterparts.

As jejune as this sounds, bureaucratic expertise represents the other dimension of the historical memory discussed in chapter 8. Those memory cells are not laden with foreign policy details. Historical memory stands in a strategic rather than tactical relationship to practical foreign policy issues. The continuity of foreign policy expertise—which any foreign ministry embodies—provides the complementary tactical role of laying out the facts and options: Does North Korea have a bomb? Is Russia seeking a new empire? Which countries harbor terrorists? This expertise thus remains vital for the effective implementation of policy. And this leadership comes best from the repository of continuity, rather than from quick-fix outsiders.

Achieving a new public consensus for America's new post–Cold War foreign policy is proving difficult enough without the nation having to suffer the self-inflicted wound of a bureaucratic structure that obstructs the full exploitation of the Foreign Service professionals.

Bureaucratic reform will not, of itself, provide a first-class foreign policy. We have submitted only two proposals to improve the structure by increasing its efficiency. But today's foreign policy process suffers from too much inter-departmental buck-passing and lacks team work. If professionalism can mesh with accountability within traditional channels of responsibility, some progress can be made in equipping the United States with government structures that can meet the foreign policy demands of the day.

Chapter 12

New Directions

Policy, like strategy is an act in which everything
depends on execution. Everything about it is simple,
but the simple is always difficult.
                    — attributed to Napoleon Bonaparte

Over the past chapters we have tried to take a hard look
at the underlying state of American foreign policy. Where
we have detected deficiencies, we have pointed to them,
but always trying to move beyond mere criticism to develop new ideas for reforming military and bureaucratic
structures and for reinvigorating the concept of national
interest. We have also tried to open up the foreign policy
process, stressing that, as the United States has to make
its way in an increasingly competitive world, Americans
need to understand that they have a stake in the quality
of foreign policy decisions—just as they do in other fields
of public policy. We have sought ways, therefore, for rediscovering a sense of strong and united national purpose.

In these last two chapters, we turn our eyes firmly to
the future. In this chapter, we set out some behavioral

151

ground rules aimed at avoiding basic diplomatic mistakes and at enhancing the opportunities for effective diplomacy. In the final chapter, we take a shot at fitting these rules to practical policies and hard politics.

It hardly needs mention by the authors—both longtime expatriates—that the United States should continue to be an effective player in world politics. This is not just a matter of handyman's habits, of keeping the global machinery running smoothly. The good old-fashioned reason is good enough for us: American ascendancy improves the chance that Americans will live prosperous, safe lives. That has seemed an American birthright for many decades, but there is no longer any inevitability about it. The poodles that once trotted deferentially next to Uncle Sam's heels— the Japans, Germanies, Koreas—have grown up into well-muscled Alsatians. We may no longer be staring at thousands of Soviet missiles, but the world is now a more equal and therefore more competitive place. American welfare cannot be taken for granted.

The rules of the game have changed from their writing at the post–World War II settlement. At that time the United States spoke and the rest of the world snapped to attention. Complacent reliance on habits inherited from that period will gradually consign the United States to second-class status—not perhaps in the lifetime of the present crop of foreign policy experts, but their children may not be so lucky.

To prosper in this world, American diplomacy needs to be smart, farsighted, and, most of all, realistic. To this end, there are no quick fixes. On the contrary, the essence of our book is that diplomatic *Blitzkrieg* no longer works. Instead, we have tried to map out a more complex process for the foreign policy leadership to seek fresh inspiration for their task from America's historical memory. To this end we have developed ten injunctions: five positive and five negative. We start with the negatives.

The Negative Injunctions

1. Don't Chase after Ghosts from the Past

The Book of Exodus warns that the "iniquity of the fathers shall be visited upon the children unto the third and fourth generation."[1] Give or take a generation, many of today's policy makers and commentators appear locked in this ancient cycle of atonement.

To hear their speeches and read their writings, they seem consumed by a desire to expiate two all-encompassing sins: Munich—the symbol of appeasement, of not doing enough—and Vietnam—the emblem of quagmire, of trying to do too much.

These symbols pull in opposite directions. The former leads to belligerence—as exhibited in 1994 by Senator John McCain when advocating a tough policy against North Korea: "history is replete with evidence to support my view that appeasement of tyrants makes war more, not less likely," he said.[2] The latter symbol results in irresolute nervousness, as evidenced by the short-order withdrawal from Somalia and the panic-laden expectation of the first American combat death in Haiti.

Both positions contain strong points. And historical knowledge is an indispensable component of sound foreign policy. In the country at large, however, Americans are finding it hard to accept that two alleged sins of omission or commission by previous generations should set the terms of today's foreign policy debate, let alone decide the outcome of tomorrow's. Whether or not British, French, and American statesmen were right or wrong not to take action against Germany in the mid-1930s does not mean that every Arab or Balkan dictator is a new Hitler. Nor do the political and military miscalculations of Vietnam mean that every subsequent foreign deployment is fated to replay that tragedy.

Yet by interpreting today's issues through easily assimilated historical snapshots, policymakers have made themselves prisoners of historical cliché—what the writer Michael Lind has called the "op-ed history of America."[3] For the truth is that American history plays out on a wider tapestry than the bannered mistakes associated with the rise of Nazism or the Vietnam war. In today's world, the

United States faces a constantly shifting pattern of graduated challenges and opportunities. Responses need to be flexible and diverse. To shoehorn choices into mutually exclusive categories of guilty aggressiveness or defeatist withdrawal offers us little creativity and even less imagination.

2. Don't Overestimate Your Enemies

The Cold War accustomed us to think of the world as divided into two mutually antagonistic camps: the free world and the Communists. This way of thinking became so ingrained that we have forgotten how unnatural it is. Washington, Jefferson, Madison, Polk, Lincoln, McKinley, the Roosevelts—all these presidents and more were attuned to foreign threats, but—until the advent of Nazism—none divided the world into good and evil.

Unfortunately, unreconstructed habits of thought keep us tethered to the rails outside the familiar old saloon where gunslingers in white or black hats still stare each other down at high noon. We deal in enemies. Sometimes, it seems, the more, the merrier. Around budget time, congressional representatives from military districts, ambassadors, and generals appear armed with maps on which the world's hot spots flash out in red. From Abkhazia to Zaire, a motley collection of villains is paraded before the C-SPAN cameras as though all these undesirables were not merely local thugs but also sworn enemies of our way of life.

Without a Cold War demonology, little justification exists for this attitude today. Opponents of the United States abound, but none has even a sliver of the USSR's passion, power, and dedication to challenge the American dream. So why produce new enemies based on a straight-line extrapolation from the USSR? The labels backlash, outlaw, or rogue may roll off the tongue as descriptions of nations like Iraq, Libya, Iran, and North Korea. Syria used to be a member of this select company until the dynamics of the Arab-Israeli peace process prompted two meetings between the Syrian and American presidents in 1993 and 1994. Does this sort of language contribute to good policy? Or does it simply distract?

With few apologists outside a committed few, almost no points of sympathy exist between these nations and the United States. Rightly so, but should we sever *all* contact with them? Twenty years ago, Iran was one of America's closest partners in the Middle East. Does no vestige of the geopolitical reasons for that relationship still exist today? Although it may sound like heresy, a viable Iran shields central Asia from virulent attentions from the Middle East. Regarding Iraq, will we some day need Iraqi oil? If so, will the hatreds that are compounding today deny this to us on reasonable terms?[4] In the same way, events in 1994 forced the United States to have dealings with both Cuba and North Korea. These showed that we don't have to love these zealots in order to deal with them; we don't even need to like them. But we can avoid the type of ineffectual rhetoric that only strengthens the zealots' grip on state power while doing nothing to alter facts on the ground.

An approach that prolongs the division of the world between the good and the irredeemably bad seems ill calculated to serve the intended goal of transforming enemies into friends. Instead of deflating enemies, it puffs them up, giving them extra years of life. Local bullyboys like Saddam Hussein, Fidel Castro, and Kim Jung Il gratefully revel in their pariah status; far from loosening their grip on power, it provides them with a ready-made excuse to continue the intimidation of their people. Further, it blinds us to rational analysis of their actions.[5]

Our concern here is not to diminish the actuality of enemy threats—everyone shudders at the prospect of a nuclear-tipped Qaddafi—but to question the tactics employed in addressing them. By applying too liberally the word *enemy*, we may be condemning ourselves to pick quarrels or create confrontations. Nazi Germany, Imperial Japan, and the Soviet Union lived up to the term in full measure, but can the same be said of their latter-day successors? They seem very small fry.

In practical terms, our suggestion here is that we return to traditional American habits of dealing with the world. This means keeping an eagle eye open for possible challenges, *retaining the strength to deal with the unexpected*, but at the same time remaining open to the good or at least the potential for improvement in the countries of the world. Labels that seem to rule out any virtue just make enemies more intractable. "A thousand friends, too few; a single enemy, too many"—so runs an old Chinese proverb. It is an old proverb precisely because it has stood the test of time.

3. Don't Underestimate Your Friends

As we all know, the United States has become by far the world's largest single repository of military force. In contests as far removed as World War I, World War II, or the Gulf War, the United States provided the decisive power that made victory possible. This has bred a unilateralist frame of mind according to which, when the chips are down, the United States has to do things by itself with only token support from allies. The Pentagon's Two-War scenario bases American military requirements around the assumption that only minimal allied help will be available.

In some cases this remains true. In the event of, let's say, serious unrest in Mexico leading to pressure on the American border, the United States would be unlikely to receive significant physical support from friends. Nor is anyone going to build a shield against missile attack for the United States.

But, this go-it-alone assumption is less true elsewhere. In many parts of the world, the interests and actions of America's friends dovetail with the interests of the United States. In eastern Europe, for example, the European

Union—and Germany in particular—has provided some 90 percent of financial assistance to former members of the Warsaw Pact. In Asia, Japan has now far outstripped the United States as the major donor of developmental aid. In terms of international peacekeeping, the efforts of other countries now have to compensate for American reluctance to commit troops and money to UN operations. On transnational issues, such as drugs, immigration, and the environment, the United States by definition must co-operate on a multilateral basis.

So, from the American perspective, the world is *not* a hostile place; friends greatly outnumber enemies. The world is not one big happy family, but neither are foreigners engaged in a gigantic conspiracy to shortchange American interests. On the contrary, they share many American values and goals. Nuclear nonproliferation, regional stability, stopping terrorism, checking aggression, immigration, population growth, human rights are not exclusively American concerns. On all these issues, the United States can expect to work with (and not against) the grain of the international community.

To be sure, tactical differences will frequently emerge between the United States and its overseas partners. The American emphasis on moral values as a central component of foreign policy is very unusual. Neither Asians nor Europeans, for example, share America's hard-driving approach to human rights. This should not, however, lead American policymakers to dismiss them as waverers on the other side of the fence. In a similar way, Europeans and Americans frequently quarrel on specific trade matters, but this does not obscure the fact that they remain each other's best allies on the question of open markets.

By regarding its friends as *multipliers* of American policy goals, the United States will be able to move much of the diplomatic burden of world responsibility off its own shoulders, leaving the nation better able to concentrate on those interests that really are central to its well-being.

4. Don't Concentrate on Personalities

In his celebrated epilogue to *War and Peace*, Leo Tolstoy offers a compelling literary analysis of the forces of history.[6] What causes events? Great men like Napoleon and Louis XIV? Or humanity coming together in a collective effort? Tolstoy's sensible conclusion—that an interdependence exists between the two factors—is less important for our purposes than the fact that he highlights the common tendency to focus on prominent people rather than on broader forces.

This is certainly true of many foreign policy analysts today. They at one point stated that Russia's future depended on Mikhail Gorbachev. Later, when the political tides swept him away, they transferred their affections to Boris Yeltsin. This man, whom the Bush administration deliberately set out to belittle as a boorish drunk, now (according to the Heritage Foundation) stands alone against the prospect of the re-emergence of an anti-American dictatorship. In China, the fate of over a billion people is said to depend on who emerges as successor to Deng Xiaoping. Elsewhere, the entire American approach to certain countries is built around the personalities of strong men like Saddam Hussein and Kim Il Sung (now transferred to his son Kim Jong Il). Overseas, we can be sure that foreign observers are making the same mistake by focusing minutely on the characters of the president and secretary of state in drawing their conclusions about the likely trends of American policy.

Without reopening Tolstoy's debate, we have reason to believe that this particularly American focus on prominent individuals distorts foreign policy by its overnarrow concentration on a factor which, after all, is only a heartbeat, assassin's bullet, or sexual scandal away from oblivion. In Somalia, for example, the American engagement started to go awry in direct proportion to the focus of effort on Mohammed Farah Aideed. The analytic mistake, compounded by UN commanders, was that if he were somehow removed from the scene, gang warfare would cease.

This analysis failed to give proper weight to the much larger forces of Somali tribal politics. On the more positive side, certain hair-brained schemes to assassinate Saddam Hussein after the Gulf War were put on hold following calculations that his demise might produce an even more repressive representative of the Tikrit clan.

Concentrating on individuals rather than societies as a whole makes for easier analysis. Individuals stand out from the crowd with actions that can be described and attitudes that can be analyzed; they are, after all, the people American officials meet and do business with. On television, people rather than issues make for compelling viewing. The demonization of Saddam Hussein provided a readily grasped shorthand justification for the Gulf War. At best, however, people represent only half the picture—and a half that can be very misleading.

In Russia, nationalist concern for the 23 million ethnic Russians stranded abroad by the breakup of the USSR has come to be identified with the personality of Vladimir Zhirinovsky. The next step is to label him alternately as a harmless clown or a dangerous lunatic. He is easy to banish from the salons of civilization. Visiting statesmen can feel good as they snub him. The trouble with this approach is that it treats the messenger as the message. People come and go, but issues continue as potent and complex forces.

We are never going to get away from people. But American policy cannot be allowed to rest there. If it is to be successful over time and resistant to the whims of health or political change abroad, it must base itself around the longer term trends in the society of foreign countries.

5. Hold Those Bumper Stickers! Avoid that Bluster!

Immediately following his visit to Moscow in January 1994, President Clinton found himself threatened by the collapse of his Russia policy when several prominent reformers from Boris Yeltsin's cabinet abruptly resigned. Vice President Al Gore and Ambassador-at-Large Strobe Talbott seemed to adopt contradictory positions. Asked by reporters about this discrepancy, Clinton admitted that his administration was having difficulty coming up with the right bumper sticker in which the right balance of shock and therapy could be distilled into a memorable jingle.[7]

Everyone will have sympathy with efforts to reduce complex and exotic situations to more readily understandable language. Even the revered icons of European diplomacy—Metternich, Talleyrand, and Castelreagh—were not immune from christening their diplomatic system with the catchy title of the Concert of Europe. This title led to momentary confusion in Peking's Forbidden City as courtiers of the declining Manchu dynasty struggled to understand, when they first heard the term literally translated, why the foreign barbarians had formed a musical orchestra!

Our worry is that symbols and substance have reversed their positions in the process of policy formation. From New World Order to Enlargement of Democracy it seems that policymakers prefer an approach scripted by a Madison Avenue creative writing department than building practical structures within which American interests can prosper.

What starts out as a harmless exercise in media marketing all too often becomes a blunderbuss for self-inflicted wounds. Officials come to believe that mere words will achieve policy objectives. Human rights make an attractive centerpiece for a stem-winder speech on the Senate floor but, unless this is backed up by a pragmatic strategy designed to bring about the desired effect, it soon loses its sheen. Unacceptable. Intolerable. These may sound like impressive rebukes to lesser powers but, once again, without a strategy for changing the unwelcome behavior, the speaker and the country are left looking weak and foolish.

Policy making by slogan lends an unserious air to American pronouncements. When an American official says that "if 1993 was Russia's year, 1994 will be the year of Ukraine," what are citizens of either country expected to make of the longevity of American purposes?[8]

The problem lies in our politicians' unwillingness to distinguish between domestic and foreign affairs. In the domestic political maelstrom, harsh or misplaced words can become lost against the background cacophony. This is not so in the foreign policy of a great power. Foreigners listen, analyze, and remember. They maintain small armies of diplomats in Washington and around the nation to report each and every word uttered by the administration and other relevant foreign policy figures. If the word goes back to capitals that American rhetoric is constantly simplistic, empty, or self-contradictory, who can blame foreign leaders if they shed their sense of awe or think, at the wrong moment, that the United States doesn't really mean it?

Inevitably, the United States loses credibility. Like the boy who cried wolf, this can have dire consequences. How does the United States signal that it really means business? What, for example, did Kim Il Sung make of the barrage of rhetoric launched against him in 1993? Was it intended as a substitute for action, as over Bosnia? Or was it the real thing? Miscalculation by either side could have been exceedingly dangerous. The way out of this trap is to leave the advertising copy writers in the waiting room until the real job of discovering the foreign policy substance is complete.

The Positive Injunctions

1. Organize. Have a Strategy

In admitting that he had a problem with the "vision thing," George Bush managed to turn that concept into an all-time object of derision. Fair enough. That arch cynic Harold Macmillan, British Prime Minister from 1957–63, once told a young backbencher that as a politician he did not deal in a "sense of purpose," delegating that activity to archbishops.[9] So, let's drop the word and leave aside the search for an overarching theme.

But what about organization? What about a strategy? Is there no place for these concepts? Of course there is. Supposing that foreign policy can be handled on an as-it-comes basis comes close to mimicking the intellectual laziness of those who mistakenly think that Cold War foreign policy was absurdly easy. For them, it was a one word job: Containment. Five minutes of the president's or secretary of state's time each day sufficed, they allege, to get the job done of checking that the missiles were still armed and that the military had plenty of money.[10] How absurd. And so is any strategy based on simply coming in each day and checking what's in the in-box.

Whatever the specific strategy should be, it must rest on a cold-eyed assessment of the means to carry it out. In 1909, Herbert Croly said that "the American habit is to proclaim doctrines and policies without considering either the implications, the machinery necessary to carry them out, or the weight of the resulting responsibilities."[11] He was quite right. Strategy does not consist simply of a statement of desirable objectives in some rough order of priority. Reform in Russia, an opening of Japanese markets, a slow-down in rain forest loss in Latin America, or the myriad other items cramming official briefing books all represent worthy aims. Yet, they have little practical relevance unless they carry with them some sort of flow chart setting out the *means* to reach these objectives. As George Kennan has written, in foreign policy the what cannot be separated from the how.[12]

A good example might be the Partnership for Peace program for integrating NATO with the former Warsaw Pact. This may not represent the best way of setting a new security regime for Europe and it has encountered Russian intransigence, but at least it has the shape of an honest nuts-and-bolts program going beyond declarative statement.

If this or any administration can successfully combine the how and the what in Europe, it can do so elsewhere.

Strategy makes for difficult work, both intellectually and during the administrative grind of fitting means to ends, but there is no substitute for it.

2. See Situations in the Round

In the American system, strong secretaries of state tend to be controversial figures. John Foster Dulles and Henry Kissinger certainly fit this description. History, however, has its own ways of cutting people down to size. As history's wheels grind over Kissinger's record, we still remember that, for all his faults, he did possess at least one great virtue: the ability to see the connecting threads that make up the foreign policy weave. In designing the opening to China in 1970–71, for example, he drew together an immense diversity of factors. In addition to China itself, relations with the USSR, Taiwan, Pakistan, Japan, Korea, and Romania were also involved, each championed by conflicting lobbies in Washington. There were the Slavophiles, who did not want to upset the Soviets, and also the Free China backers of Chiang Kai-shek. Each had a place in Kissinger's achievement of overall congruence of policy.

This ability to integrate interests and achieve an overall net gain seems now to be missing. We do not detect much evidence that senior administration figures perceive the trade-offs between, say, accepting a dramatic accretion of centralized presidential authority in Russia and the future course of democratic reform. Or the trade-off between bashing Japan on trade or China on human rights while needing both as strategic partners in East Asia. Or between raising Third World imports and moderating the population explosion in developing countries through resultant economic growth. A trade-off also exists between a unilateral lifting of the arms embargo on Yugoslavia and respect for international law.

Part of the explanation for this loss of what might be called the Comprehensive Viewpoint is the disorganized character of the American official machinery. Too many fiefdoms exist, all shouting for their pound of flesh. We have recommended earlier the reestablishment of greater accountability by restoring the secretary of state's authority over foreign affairs.

Administrative reforms like this count for nothing without a change of mental attitude. In his book, *The Endangered American Dream*, Edward Luttwak has presented a trenchant case against the overinfluence of the legal profession on American government. His criticisms apply, in part, to the foreign policy process. Here, the large number of lawyers encourages the case by case approach typical of the law—even as practiced in the corporate environment. Officials speak of interest groups as clients. They pick up the human rights docket, argue from it, and then move on to the security dossier and make a totally separate presentation. This approach works in a court of law, where cases are argued before different judges and different juries, with each case being argued on its specific merits with no spillage from one to the next.

But it does not work in foreign affairs. Here the judge and jury stay the same. After placing the Japanese prime minister at the top of an international hit list for trade intransigence, one does not simply move into the next court room and sit down with a different prime minister for talks about Asian nuclear weapons. It's the same guy. And the Japanese voters act as jury to both cases.

In general, sports analogies bear little relevance to foreign affairs. In the life of nations, there is no final whistle, no toting-up of a final score; but, if forced to take a metaphor from the athletic world, we would say that foreign affairs resembles golf much more than football. In the latter, one can match one's opponent's touchdown with one of your own. In golf, a bad score on one hole stays on the score card the whole round. Two bad holes and you may be out of contention. The most successful golfers aim for consistency over the long haul. Our foreign policy makers could learn from this.

3. Stay in Touch with the American People

The classic manuals of diplomacy devote little space to the role of public opinion. As the Chinese thinker Sun Tzu asserts, good strategy required the leaders to be in harmony with the people, but career diplomats normally view public opinion as a bit of a nuisance, at best a sort of elevator mood music. At worst, it is a dangerous distraction from their true tasks.

This attitude is not very surprising. Diplomacy grew to maturity as a princely practice in the European states system of the seventeenth century. Diplomatic works of that period bear titles such as *De Systematibus Civitatum* or *Discorsi politici ai principi d'Italia*.[13] Their contents are as dense and elitist as their titles are imposing. Most diplomats, in short, regard their calling as something well elevated above the distasteful hurly-burly of domestic horse-trading.

A central theme of this book has been to reject this aristocratic model of foreign affairs as unworkable in the United States. This theme present a dilemma for the foreign policy establishment. Not anti-democratic by orientation, but, accustomed to a half century's consensus on foreign policy fundamentals, the establishment has lost the habit of inviting the public to join the policy-making debate.

This may be a costly mistake. With the exception of the Gulf War, foreign policy actions since 1989 have been marked by successive false starts, embarrassing retreats, and halfhearted advances. (Without this background uncertainty, former President Jimmy Carter would never have been able to carve out for himself a role as an international mediator). True, the bookshelves groan with guidance for the twenty-first century. But much misses that vital connection between what diplomats seek and what Americans are prepared to support with real resources and real lives. Successively, Bosnia, aid for Russia, Somali reconstruction, human rights in China, democratic restoration in Haiti,

North Korea's nuclear program—all these have been trumpeted as vital to American interests. Yet the execution of purported strategies to achieve these ends has been consistently limp. Americans simply don't buy into this all-purpose activism.

We would thus prefer to see policy formation start with public opinion rather than end with it as an afterthought. To start with, public opinion does not entail government by electronic town meetings. It does not mean daily opinion polls or abrupt turnarounds in response to emotional scenes on television. Nor do we advocate abandoning leadership or expertise. We simply mean that Americans retain good gut instincts about what is reasonable in foreign affairs when set against a long historical perspective. Our recommendation to policymakers is to spend more time on the road talking to Americans and reestablishing contact with these same gut instincts. (This task, incidentally, is harder than it sounds for—unlike other commentators who urge dispersal from Washington—we do not believe that these instincts can be easily measured by referenda and telephone bank polls).[14] If you believe that you can tabulate these instincts mathematically or derive them from the soundings of a hired pollster, even your best efforts will falter.

4. Keep Foreign Policy Open

So many of the problems facing the United States today do not conform to the traditional, nation-on-nation issues, but rather involve ethnic, cultural, and religious clashes. The concern over Islamic fundamentalism is a classic example.

Two concerns arise. Within government departments valuable reserves of expertise exist in these frequently complex areas. All too often, however, a perverse form of political correctness imposes a weird discipline over policy formation, and those who do not share a particular party line find themselves excluded from the process. Such exclusion may have worked during the Cold War when strategy occasioned less dispute than tactics, but in the new, messier circumstances, a full range of administrative expertise needs to be brought to bear.

Seeking expertise from outside government will be just as important. We are thinking here particularly of noncentral government organizations like charitable agencies or political foundations, which may be better equipped to provide advice on issues like famine relief or nation building than the central government.

5. Above All, Be Realistic

Many professions depend on the application of heavy doses of realism. A high school college counsellor must dole out plenty of it. Don't apply to MIT or Caltech, he or she will advise, if your SAT scores only qualify you for less academically challenging pastures. Normally, students express gratitude for this honest advice, which spares them from the subsequent rejection slips.

In the political game, realism is a poor relation. The ethos of professional politicians the world over is to offer instant gratification, hoping for the best on the well-tested experience that no one believes political promises. In foreign policy, leaders regularly promise that they will bring about world peace, rout the nation's enemies, and provide unlimited markets for American goods. All harmless fun, many will say. No one really expects this to happen.

Unfortunately, penalties become harsher in the foreign arena. At home, Washington insider games may leave the net national welfare little changed. But foreign nations are able take advantage of weak foreign policy to extract costs in terms of net transfers of advantage away from the United States to themselves.

Foreign policy practitioners need to be brutally realistic about the country's strengths. The greatest disservice is to expose the country as a paper tiger, a risk which arises from choosing tactics more suitable to a rug merchant than to a diplomat. The former sets out with an impossibly high price, knowing that he will have to make concessions in the subsequent negotiations but hoping to come out with a satisfactory profit. Occasionally this tactic may work against the inexperienced; applied to diplomacy, however, it will more often lay bare American weaknesses.

Over the long term, America's best strategy must be to look objectives straight in the eye and then adjust American aims to reality. To take nuclear nonproliferation as an example, is it realistic to expect that the number of non-nuclear powers will not increase? Writing in 1977—well before the current crop of second and third-tier powers acceded to nuclear status—the late Oxford Professor Hedley Bull poured doubt on this assumption.[15] Should, therefore, American policy continue, as at present, to focus on containing the spread of nuclear weapons? Or should it turn to devising systems to protect American and global security in an environment where significantly more nuclear powers will exist than at present? We cannot suggest firm answers to these questions, but they need to be asked.[16]

In the resuscitation of realism, leadership comes into its own. The role we envision for public sentiment lies only in the strategic sphere. It sets general directions, and cannot—should not—set tactics. Only the foreign policy leadership can possess the full range of information about the challenges the country faces and only it can marshall the resources to meet them.

Foreign policy can never be a mathematically precise business. No one will object to an additional 15-20 percent on the top of policy pronouncements for rhetorical flourish—just as the high school counsellor will encourage students to be ambitious in their college selections. But anything more begins to look like a dangerous gamble with realism and, thus, with national welfare.

Chapter 13

The Roads
Best Traveled

Anjing menggonggong, kafilah lalu
The dogs bark, but the caravan moves on.
— Indonesian proverb

And now that we have reached the last chapter of our essay, we have a staging point from which to draw on earlier precepts and set down a typology of interests having a direct, immediate, and recognizable importance for the United States and her people. That is, after saying a lot about what's wrong since 1989, we can now identify the principal superhighways of foreign policy and, by corollary, save ourselves from getting lost on suburban back streets.

However, this chapter gives us pause. Anyone writing critically about America's meandering since the end of the Cold War must feel a bit like the Indonesian village watchdogs in the proverb above—the barks of warning go unheeded, as the caravan of American foreign policy plods across the plain.

We have few illusions about this little yelp of protest.

It may be just another howl in the canine cacophony, but we hope the caravan's scouts will hear a note of encouragement, rather than alarm, in our bark. And thus we close these pages by sketching the issues out there that we think really do matter and deserve time, analysis, patience, leadership, and resources.

To start with a caveat—ideologues, bleeding hearts, militarists, messianic democracy enthusiasts, *Realpolitik* devotees, or planetary ecocampaigners will find few endorsements for their pet agendas in the following section. In keeping with our theme that we face a world regained rather than something totally new, our thoughts on more effective diplomacy center around a selective and a somewhat old-fashioned manual for America's procession into the twenty-first century. Those hoping for arguments in favor of new bureaucratic empires will also go unrequited.

We do *not* seek exotic destinations for the foreign policy caravan. We regard the Cold War's global engagement as in some ways a *diversion* from the republic's earlier compass bearings and do *not* want to see this continue for another half-century. We do *not* welcome distractions from the vital business of mustering support to restrain real enemies and preserve real advantages that, now more than ever, are so easily lost to competitors. We hope *not* to see an America playing either on-call gendarme or civics schoolmaster to the world.

The Main Games

This country's security rides on issues that are, at once, both local and global. For example, the United States depends for its commercial health on far-flung transit routes yet, also, in a different and quite old-fashioned, often forgotten, way, on a stable Mexico and coherent Canada. These countries, in turn, rely on most of the same set of global circumstances as do we. A complex interdependence entwines apparently heterogenous issues, such as immigration and trade policy, into the same bundle. It is all maddeningly difficult.

Nonetheless, certain *global* issues (that is, circumstances that take the same form wherever in the world we find them) stand out as commanding the foreign policy agenda. These issues are the ones that American policy must seek to retain with the same essentially favorable orientation they now have for this country for the indefinite future. The United States enjoys a favorable position on the following issues:

- a world trading system progressively freer of unfavorable distortions

- an essentially very favorable global nuclear weapons balance

- the still favorable (or at least not yet distinctly unfavorable) tripartite concentration of global industrial power

- maintenance of the current levels of security of energy supply and of freedom of navigation

- the existing multilateral security and financial machinery, now embedded in the state system, which serves us rather indifferently (mostly because of our lack of imagination about, and ambivalence toward, the very multilateral institutions we helped create 50 years ago)

Economics and the American Livelihood

The post–1945 free trade and free-exchange regime, which first contested and then utterly triumphed over the totalitarian socialist challenge, provides and will continue to provide the very best set of externalities to enable America, which by 1994 was exporting a greater percentage of her GDP than Japan, to perform more competitively in world markets.

Some writers have responded to this centrality of economic imperatives by inventing a new branch of international competition called geoeconomics—what MIT professor Lester Thurow calls "head-to-head" conflict over market share, technological edge, and comparative dynamics.[1] They urge that the United States should gird itself to fight World War III with letters of credit, industrial policy, and patent lawyers.

We do not feel very comfortable with this approach—or at least we do not share its central thesis that the inexorability of mutual confrontation is a new element in international intercourse. Competition over commercial advantage was an entirely familiar theme to the city states of ancient Greece and the Italian principalities of the sixteenth century.[2] We accept without quibble that economic considerations must occupy a central position in today's foreign policy, but reject the notion that the United States should confront Japan or the European Union with the same mindset of confrontation that it brought to the Soviet Union during the Cold War.

To be sure, we accept that the increasing American pressure since the mid-1980s to prize open markets—stymied by open national preference as in Europe or by informal barriers and local lobbies as in Asia—must continue unabated. A *sine qua non* must be what we might call the Motorola Proviso—that is, a state of affairs in which, other things being equal, American firms capable of selling competitive, high-quality, market-proven products must be allowed to compete on level terms without being shut out of the action—as Motorola's cellular telephones were shut out of Japan and still in 1995 faced labyrinthine, officially connived obstacles to entering that marketplace.[3]

One of the larger errors of the Bush administration after its Gulf War success occurred when it continued to give every appearance—an inaccurate impression as it turned out—of not taking economics seriously *in our foreign relations*. In fact, the change among Foreign Service professionals—who once viewed commercial office staff as a vulgar add-on to an embassy's work—had already begun.

In the year before Bush's electoral defeat, Acting Secretary of State Lawrence Eagleburger wrote a strong memo to all heads of U.S. missions abroad, stressing the shift in priorities and making it abundantly clear that advocacy of business interests should come at the top of an ambassador's checklist.[4] Also unknown at the time, President Bush had done his own spade work when, for example, he put in several phone calls to Indonesia's President Suharto to help AT&T participate in a major telecommunication modernization program in that country that seemed locked up by the Japanese giant NTT, until Bush lobbied. The Clinton administration's record in this area of diplomacy has followed this example. Clinton's personal interest in going an extra mile or two for American firms selling abroad can be seen in his close stewardship of American pressure on the Saudi Arabians and other allies to purchase American aircraft.

Going to bat on behalf of individual companies or in specific countries is important, but is only half the battle. Far more significant are the efforts needed to counter the tide of protectionism which, given the slightest encouragement, threatens to undo the gains of the past fifty years. A powerful reason for continuing the pressure against protectionism is an across-the-board *widening* of the range of U.S. export goods well beyond the current, rather oddball, First World/Third World mix of things we now sell abroad—from soybeans, forest products, and scrap metal to business machines, airplanes, and such high value-added items as films, music, and computer software.

Pursuing global economic interests requires sustained, steady pressure, and continuous monitoring by the president. Short of this, derailment is a constant danger, as the 1993 NAFTA debate and the choppy waters through which the legislative deliberations on the incorporation of the GATT agreement into United States law had to pass in

December 1994 show. We would therefore urge that the maintenance of the open trading system—the Open Door policy of McKinley's Secretary of State, John Hay—occupies a place of honor at the top of the foreign policy agenda.

In doing this, policymakers should note that trade has its own, proper area of discussion, with trade officials, industry groups, and industrial associations. It does not fit into an inappropriate arena, as the fiasco over linking extension of China's MFN status to its human rights performance vividly shows. Other inapposite connections between essentially economic issues have confused diplomacy and obscured the real economic differences. In 1994, the United States committed this error with practically all its Asian partners. Assistant Secretary of State Winston Lord commented in an internal State Department memorandum in April 1994 that a "host of other frictions" bedeviled U.S. foreign policy in Asia. Lord, who has responsibility for East Asia and the Pacific, noted "our attempt to interject workers' rights issues into the World Trade Organization has been universally opposed by Asians and non-Asians alike. . . . it [also] threatened to mar the trade ministers meeting" [then planned to convene in Morocco].

"A common thread," Lord continued, "is the question of how we pursue global agenda issues in our bilateral relations. In most instances, we have sought to use trade measures to achieve non-trade objectives," and he added that "we must weigh the impact of pursuing specific short-term goals on our overall long-term interests in East Asia and the Pacific [including] tapping Asia's huge economic potential . . . "[5]

Quite rightly, Lord follows Kennan in drawing attention to the how. In an age when gunboats no longer deliver market access, American diplomacy needs to be subtle. Crude threats, as were tried against the Japanese in early 1994, and which the dollar crisis of the mid-summer showed to be mere gossamer, should have no place in this scheme. But joint European-American pressure on Japan and joint Japanese-American pressure on Europe just might deliver what is required.

U.S. Nuclear Supremacy

At the close of a 1994 television interview, the British war historian John Keegan, whom we quoted in chapter 5, asked rhetorically why people had forgotten about nuclear weapons. Some significant reduction in the arsenal occurred in the last spate of arms control agreements just before the Soviet Union's demise; the standing down of high alert has soothed the waters.

Yet nuclear weapons states other than the United States exist, two of whom, Russia and China, are not full members of the Western camp, nor perhaps are ever likely to be. At the same time, new nuclear programs proliferate around the world, both in countries like North Korea of which we do not approve and in countries like Japan, with whom we maintain the closest possible links and which is not at present a nuclear power but could within months become one given a political decision to that effect.

To start with Russia and China. These states call for very different tactical approaches, but the Superhighway imperative for the United States is clear. It must place at the top of its list of priorities the strategic integration of Russia and China into a network of relationships and commitments that both increases the incentives for favorable behavior and stiffens the penalties for noncompliance. Some form of Strategic Partnership—perhaps in combination with the European Union (EU) might be contemplated. The simple point here is that, when countries or groups of countries have the capacity to inflict immense harm on one another, they should seek inclusionary arrangements for working out their differences, rather than eyeing each other warily from mutually exclusive encampments.

The truth is, no one can rewind the tape in the development and acquisition of nuclear weaponry. The genie is well and truly out of the bottle. It is futile to insist—as did the United States in Pakistan—that the nuclear weapons program be halted and reversed, in exchange for unfreezing a sale of fighter aircraft. In the short term, the present policy of minimizing the spread of nuclear weaponry may exercise a certain palliative effect, especially on smaller, backward states like North Korea or impoverished nations like Ukraine. These efforts, especially the successful incentives offered to the three non-Russian nuclear states of the former Soviet Union, should continue and be reinforced at the 1995 review of the 1970 Non-Proliferation Treaty. At the national level, this means marshalling every bit of operational capability possessed by the intelligence agencies, to ensure that weapons locations remain known and monitored.

Looking further ahead, however, to a day when large countries like Brazil, Algeria, or Iran, which are less susceptible to the pressure of sanctions, may be tempted along the nuclear path, the United States should work now to lessen the regional tensions that lead in the nuclear direction. In some areas, first and foremost concerning Israel, the United States is already bringing the correct level of energy, creativity, and commitment to bear.

But elsewhere, notably in the wider Middle East, and Northeast Asia, more could be done.

In the Middle East, the nuclear issue adds emphasis to the fact—already manifest for a number of separate reasons like energy access and the fight against terrorism—that the time is overdue for a more enlightened policy toward Islam. This does not mean that the United States should embrace zealots or fanatics but we should be much more sparing of those labels. At present, the United States risks presenting itself as the enemy of Islam and thus as the legitimate target of nuclear dreamers, whether against the United States itself or to cleanse American influence from client states like Egypt and Saudi Arabia. We would urge an intense effort, not necessarily government-to-government but perhaps better through nongovernment mechanisms, to reach out to Islam.

Still in the Middle East, the unremitting hostility to Iran and Iraq strikes us as overdone. We doubt that either of these nations will become again the Western satrapies they were in the 1950s, but neither should they be allowed to fester in a sort of diplomatic no-go area—no matter the petty, or not so petty, provocations that either country may from time to time instigate. Both countries weigh heavily in the volatile politics of the Middle East. At some point in the future we are going to need their cooperation. Permanent exile from respectable society will only breed the hatred that will fatally compromise the prospects for collaboration. This mistake could one day lead to nuclear disaster. We suggest, therefore, slow, modest efforts to coax both Iran and Iraq back into the international community.

In South Asia, the classic conditions for nuclear conflict present themselves: an intensely nationalistic dispute over Kashmir, cultural enmity between Hindus and Muslims, one state (Pakistan) willing and able to equalize the conventional military superiority of another (India) with a nuclear bomb. Here, two forms of American activity suggest themselves:

The first is to use good offices as was done in April 1990 by the then deputy National Security Adviser Robert M. Gates, brokering a resolution to the continuing Kashmir imbroglio (this means, among other things, appointing and maintaining an effective American ambassador in New Delhi, a post that lay vacant for nearly two years of the Clinton administration!).[6]

The second is sharing with India and Pakistan the immense wealth of American and Russian knowledge of nuclear command and control systems built up during the Cold War together with their experience of confidence building measures that played such a crucial role in the Cold War endgame. These systems provided the cornerstones of what writers like James Schlesinger mean when they refer to the unique discipline of that era. If these systems worked and continue to work in the superpower confrontation, they can be adapted for service in regional contexts.

In Northeast Asia, the main nuclear threat over the medium term will arise from the security vacuum that will emerge as the American defense commitment to Asia declines. (It may be controversial, but we assume that this is likely to happen for good reasons—the region is becoming more prosperous, more integrated, and less tense—and for bad ones—American will and resources continue to decrease.) Rather than passively waiting for these factors to take their toll, the United States should start today working toward a Northeast Asian security organization—modelled perhaps on the OSCE—that would comprise all the states of that area. The purpose of this organization would be to enhance transparency about national strategy and promote mutual confidence—thus rendering the possession of nuclear weapons unnecessary.

*The Advantages of the Tripartite
Concentration of World Power*

As nuclear theorists realize, possessing nuclear weapons often adds little to a country's influence while saddling it with the deadweight of an omnipresent security apparatus, expensive public spending on weapons upgrading and research—in addition to the costs of development, training and productionizing. Many of the world's most influential countries—Germany, Japan, South Korea and Taiwan—project their power through their economies, not through their weapons.

North America, the EU, and the aggregate of Asian dynamism concentrated in Northeast Asia (China, Korea, Japan, and Taiwan) together account for 85 percent of the global GDP. Playing to fears in Europe or Asia, recent writing has tended to depict these areas as embryonic blocs, each dominated by a respective core economy—the United States, Germany, and Japan, respectively. Reality is a little more complicated, however: None of these core economies, let alone adjacent economies within each respective region, want to be confined within a bloc. Economies of scale for key industrial sectors—aviation, electronics, computer software, capital equipment for energy generation, and the motor transport industry—result only from access to the global market. The Ford Motor Company has pioneered the concept of a world car. Further, each of these alleged blocs depends crucially on access to the other blocs for their economic wellbeing.

What does this imply for American policy? First, primary effort should go into the development of a solidly based economic community within North America (NAFTA). This will increase both the size of the market and the amount of leverage for market-access diplomacy elsewhere. Linkage can never be crude, but the Japanese obsession with their own lack of a hinterland can and should be turned to good account: NAFTA already had prompted, by June 1994, the TV maker Hitachi to move production for North America from Malaysia to Mexico.[7] In the same way, the German car manufacturer BMW was prompted in 1993 to locate a factory in the United States to take advantage of the growing north American market.

The American interest in this tripartite division of the world's wealth is clear. Given improved competitiveness—which depends absolutely on improved savings and reinvestment in social capital at home—the expansion of wealth and markets in these other regions complements our drive to broaden and deepen these markets in North America. The task, then, is to devote much energy and expend presidential capital to emphasize the importance of our NAFTA partners. Institution-building is already underway and some American sovereignty already has been compromised under the dispute-resolution procedures of the Canada-United States Free Trade Agreement.

Building on NAFTA, the United States should seek to construct a set of legally anchored commercial relationships below the global GATT level. A point of departure might be to negotiate a treaty relationship with the EU. At present, the United States is tied to Europe through the NATO treaty, but nothing comparable exists on the economic front. This needs to be rectified.

The policies that best ensure the viability of the North American experiment—financing improved communications and transport and rewarding investment at home, that is, within North America—will take precedence in White House strategies. In this case, an apposite slogan would be: Come Home, *North* America.

An Old, Familiar Tune—
Secure Oil and Secure Seas

The world remains a familiar place, despite the disappearance of the Red Giant. The need to maintain freedom of navigation and retain our preferential access to petroleum remains high on the list of essential American interests that have global implications. As long as the United States retains its dependence on imported petroleum (itself an assumption with strategic implications that are best reviewed as an aspect of domestic policy), the area of primary reserve supply will remain of central importance to the United States.

At present, the United States finds itself in an awkward posture. On the one hand, many of its relationships and interests depend on friendly, but, let's be honest, reactionary Gulf monarchies whose values are very different from those the United States champions. On the other hand, these states are vulnerable to forces that openly avow anti-American hostility. We think American policy should work on both sides of this equation both to moderate autocratic practices that feed popular resentment and to reposition the nation with regard to Islam. This delicate process of evolution will require exceptional diplomatic and military skills.

The freedom of navigation remains one of the oldest continuing preoccupations of American foreign policy. Since the inception of the young republic's navy in the 1790s running straight up to the present, America has insisted on passageways for its warships. Given that American power projection will depend even more, in coming years, on a navy able to go anywhere it wants, the free-dom-of-the-seas arguments stand as compellingly as ever. The rising importance of the Asia-Pacific region, where, in contrast to Europe, the ocean occupies so much geographi-cal space, drives this point home.

In a policy sense, this means retaining influence in unfamiliar places, such as Indonesia, where serious efforts to deny our transit through the Malacca or Lombok straits would cripple our navy's operational stance. It also means a continuation of unobtrusive efforts, such as admirably achieved during the last two years of the Bush adminis-tration, to obtain onshore facilities for ship repair and resupply.

Multilateral Machinery

The Clinton administration entered office pitching a far too elaborate argument in favor of subordinating Ameri-can unilateralism to a UN-orchestrated multilateralism—"assertive multilateralism" it was called. A series of events—the tragedy in Somalia, disagreement with Euro-pean allies over Bosnia and with Asian partners over North Korea, Pentagon reservations about non-American command of American forces, the extraordinarily high cost of UN peacekeeping (for which the United States has con-tracted to pay 30 percent)—have contributed to a souring of the atmosphere for multilateralism. The latest doctrine on American cooperative intervention overseas (Presiden-tial Decision Document 13) sets up a series of roadblocks against such efforts.[8]

We regard this negative attitude as unfortunate and suggest that policymakers should seek to reverse it. While we certainly do not seek increased opportunities for American intervention abroad, we do see occasions when intervention will be necessary and when multilateral ma-chinery will facilitate rather than impair the safeguarding of American interests. Indeed, as American resources for overseas missions continue to shrink and as popular resistance to accepting overseas fatalities is maintained, some form of multilateral cooperation becomes absolutely essential.

In chapter 7, we set out the arguments for applying local and then regional approaches to peacekeeping and dispute resolution. Two policy consequences for this approach flow out rather obviously: increased support, which does not necessarily mean additional American security commitments, for regional groupings such as the OSCE, Gulf Cooperation Council, SAARC, ECOWAS or ASEAN, and an application of a clear sense of what the UN can, and cannot, do.

Alongside these issues, another looms in importance—how to enlarge the Security Council. It becomes harder the longer it is postponed. The United States has already moved to support the addition of Japan to the permanent membership of the council, but this will not be enough. The mismatch between the concentration of economic power and political influence in the G-7 and the Security Council's (from which important G-7 countries are absent) position as the formal repository of legitimized compulsion, has become too glaring.

The avenue of permanent membership (leaving open whether this should be with or without a veto) should be explored, for Germany, Japan and—perhaps—India, realizing that the list of claimants includes Nigeria, South Africa, Indonesia, and Brazil as well.

Multilaterally, but not within the UN, the United States must also ensure that the World Bank system, the emerging World Trade Organization, and the IMF retain their clout and prestige in the vast swath of the world that does not now figure as lying within America's primary circle of interests. In a range of work, from promoting better environmental standards to enforcing stricter human rights standards, the quiet but effective application of financial conditionality has already made interesting inroads into World Bank, IMF, and other operations.

The World Bank's role as the single most important and well-seasoned repository of development experience tends to be overlooked, especially in the United States, and, more especially still, in Washington. The Bank's emergence from a tight-lipped reactive role needs to be accelerated. The preeminent position of the United States within the Bank system can help achieve this. The Bank can and should promote the real stuff of development funding in the twenty-first century—that is, regional solutions to urgent development issues once seen as strictly national in scope, as in water and electricity supply or in cheaper transport.

In summary, close attention to these guidelines would allow the United States to achieve the following objectives:

- avoiding costly interventions abroad
- reducing its role as an overworked global handyman
- shifting responsibility and financial cost to allies
- projecting conventional power around the world
- retaining unchallengeable nuclear superiority
- applying pressure more creatively via multilateral channels, and
- retaining security of energy supplies

Imagine what might have occurred, and what might *not* have occurred, if America's foreign policy after the fall of the Berlin Wall had followed some of these priorities. To our minds, it might have resulted in the following:

- Two major mistakes would have been avoided. President George Bush would have seen that, although he was right to take the country to war against Iraq, he was wrong to insist that foreign policy should retain its Cold War primacy. For his part, President Bill Clinton would see—there is still time—that, although his instinct that domestic renewal should take precedence is correct, he too falls into error by imagining that foreign policy can be handled on a casual basis. It cannot. Presidential leadership is essential. This need not be full-time, but on the three or four things that are central to American welfare, presidential performance needs to be *consistent and considered.*

- A more realistic appreciation of American interests and public resolve would have reduced the Somalia intervention to much smaller scale, possibly to support for intensified civilian efforts to deliver food or to protection of limited safe havens, a course of events that was already successfully in train at the time of the military landing. By avoiding the American tragedy in Somalia, similar humanitarian missions in other areas of pressing need, for example in Sudan or Rwanda, might have remained within the realm of the politically doable—to the benefit of America's humanitarian agenda.

- In Bosnia, the United States would have understood that, determined as it was not to commit ground troops, the best hope for resolving the war lay in giving full and early support to European efforts to produce a peace—however flawed or fragile. In late 1992, peace of a sorts lay within the grasp of the European negotiators, but eluded them as hopes for American intervention hardened attitudes at the negotiating table. Had the war ended then—clearly a debatable assumption—two years or more of war with all its attendant horrors would have been avoided.

- On Japan, and trade matters generally, pressure for market access on the basis of mutually agreed, fair rules would continue to be intense, but the methods of achieving access would be consistent with American capabilities to make them stick. Partners would not be threatened with reprisals like dollar devaluations or price rises on domestically sold products, the effect of which would be worse in the United States than abroad.

- On China, policymakers would have recognized it as potentially the United States' most complex bilateral challenge. As a partner, China would be an invaluable force for Asian stability and offers immense commercial potential. Yet the list of potential bilateral irritants is daunting: missile sales, human rights, illegal immigration, prison labor, unfair trade practices, narcotics transshipment trade, and Tibet. Under our guidelines, the idea that *one* aspect of *one* of these issues—Chinese treatment of a small number of Western-inclined dissidents—should emerge with the ability to hold all other aspects hostage would have been preposterous. Instead, a strategic approach that attempted to integrate or at least balance these questions would have held sway. In this way, the loss of American credibility would have been avoided and, indeed, quiet diplomacy might have produced an amelioration of the very human rights that the United States was seeking to enhance.

- In Haiti, the United States would not have allowed a small regional problem to assume the proportions of a major objective of its foreign policy. Ultimately, Haiti's fate lies with the Haitians themselves, rather than with American efforts to restore a particular person to office. Acting on this basis, the United States would not have drifted into a no-win choice between an invasion of Haiti and a humiliating back down.

- In the Middle East, support for Israel—as long as its commitment to the peace process continued—would remain firm, but a more creative approach to Islam would be in progress. In particular, the policy of dual containment of Iran and Iraq would never have been put in place, and Israel would be served notice that balance-of-payments support cannot last forever.

- On North Korea, the United States held all the high cards but, by reckless overbidding, in particular by loose talk of war, transferred the initiative to the much weaker North Koreans. This was and is an important issue for the United States, yet it is making the same mistake of threatening what it cannot deliver. A decision in favor of quiet, persistent diplomacy in concert with its Asian partners (of the kind displayed at the end of 1994 in obtaining the release of the downed American helicopter pilot) might over the years have produced North Korean compliance with its NPT obligations without the need to have made such public concessions on high-level talks and military exercises.

- On UN peacekeeping, the early overpassionate embrace of too much multilateralism and the later espousal of too little would have been avoided. In 1993, after six years in gestation, the United States Commission on Improving the Effectiveness of the United Nations presented a report containing a wide range of ideas for improving UN performance. The UN is unlikely ever to provide a full answer to American peacekeeping needs, but it will often form an important part of the institutional mix. A steadier approach to overall foreign policy would have avoided the wide swings in mood about the UN.

✳   ✳   ✳   ✳   ✳

These, then, are our instruments, the toolkit to which we alluded at this book's beginning. By using them in the future, the United States can attain an effective, well-balanced, and strategically coherent foreign policy. Had these basic tools been applied since 1989, the damaging erosion of American credibility might not have occurred.

It comes as a bracing surprise to remember that the world still presents, after all, a very favorable face to the United States. American mettle does not face crucial tests, nor are the penalties for the current underperformance in foreign policy making themselves felt. Not yet, anyway. For the time being, the caravan still continues its stately procession across the duned horizon. There is still time to listen to the watchdogs' warnings before both princes and packhorses lurch into quicksand.

Notes

Preface

1. See John F. Kennedy, *Public Papers.* 3 vols. Washington, D.C.: 1963–4 I, p. 1ff.
2. Godfrey Hodgson, *In Our Time: America from World War II to Nixon* (London: Macmillan, 1976), p. 119. For an irreverent deconstruction of foreign policy pretensions, see Michael Lewis, "The Case Against Abroad: The Strange Snobbery of Foreign Affairs Wonks," *New Republic* 211, no. 24 (December 12, 1994): pp. 21–3.
3. See Warren Christopher, "Securing US interests While Supporting Russian Reform," U.S. Department of State *Dispatch* 4, no. 13 (March 29, 1993): p. 173; for a good example of this kind of multiple agenda, see John Lancaster and Barton Gellman, "National Security Strategy Paper Arouses Pentagon, State Department Debate," *Washington Post*, March 3, 1994, p. A 14.

Introduction

1. Lo Hui-min, ed., *The Correspondence of G. E. Morrison*, vol. 1 (Cambridge, England: Cambridge University Press, 1976), p. x, (emphasis added).
2. In talking about the Prussian-Austrian War of 1866, German

Chancellor Otto von Bismarck made the same point when he said, "Austria was no more in the wrong for opposing our claims than we were in making them." See A. J. P. Taylor, *The Origins of the Second World War* (London: Penguin Books, 1964), p. 9. Post-Hitlerian American tradition has, in contrast, played up the Manichaean aspects of international competition. See, for example, Richard Nixon, *The Real War* (New York: Warner Books, 1980), p. 314; Robert Johnson, "Cold War Games Again," *New York Times*, September 23, 1994, p. A 35, shows that the Clinton administration also tends to view the world as divided into mutually antagonistic camps of good and evil. For a general discussion of international evil, see Daniel Chirot, *Modern Tyrants: The Power and Prevalence of Evil in Our Age* (New York, The Free Press, 1994).

3. For a presentation of these continuities, see F. H. Hinsley, *Power and the Pursuit of Peace* (Cambridge, England: Cambridge University Press, 1963), pp. 275–87.

4. George Bush, "The U.N.: World Parliament of Peace," Address to the U.N. General Assembly, October 1, 1990, U.S. Department of State Dispatch 1, no. 6 (October 8, 1990): p. 152; for an analysis of the new world order concept, see Robert W. Tucker and David C. Hendrickson, *The Imperial Temptation* (New York: Council on Foreign Relations, 1993), pp. 21–53.

5. Samuel Eliot Morison, *The Oxford History of the American People* (New York: Oxford University Press, 1965), p. 885; see also Jeane Kirkpatrick, "Normal Country in a Normal Time," *National Interest*, Fall 1990, pp. 40–4, and David Hendrickson, "The Renovation of American Foreign Policy," *Foreign Affairs* 71, no. 2 (Spring 1992): pp. 48–63.

6. Ironically, the United States remains by far the largest supplier of conventional weapons to third-world markets. See Mark Kramer, "The Golbal Arms Trade after the Cold War," *Security Studies* 2, no. 2 (Winter 1993): p. 263. When American arms sales declined drastically in 1993, export regulations were rewritten to facilitate weapons exports. See Eric Schmitt, "Clinton Devises New Guidelines on Arms Sales," *New York Times*, November 16, 1994, p. A 14.

7. Zbigniew Brzezinski, *Out of Control: Global Turmoil on the Eve of the Twenty-First Century* (New York: Scribners, 1993), p. x.

8. See, for example, the wide range of views held by a group of international scholars in Michael Hogan, ed., *The End of the Cold War: Its Meaning and Implications* (New York: Cambridge University Press, 1992); a typically iconoclastic interpretation of the genre may be found in Noam Chomsky, *World Orders New and Old* (New York: Columbia University Press, 1994), pp. 157–88.

9. Eugene V. Rostow, *Managed Peace* (New Haven, Conn.: Yale University Press, 1993), p. 362. This same spirit of activism permeates the National Security Council's 1994 publication *The National Security Strat-*

egy of Engagement and Enlargement 040-000-00642-7 (Washington, D.C.: GPO, 1994).

10. Graham Allison and Gregory Treverton, *Rethinking America's Security* (New York: W. W. Norton in association with the Council on Foreign Relations, 1992), p. 16; Henry Kissinger, *Diplomacy* (New York: Simon and Schuster, 1994), p. 833.

11. Kim R. Holmes, ed., *A Safe and Prosperous America*, 2d edition (Washington, D.C.: Heritage Foundation, 1994), p. 3.

12. See Ainslie T. Embree, *Imagining India: Essays on Indian History* (New York: Oxford University Press, 1989). For further reading on masterly inactivity, see Peter Hopkirk, *The Great Game: The Struggle for Empire in Central Asia* (New York: Kodansha, 1990), pp. 306–38.

13. David Marash, "Their War, Not Ours," *Media Studies Journal* 7, no. 4 (Fall 1993): p. 159.

14. On the general influence of television, see Shanto Iyengar, *Is Anyone Responsible: How Television Frames Political Issues* (Chicago: University of Chicago Press, 1991), pp. 7110.

15. Theodore H. White, "The Action Intellectuals," *Life*, June 9, 1967, p. 43.

16. The phrase "feel-good diplomacy" is used by Robert Manning, a former special adviser in the State Department's East Asia and Pacific Bureau, in Robert Manning, "The Big Trade-Off: Clinton's Asia Policy Stresses Human Rights and Economics," *Los Angeles Times*, March 13, 1994, p. M 2. The phrase had been in common currency during the Reagan administrations.

17. Henry Kissinger, *Diplomacy*, p. 810; Boutros Boutros-Ghali, Commencement Speech at Georgetown University, Washington D.C., UN document S9/SM/5306, (New York: United Nations, May 27, 1994), p. 1.

18. H. G. Sparrow, "Ecoquiz II: How Environmentally Correct Can You Be?" *Washington Post*, June 5, 1994, p. C 3.

19. For a paean to Wilsonianism, see Tony Smith, *America's Mission: The United States and the Worldwide Struggle for Democracy in the Twentieth Century* (Princeton, N.J.: Twentieth Century Fund, 1994), pp. 84–109.

20. Bradley Graham, "Air Force Chief on Attack," *Washington Post* October 24, 1994, p. A 1.

21. See Daniel Williams and Ann Devroy, "U.S. Applies Dual Policy to Use Force," *Washington Post*, October 16, 1994, p. A 1.

Chapter One
Looking for that Hole in the Doughnut

1. Henry Stimson, "The Challenge to Americans," *Foreign Affairs* 26, no. 1 (October 1947): p. 5. Other writers from the same period also

sound themes that are hauntingly familiar to those that fill today's foreign policy volumes. See, for example, the introduction to Walter Lippmann's *U.S. Foreign Policy: The Shield of the Republic* (Boston: Little, Brown, 1943), pp. 3–9.

2. For example, in his address to the UN General Assembly on September 26, 1994, President Clinton used in quick succession the images of contest, struggle, and fight to describe the foreign policy tasks facing the United States. William J. Clinton, "Building A Secure Future as the Foundation for Democracy," Address to the UN General Assembly, September 26, 1994, U.S. Department of State *Dispatch* 5, no. 39 (September 26, 1994): pp. 633–6.

3. Robert D. Kaplan, "The Coming Anarchy," *Atlantic Monthly* 273, no. 2 (February 1994): pp. 44–76; Matthew Connelly and Paul Kennedy, "Must it be the Rest against the West?" *Atlantic Monthly* 274, no. 6 (December 1994): pp. 61–84. The British historian M. R. D. Foot describes such doom-laden tracts as the work of "outgribing [sic] futurologues" who neglect the force of human character in shaping history. M. R. D. Foot *Resistance: European Resistance to Nazism 1940–45* (London: Eyre Methuen, 1976), p. 320.

4. Michael Mandelbaum as quoted in Benjamin Bradlee, "America's Tooth-Ache," *Washington Post*, November 17, 1991, p. C 4.

5. "Islam and the West," *Economist* 332, no. 7875 (August 6, 1994): p. 6; Martin M. Sieff, "New Challenges for West: Islamic Fundamentalism," *Washington Times*, February 16, 1992, p. A 19.

6. Ronald D. Asmus, Richard L. Kugler, F. Stephen Larrabee, "Building a New NATO," *Foreign Affairs* 72, no. 4 (September-October 1993): p. 30.

7. Samuel P. Huntington, "The Clash of Civilizations?" *Foreign Affairs* 72, no. 3 (Summer 1993): pp. 22–49.

8. Linton F. Brooks and Arnold Kanter, eds., *U.S. Intervention Policy for the Post-Cold War World* (New York: The American Assembly, 1994).

9. Any review of this kind is bound to be arbitrary, but we have tried to draw on a wide spread of opinion, not simply on the extremists. Although we disagree both with David Callahan's diagnosis of the ills of American foreign policy as consisting of an over-consumption of realism and with his antidote as lying in a dose of idealism, he provides an excellent review of the mainstream post–Cold War foreign policy literature in David Callahan, *Between Two Worlds: Realism, Idealism, and American Foreign Policy After the Cold War* (New York: HarperCollins, 1994). His analysis (see page 64) shows that, in their respective responses to the end of the Cold War, public and expert opinion took diametrically opposed directions.

10. Morton Halperin, "Guaranteeing Democracies," *Foreign Policy* 91 (Summer 1993): pp. 105–22.

11. Edward Luttwak, *The Endangered American Dream* (New York: Simon and Schuster, 1993), pp. 117–27.

Notes 193

12. James Schlesinger, "Quest for a Post-Cold War Foreign Policy," *Foreign Affairs* 72, no. 1 (January 1992): p. 28.
13. Francis Fukuyama, "The End of History," *National Interest* 16 (Summer 1991): pp. 3–18
14. For examples of this genre see Jessica Mathews "Redefining Security" *Foreign Affairs* 68, no. 2 (Spring 1989): pp. 162–77 and Thomas W. Lippmann, "Population Control is Called a Top Priority in Foreign Policy," *Washington Post,* January 12, 1994, p. A 4.
15. Anthony Lake, "From Containment to Enlargement," Remarks at Johns Hopkins University, School of Advanced International Studies, September 21, 1993, U.S. Department of State *Dispatch* 4, no. 39 (September 27, 1993): pp. 658–64; similar advocacy of America's mission to promote democracy—even forcibly—may also be found in conservative commentators. See Joshua Muravchik, *Exporting Democracy: Fulfilling America's Destiny* (Washington, D.C.: American Enterprise Institute, 1991), pp. 1–16 and 91–118.
16. Anthony Lake, "The Reach of Democracy," *New York Times,* September 23, 1994, p. A 35. For an academic underpinning of the moral components of this approach, see Lea Brilmayer, *American Hegemony: Morality in the One Superpower World* (New Haven, Conn.: Yale University Press, 1994), pp. 141–72.
17. James Schlesinger, "Quest," p. 17.
18. Steven R. Ratner and Gerald B. Helman, "Saving Failed States," *Foreign Policy* 89 (Winter 1992): pp. 3–20; Steven Ratner, "The United Nations in Cambodia: A Model for Resolution of Internal Conflicts?" *Enforcing Restraint,* ed. Lori Fisler Damrosch (New York: Council on Foreign Relations, 1993), p. 260.
19. See, for example, Stanley Hoffmann, "What Should American Foreign Policy Be?" *Dissent* (Fall 1994): p. 498.
20. Ambassador Madeleine K. Albright, Remarks to the National Defense University, September 23, 1993, U.S. Department of State *Dispatch* 4, no. 39 (September 27, 1993): pp. 665–68.
21. Elaine Sciolino, "The Reluctant Policeman is Still Picky About His Beat," *New York Times,* October 16, 1994, p. E 4.
22. See, for example, Ethan B. Kapstein, *Governing the Global Economy* (Cambridge, Mass.: Harvard University Press, 1994).
23. Strobe Talbott, "Journey Without Maps," *Time* 138, no. 12 (September 23, 1991): p. 34.
24. Dimitri Simes, "Clinton's Innocence Abroad," *Washington Post,* January 9, 1994, p. C 1.
25. William Pfaff, *The Wrath of Nations: Civilization and the Fury of Nationalism* (New York: Simon and Schuster, 1993), p. 158. Pfaff has repeated this call for intervention in foreign disputes in his article, "Invitation to War," *Foreign Affairs* 72, no. 3 (Summer 1993): p. 97.
26. Conor Cruise O'Brien, "The Wrath of Ages: Nationalism's Primordial Roots," *Foreign Affairs* 72, no. 5 (September 1993): pp. 142–9.

194 *Notes*

27. Colman McCarthy, "Powell Blinds with a Big Gun's Flash," *Washington Post*, October 12, 1993, p. C 11.
28. O'Brien, "The Wrath of Ages," p. 146.
29. Felix Gilbert, *To the Farewell Address: Ideas of Early American Foreign Policy* (Princeton, N.J.: Princeton University Press, 1961), pp. 144–7.
30. Anthony M. Lake, "Confronting Backlash States," *Foreign Affairs* 73, no. 2 (March 1994): pp. 45–55.
31. These motives are at work in, for example, Michael Lind, "One Nation, One Vote? That's Not Fair," *New York Times*, November 23, 1994, p. A 23.
32. Daniel Patrick Moynihan, *A Dangerous Place* (New York: Secker and Warburg, 1979), p. 17. For a study of the collison between ambition and reality under Johnson, see H. W. Brands, *The Wages of Globalism: Lyndon Johnson and the Limits of American Power* (New York: Oxford University Press, 1995), pp. 3–29.

Chapter 2
What Kind of World?

1. Leslie Gelb, "Can Clinton Deal with the World?" *Washington Post*, March 6, 1994, p. C 1.
2. "Indiana Jim and the Temple of Spooks," *Economist* 326, no. 7803 (March 20, 1993): p. 34.
3. This was a favorite phrase of Gates that he used at diplomatic gatherings, such as one attended by one of the authors.
4. Leslie Gelb, "Can Clinton Deal," p. C 1.
5. Compare the remark of Deputy Army Secretary John Deutch that "readiness is as high as it ever has been" (Bradley Graham, "Gulf Operations Reassure Pentagon," *Washington Post*, October 15, 1994, p. A 37) with Defense Secretary William Perry's contrary position following the November 1994 elections. See Bradley Graham and John F. Harris, "Army's Combat Readiness Overstated, Perry Admits," *Washington Post*, November 16, 1994, p. A 1. Six weeks later, in remarks to the National Press Club, Washington, D.C., on January 5, 1995, Perry reversed himself again, declaring that the United States was fully ready to fight two simultaneous wars.
6. Michael Gordon, "Christopher, In Unusual Cable, Defends State Department," *New York Times*, June 16, 1993, p. 13.
7. Daniel Patrick Moynihan, *Pandaemonium: Ethnicity in International Politics* (New York: Oxford University Press, 1993), p. 143; this description of the contemporary world in terms of chaos has also entered the literary world. See Harold Bloom, *The Western Canon* (New York: Harcourt, Brace, 1994), p. 369.

Notes 195

8. Adam Clymer, "State of the Union: the Republicans," *New York Times*, January 26, 1994, p. 15.

9. William Hyland, "Foreign Policy: The Agenda is Easy," *Washington Post*, January 24, 1993, p. C 9. For a similarly moderate apporach, see Charles William Maynes, "A Workable Clinton Doctrine," *Foreign Policy* no. 93 (Winter 1993–94): pp. 3–20.

10. "Looking Back from 2992," *Economist* 325, no. 7791 (December 26, 1992): pp 17–19. In this article the author set himself a test similar to that in which we invite our readers to participate in chapter 7.

11. George Bush, remarks before the Supreme Soviet of the Ukrainian Soviet Socialist Republic, August 1, 1991, U.S. Department of State *Dispatch* 2, no. 32 (August 12, 1991): p. 32; and Daniel Williams, "Christopher Supports Ukraine in Feud over Crimea," *Washington Post*, May 24, 1994, p. A 14.

12. Henry Brandon, "The United States and the New Europe," *In Search of a New World Order*, ed. Henry Brandon (Washington, D.C.: Brookings Institution, 1993), p. 4.

13. Sam Nunn and Richard Lugar, "Still a Soviet Threat," *Washington Post*, December 22, 1992, p. A 21

14. Paul Johnson, *A History of the Modern World* (London: Weidenfeld and Nicolson, 1983), p. 615.

15. Louis Freeh, Speech at Rotes Rathaus, Berlin, Germany, on January 28, 1994, p. 4; when, in the search for savings in federal expenditure, attention turned to the FBI, Freeh wrote in protest to Attorney General Janet Reno. See Pierre Thomas, "Heads of FBI, DEA Say Proposed Cuts Would Undermine Anti-Crime Missions," *Washington Post*, December 20, 1994, p. A 17.

16. Lake, "From Containment to Enlargement," p. 662.

17. Stephen E. Ambrose, *Eisenhower: Soldier and President* (New York: Simon and Schuster, 1990), p. 233. For a detailed exposition of how the Truman administration perceived the Soviet threat as all-encompassing in terms of domestic U.S. arrangements, see Melvyn Leffler, *A Preponderance of Power: National Security, the Truman Administration, and the Cold War* (Stanford, Calif.: Stanford University Press, 1992), p. 13.

18. Dean Acheson, *Present at the Creation* (New York: W. W. Norton, 1969), p. 219.

19. Gordon, "Christopher," p. 13.

20. Arthur M. Schlesinger, Jr., *The Cycles of American History* (Boston: Houghton Mifflin, 1986), p. 53.

21. Warren Christopher, "The Importance of American Engagement," U.S. Department of State *Dispatch* 5, no. 31 (August 1, 1994): p. 519.

22. James Schlesinger, "Quest for a post-Cold War Foreign Policy," *Foreign Affairs* 72, no. 1 (January, 1992): p. 27

23. Martin Walker, *The Cold War: A History* (New York: Henry Holt, 1994), pp. 1–7. For a similar treatment of the Cold War, see Roger A.

Kanet, "The Cold War as Cooperation," *The Cold War as Cooperation*, ed. Edward A. Kolodziej (Baltimore: Johns Hopkins Press, 1991), pp. 3–30.

24.   Ann Devroy and R. Jeffrey Smith, "Clinton Reexamines Foreign Policy Under Siege" *Washington Post*, October 17, 1993, p. A 1.

25.   Willy Brandt, *My Life in Politics* (New York: Viking Penguin, 1994), pp. 9–26.

26.   David Welsh, "Domestic Politics and Ethnic Conflict," *Ethnic Conflict and International Security*, ed. Michael Brown (Princeton, N.J.: Princeton University Press, 1993), p. 43.

27.   William Hyland, *The Cold War is Over* (New York: Time Books/Random House, 1990), p. 205.

28.   Kim R. Holmes, ed., *A Safe and Prosperous America* (Washington, D.C.: Heritage Foundation, 1993), p. 1.

29.   For details of the agreement with North Korea, see Warren Christopher, "Ensuring Peace and Stability on the Korean Peninsula," U.S. Department of State *Dispatch* 5, no. 46 (November 14, 1994): pp. 757–60.

30.   John Lancaster, "Pentagon Issues Plans for Future," *Washington Post*, September 2, 1993, p. A 1.

31.   Richard Nixon, *The Real War* (New York: Warner Books, 1980), p. 17. Nixon returned to this theme in *No More Vietnams* (New York: Arbor House, 1985), p. 212.

32.   U.S. Ambassador to the UN Madeleine Albright made a similar point with regard to Haiti. Jim Hoagland, "Big Deal, Bigger Questions," *Washington Post*, September 20, 1994, p. A 21.

33.   Zbigniew Brzezinski, "The Cold War and its Aftermath," *Foreign Affairs* 71, no. 4 (Fall 1992): pp. 31–49.

34.   Jaques Attali, "An Age of Yugoslavias," *Harper's*, January 1993, pp. 20–22.

Chapter 3
The Gap between Resources and Aspirations

1.   George Bush, Inaugural Address, January 20, 1989 U.S. Department of State *Bulletin* 89, no. 2145 (April 1989), p. 2.

2.   Paul Kennedy, *The Rise and Fall of the Great Powers* (New York: Random House, 1987), pp. 514–35.

3.   Clyde Prestowitz, *Trading Places: How We Allowed Japan to Take the Lead* (New York: Basic Books, 1988).

4.   Joseph S. Nye, *Bound to Lead: The Changing Nature of American Power* (New York: Basic Books, 1990); Daniel Patrick Moynihan and James Schlesinger, "Debunking the Myth of Decline," *New York Times Magazine*, June 19, 1988, pp. 34–6.

5.   Alfredo Valladão, *Le XXIème Siècle Sera Américain* (Paris: Éditions la Découverte, 1993), pp. 165–77. For a more sober assessment

of the shifts in relative U.S. and European economic weighting, see Kevin Featherstone and Roy H. Ginsberg, *The United States and the European Community in the 1990s* (New York: St. Martin's Press, 1993), pp. 47–74.

6. "Excerpts from President Clinton's Press Conference," *Washington Post*, April 24, 1993, p. A 16; President George Bush had voiced the same view on many occasions. See George Bush, "America's Role in the World," U.S. Department of State *Dispatch* 4, no. 2 (January 11, 1993): p. 13. A powerful statement of this thesis may be found in Charles Krauthammer, "The Unipolar Moment," *Foreign Affairs* 70, no. 1 (Winter 1990/91): pp. 23–30.

7. Hobart Rowen, "Baker Sticks with Aid Plan for Republics," *Washington Post*, January 19, 1992, p. H 1; on the same theme see Charles Krauthammer, "The Anti-Superpower Fallacy," *Washington Post*, April 10, 1992, page A 27.

8. Daniel Williams and John Goshko, "Reduced U.S. World Role Outlined but Soon Altered," *Washington Post*, May 25, 1993, p. A 1; Daniel Williams, "Administration Rushes to 'Clarify' Policy Remarks by 'Brand X' Official," *Washington Post*, March 27, 1993, p. A 45.

9. Michael Mandelbaum, "Like It or Not, We Must Lead," *New York Times*, June 9, 1993, p. A 21.

10. Johanna Neumann, "Christopher: U.S. will Lead, but Not in Bosnia," *USA Today*, May 28, 1993, p. A 6.

11. Letter from Lodge to Roosevelt quoted in John Blum et al., eds., *The National Experience* (New York: Harcourt, Brace, Jovanovich, 1989), p. 489.

12. The Clinton administration's ironic reward for these efforts was a cover article in *The Economist* entitled "Meet Jimmy Clinton," *Economist* 332, no. 7882 (September 24, 1994): p. 13.

13. Jeane Kirkpatrick, "Where is our Foreign Policy?" *Washington Post*, August 30, 1993, p. A 19.

14. In two variants, this chant even appears as chapter titles in Callahan, *Between Two Worlds*, pp. 7 and 64.

15. Kennedy, *The Rise and Fall*, p. 535.

16. Arthur M. Schlesinger, Jr., *The Disuniting of America* (Knoxville, Tenn.: Whittle Books, 1991); Seymour W. Itzkoff, *The Decline of Intelligence in America* (Westport, Conn.: Praeger, 1994), pp. 65–79.

17. Paul Lewis, "U.S. Reverses Position at U.N. on Funding Troops to Bosnia," *New York Times*, April 1, 1994, p. A 2; Report of the Bread for the World Institute, quoted in *Washington Post*, October 15, 1994, p. A 3.

18. Stimson, "The Challenge to Americans," p. 6.

19. Quoted in Godfrey Hodgson, *In Our Time* (London: Macmillan, 1976), p. 37.

20. Henry Kissinger, *The White House Years* (London: Weidenfeld and Nicolson, 1979), p. 57.

21. The humanitarian relief operation to Rwanda illustrates the gap between promise and delivery. See R. Jeffrey Smith, "U.S. Mission to Rwanda Criticized," *Washington Post*, September 5, 1994, p. A 1.
22. Paul Johnson, *A History of the Modern World* (London: Weidenfeld and Nicolson, 1983) p. 599.
23. *Ibid.*, p. 599.
24. Desmond Dinan, *An Ever Close Union* (Boulder, Colo.: Lynne Riener, 1994), p. 112.
25. Jagdish Bhagwati, "Samurais No Longer," *Foreign Affairs* 73, no. 3 (May 1994): p. 7.
26. "Big Deal," *Economist* 333, no. 7884 (October 8, 1994): p. 76.
27. "In the Words of the President: the Reasons Why the U.S. May Invade," *New York Times*, September 16, 1994, p. A 10.
28. Clay Chandler, "Taking on Japanese Bureaucracy," *New York Times*, February 12, 1994, p. A 16.
29. Both in the run-up to the Blair House Agreement on agricultural products in November 1992 and in the final stages of the Uruguay Round in November 1993, the French received vitriolic criticism from United States officials. See Tom Burns, "EU and US in Crucial GATT Talks," *Financial Times*, November 22, 1993, p. 6.
30. *Economist* 332, no. 7871 (July 9, 1994): p. 106; it is instructive, however, to note that the illusion that aid represents a significant element in the federal budget (and by extension is thus a major foreign policy weapon) is widely shared both in Congress and among the wider electorate. See Robin Toner, "Pollsters See a Silent Storm that Swept away Democrats," *New York Times*, November 16, 1994, p. A 14.
31. Speech at Minnesota State Fair, September 2, 1901.
32. Elaine Sciolino, "U.S. Showing Frustration over China's Human Rights Policy," *New York Times*, March 9, 1994, p. 11.
33. Daniel Williams, "Christopher Cites Progress on Human Rights in China," *Washington Post*, May 24, 1994, p. A 1.
34. William Perry, "The Sino-U.S. Relationship and Its Impact on World Peace," Speech at National Defense University, Beijing, U.S. Department of State *Dispatch* 5, no. 46 (November 14, 1994): pp. 757–60.
35. Stephen E. Ambrose, *Eisenhower: Soldier and President* (New York: Simon and Schuster, 1990), p. 300.
36. "Excerpts from Clinton's Speech on Foreign Policy Leadership," *New York Times*, August 14, 1992, p. A 15.
37. Walter Lippmann, *U.S. War Aims* (Boston: Little, Brown, 1944), p. 41.

Chapter 4
Moral Crusading: No More Sabers to Rattle

1. The Carnegie Endowment National Commission on America and the New World, *Changing Our Ways* (Washington, D.C.: The Carnegie Endowment for International Peace, 1992), p. 1.

2. Roger Cohen, "U.N. General Opposes More Bosnia Force," *New York Times*, September 29, 1994, p. A 7.

3. John Palmer, *Europe without America: the Crisis in Atlantic Relations* (Oxford, England: Oxford University Press, 1987), pp. 59–81.

4. The Carnegie Endowment, *Changing Our Ways*, p. 81.

5. Winston Lord, "Emerging Malaise in Our Relations with Asia," unpublished State Department memo, partially excerpted in Daniel Williams and Clay Chandler, "U.S. Aide Sees Relationship with Asia in Peril," *Washington Post*, May 5, 1994, p. A 38.

6. Cornel West, *The American Evasion of Philosophy* (New York: Knopf, 1989), p. 4.

7. Speech at the National Press Club, Washington, D.C., May 12, 1994. The text is available from Kim Dae-Jung Peace Foundation for the Asia-Pacific Region, Aryung Building, Suite 701, 506-20 Changchun-Dong, Seodaemun-ku, Seoul, Korea.

8. As of 1995, commentators were beginning to question whether democracy was the right prescription for Russia. See, for example, Peter Rutland, "Has democracy Failed Russia?" *National Interest*, No. 38 (Winter 1994/95): pp. 3–12.

9. Michael H. Schuman, "Dateline Mainstreet: Local Foreign Policy," *Foreign Policy*, no. 65 (Winter 1986/87): pp. 154–75.

10. Carnegie Endowment, *Changing Our Ways*, p. 4.

Chapter 5
Prisoners of Our Own Rhetoric

1. Father J. Bryan Hehir, SJ, of Harvard University, for example, quotes the fourth-century bishop Ambrose of Milan to argue the case to "expand the reasons justifying intervention," *Dissent* (Fall 1994): p. 509.

2. Harold Nicolson, *Diplomacy* (London: Thornton Butterworth, 1939), p. 226.

3. Bill Clinton, Address by the President to the 48th Session of the UN General Assembly September 27, 1993, U.S. Department of State *Dispatch* 4, no. 39 (September 27, 1993): p. 650. At least one overseas observer pronounced himself baffled by the meaning of the fulcrum and pivot point; see Ian Davidson, "Peace In, Peacekeeping Out," *Financial Times*, October 8, 1993, p. 18.

4. See the text of President Clinton's 1994 State of the Union address and Robert Dole's reply in *Washington Post*, January 26, 1994, p. A 12.

5. Ann Devroy, "Letter from the Military Academy: 4,000 Cadets Say Farewell to the Chief," *Washington Post*, January 6, 1993, p. 21.

6. Lake, "From Containment to Enlargement," p. 658.

7. Symptomatic of the need to defend against this charge is the example of Colorado College Professor David Hendrickson, who in presenting his case for a more limited foreign policy, feels constrained to subtitle his argument "Stemming the Isolationist Impulse." See David Hendrickson, "The Recovery of Internationalism," *Foreign Affairs* 73, no. 5 (September–October 1994): pp. 26–43; on appeasement, from both ends of the political spectrum, see Richard Nixon, *Beyond Peace* (New York: Random House, 1994), pp. 165–6, and Anthony Lewis, "Beware of Munich," *New York Times*, January 8, 1993, p. 25.

8. Peter W. Rodman, *More Precious than Peace: The Cold War and the Struggle for the Third World* (New York: Scribners, 1994), p. 5.

9. John Jay, Federalist Paper Number 3 in *The Federalist Papers*, ed. Clinton Rossiter (New York: New American Library, 1961), p. 43.

10. Foster Rhea Dulles, *America's Rise to World Power* (New York: Harper, 1963), p. 3.

11. Stephen Kinzer, "Russian Troops Bid Wiedersehen to Germany: Last Russian Troops Leave Latvian and Estonian Bases," *New York Times*, September 1, 1994, p. A 3.

12. Arthur Schlesinger, *The Cycles*, p. 82.

13. The mid-nineteenth century presidency of James K. Polk is a particularly illuminating example of well-focused foreign policy. See Paul H. Bergeron, *The Presidency of James K. Polk* (Lawrence, Kansas: University of Kansas Press, 1987), pp. 113–25; further interesting insights may be found in a monograph by Anna Kasten Nelson, *Secret Agents: President Polk and The Search for Peace with Mexico* (New York: Garland, 1988), pp. 12–21.

14. Dulles, *America's Rise*, p. 15.

15. *Ibid.*, p. 42.

16. R. W. Apple, "Godfather to Pacific Era," *New York Times*, November 21, 1994, p. 14.

17. Dulles, *America's Rise*, p. 16.

18. Alfred Thayer Mahan, *The Interest of America in Sea Power* (Boston: Little, Brown, 1897), p. 6.

19. Naval Policy Board, Report 1890, Senate Executive Document, 51st Congress, Vol. 4, p. 43.

20. Mahan, *The Interest*, p. 21.

21. Arthur Schlesinger, *The Cycles*, p. 145.

22. Dulles, *America's Rise*, p. 61.

23. *Ibid.*, p. 62.

24. *Ibid.*, p. 34.

25. *Ibid.*, p. 37.

26. *Ibid.*, p. 76

27. Blum, *National Experience*, p. 490.

28. Arthur Schlesinger, *The Cycles*, p. 89.

29. Dulles, *America's Rise*, p. 3.

30. Norman A. Graebner, ed., *Ideas and Diplomacy: Readings in the Intellectual Tradition of American Foreign Policy* (New York: Oxford University Press, 1964), pp. 372–3.

31. William Pfaff, "A New Colonialism," *Foreign Affairs* 74, no. 1 (January/February 1995): pp. 2–6.

32. For Roosevelt's flourishes, see Morison, *The Oxford History*, p. 126; and for Wilson's pronouncement, see Arthur Schlesinger, *The Cycles*, p. 16.

33. For a Haitian perception of Wilson's motives see Jean-Claude Bajeux, "An Embarrassing Presence," *The New York Review of Books* XLI, no. 18, November 3, 1994, p. 37.

33. For detailed accounts of the development of the rhetorical aspects of the presidency and of how a series of modern presidents have exploited "crisis rhetoric" to sustain their positions, see Jeffrey K. Tulis, *The Rhetorical Presidency* (Princeton, N.J.: Princeton University Press, 1987), and Amos Kiewe, ed., *The Modern Presidency and Crisis Rhetoric* (Westport, Conn.: Praeger, 1994).

34. Blum, *The National Experience*, p. 534.

35. Ronald Reagan, Speech at Orlando, Fl., March 18, 1983, quoted in Arthur Schlesinger, *The Cycles*, p. 54.

36. William E. Odom, "Trapped by Desert Storm," *Washington Post*, October 16, 1994, p. C 1.

37. Samuel Francis, "Revving Up for the Transnational," *Washington Times*, January 8, 1993, p. F 1.

38. George Bush, "America's Role in the World," U.S. Department of State *Dispatch* 4, No. 2, January 11, 1993, p. 13.

39. Walter Lippmann, *The Cold War: A Study in U.S. Foreign Policy* (New York: Harper, 1947), p. 18.

40. Arthur M. Schlesinger, Jr., ed., *Dynamic of World Power: Documentary History of U.S. Foreign Policy 1945–73* (New York: McGraw-Hill, 1973), pp. 111–15.

41. William Safire, "Carrots and Sticks," *New York Times*, November 29, 1993, p. 17.

42. Kathryn Tidrick, *Empire and the English Character* (London: I. B. Tauris, 1990).

43. George Bush, "Against Aggression in the Persian Gulf," U.S. Department of State *Dispatch* 1, No. 1 (September 3, 1990): p. 54.

44. Richard Nixon, "A New America" in *Thinking About America: The United States and the 1990s*, eds. Annelise Anderson and Dennis L. Bark (Stanford, Calif.: Hoover Institution Press, 1988), p. 7.

45. Kissinger, *Diplomacy*, pp. 17–25.

46. Patrick Henry, Speech in the Virginia Convention; quoted in Bernard Bailyn, *Faces of Revolution: Personalities and Themes of American Independence* (New York: Knopf, 1990), p. 242. For an account of the

interplay between idealism and realism in American foreign relations, see Robert Endicott Osgood, *Ideals and Self-Interest in America's Foreign Relations* (Chicago: University of Chicago Press, 1953).

47. George W. Ball, *Diplomacy for a Crowded World* (London: Bodley Head, 1976), p. 56.

48. Jim Hoagland, "Fumbling for a Foreign Policy," *Washington Post*, June 14, 1993, p. A 19; Gordon, "Christopher," p. 11. For an account of the Clinton administration's gyrations on Yugoslavia, see Elizabeth Drew, *On the Edge: The Clinton Presidency* (New York: Simon and Schuster, 1994), pp. 138–73 and 273–84.

49. Mahan, *The Interest*, p. 87.

50. Bill Clinton, Inaugural Address of January 21, 1993, U.S. Department of State *Dispatch* 4, No. 4 (January 25, 1993): p. 45.

51. Paul L. Ford, ed., *The Works of Thomas Jefferson*, federal edition, 12 vols. (New York: Putnam's, 1904) I, p. 365.

Chapter 6
Military Force: To Use or Not To Use?

1. Adam Watson, *Diplomacy: The Dialogue Between States* (London: Eyre Methuen, 1982), p. 53

2. Lally Weymouth, "North Korea: Talk Means Nothing to Gangsters," *Washington Post*, December 14, 1993, p. A 25; a similar sentiment may be found in Richard Haass, "Force: A User's Guide," *Foreign Policy* 96 (Fall 1994): pp. 24–42. Eagleburger's statement may seem happily categoric, but elsewhere he has expressed entirely different sentiments. Of Yugoslavia he once said "We are against the use of force, period." David Binder, "Conflict in Yugoslavia, United Yugoslavia is U.S. Policy's Aim," *New York Times*, July 1, 1991, p. A 6. Contradictions of this sort are endemic to this debate.

3. See, for example, United Nations Security Council Resolution 940 on Haiti adopted July 31, 1994.

4. Richard N. Haass, *Intervention: The Use of American Military Force in the Post-Cold War World* (Washington, D.C.: Brookings Institution, 1994). His remarks on the increased opportunities for intervention were made to an invited audience at the Carnegie Endowment in Washington, D.C. on October 18, 1994.

5. Norman Angell, *The Great Illusion: A Study of the Relation of Military Power in Nations to their Economic and Social Advantage* (New York: Putnam's, 1941).

6. Colin Powell, "U.S. Forces: Challenges Ahead," *Foreign Affairs* 72, no. 5, (October 1992): p. 36.

7. Ann Devroy and Bradley Graham, "Clinton Seeks to Boost Defense by $25 Billion," *Washington Post*, December 2, 1994, p. A 1.

8. George Shultz, *Triumph and Turmoil* (New York: Scribner's, 1993), p. 649.

9. "Text of Clinton's Address," *Washington Post*, September 19, 1994, p. A 17.

10. Brent Scowcroft and Arnold Kanter, "Korea, Time for Action," *Washington Post*, June 15, 1994, p. 25.

11. Owen Harries, "My So-Called Foreign Policy," *The New Republic* 211, no. 15 (October 10, 1994): pp. 24–31.

12. William W. Kaufmann and John D. Steinbruner, *Decisions for Defense: Prospects for a New Order* (Washington, D.C.: Brookings Institution, 1991), pp. 42–43.

13. William E. Odom, *America's Military Revolution* (Washington, D.C.: American University Press, 1993), p. 172. On a lighter note, money was still available in late 1994 to send an Air Force plane from the U.S. to Italy to collect a single passenger. See John E. Harris, "Air Fare, Rome to Colorado, $120,000," *Washington Post*, December 9, 1994, p. A 1.

14. Daniel Williams, "U.S. Officials Hope Haiti Success Cures Somalia Syndrome," *Washington Post*, October 11, 1994, p. A 10.

15. For a useful summary of the arguments on either side of this debate, see separate articles by Andrew Krepinevich and A. J. Bacevich, "The Future of War," *National Interest*, 37 (Fall 1994): pp. 30–49.

16. Jim Hoagland, "More Donald Trump than John Wayne," *Washington Post*, January 13, 1994, p. 27; polls since 1953 indicate that, with the exception of Vietnam, presidential ratings have tended to rise following military interventions. See Ann Cronin, "Presidential Support and the Military Option," *New York Times*, September 18, 1994, pp. E 4–5.

17. "Extraordinary and Plenipotentiary," *Economist*, 332, no. 7882 (September 24, 1994): p. 30; Murray Kemp, "The Carter Mission," *New York Review of Books* XLI, no. 17 (October 20, 1994): p. 71; Michael Kramer, "The Carter Connection," *Time*, October 3, 1994, pp. 30–1.

18. Fred Barnes, "Oh, All Right Then," *The New Republic* 211, no. 15 (October 10, 1994): p. 11; Jim Hoagland, "Saddam Won't Just Fight the Same War Over Again," *Washington Post*, October 12, 1994, p. A 23.

19. Lippmann is quoted in Godfrey Hodgson, *In Our Time* (London: Macmillan, 1976), p. 117.

20. See George Shultz's comparison of Warren Christopher to Neville Chamberlain in Daniel Williams and Ann Devroy, "U.S. Policy lacks Focus, Critics Say," *Washington Post*, April 24, 1994, p. A 1; Anthony Lewis, "Beware of Munich," *New York Times*, January 8, 1993, p. 25, and Anthony Lewis, "Words and Deeds," *New York Times*, April 11, 1994, p. A 19; conservative commentators take the same tack. See William Safire, "Leadership Farewell," *New York Times*, September 29, 1994, p. A 25; Safire also likened the UN Commander in Bosnia, Sir Michael

Rose, to Chamberlain in "Robust or Bust," *New York Times*, November 28, 1994, p. A 17.

21. Brent Scowcroft, "Who can Harness History? Only the U.S.," *New York Times*, July 2, 1993, p. A 15.

22. Lake, "From Containment to Enlargement," p. 660.

23. Sherman Adams, *Firsthand Report* (New York: Harper, 1961), p. 360.

24. Kim R. Holmes, ed., *A Safe and Prosperous America: A U.S. Foreign and Defense Policy Blueprint* (Washington, D.C.: Heritage Foundation, 1993), pp. 8–13.

25. David Ignatius, "The Secret Korea Debate," *Washington Post*, June 12, 1994, p. C 1.

26. William J. Perry, "Military Action: When to Use It and How to Ensure Its Effectiveness," in *Global Engagement: Cooperation and Security in the 21st Century*, ed. Janne E. Nolan (Washington, D.C.: Brookings Institution, 1994), pp. 235–42

27. The comments of Lt. Col. Lee Gore, quoted in "U.S. Troops Study Lessons in Somalia Mission," *Washington Post*, December 8, 1993, p. A 25.

28. For an academic study of the differences between civil and interstate wars, see Hans Magnus Enzensberger, *Civil Wars: From L.A. to Bosnia* (New York: Free Press, 1994).

29. John Keegan, *A History of Warfare* (New York: Alfred A. Knopf, 1993), p. 392.

30. *Ibid.*, p. 385.

31. Rupert Smith, "War and Conflict in the Future," remarks at War Studies Group, King's College, London, September 14, 1993, para 4.

32. *Ibid.*, para 6 and 9.

33. Michael Specter, "Rebels Beat Back a Russian Force," *New York Times*, January 3, 1995, p. A 1.

34. Don Higinbottom, *The War of American Independence* (Boston: Northeastern University Press, 1983), p. 63.

35. George Shultz, *Turmoil and Triumph* (New York: Scribner's, 1993), pp. 649–50.

36. Keegan, *The History of Warfare*, p. 192.

37. Weinberger's conditions have become an object for derision for interventionists. See Shultz, *Triumph and Turmoil*, pp. 650–1. Shultz and Weinberger were on notoriously bad terms. See Robert C. McFarlane, *Special Trust* (New York: Cadell and Davis, 1994), p. 333.

38. One of these officials, George Kenney, has since recanted. See George Kenney, "Ending Bosnia's Endgame," *New York Times*, December 3, 1994, p. A 33.

39. Barton Gellman, "Somalia Hearing Examines Rejected Request for Armor," *Washington Post*, May 13, 1994, p. A 40. An even more wrenching account can be found in Fred Barnes, "Oh, All Right Then," *New Republic*, October 10, 1994, p. 11. A recent Rand Corporation report (MR-431-AF) by Benjamin C. Schwarz, *Casualties: Public Opinion*

and U.S. Military Intervention (Santa Monica, Calif.: Rand Corporation, 1994), represents an ingenious—if, in our view, unsuccessful—attempt to draw the conclusion that the American aversion to casualties can be turned into an offensive weapon.

40. Samuel B. Griffith, *Sun Tzu: The Art of War* (Oxford: Oxford University Press, 1963), p. 64.

41. The Gallup/*USA Today* poll is quoted in Daniel Yankelovich and I. M. Destler, *Beyond the Beltway: Engaging the Public in U.S. Foreign Policy* (New York: The American Assembly and Norton, 1994), p. 45; the earlier polling data appears in Godfrey Hodgson, *In Our Time*, p. 68.

42. Catherine Manegold, "Business Owners Fear Chaos at the Hands of Mob When Aristide Returns," *New York Times*, October 12, 1994, p. A 8.

43. William J. Perry "Military Action: When to Use It and How to Ensure Its Effectiveness," *Global Engagement: Cooperation and Security in the 21st Century*, ed. Janne E. Nolan (Washington, D.C.: Brookings Institution, 1994), pp. 235–42.

44. Morison, *History*, p. 860 (emphasis added).

45. Daniel C. Hallin and Todd Gitlin, "The Gulf War as Popular Culture and Television Drama," *Taken by Storm: The Media, Public Opinion, and U.S. Foreign Policy in the Gulf War*, eds. W. Lance Bennet and David L. Paletz (Chicago: University of Chicago Press, 1994), p. 155.

46. Jim Hoagland, "Even America Gets the Blues," *Washington Post*, December 14, 1993, p. A 25.

47. Eric Smitt, "Some Doubt U.S. Ability to Fight Wars on Two Fronts," *New York Times*, October 17, 1994, p. A 9.

48. Keegan, *A History of Warfare*, p. 294.

49. Jim McGee, "U.S., Russian Officials Stress Mutual Interests Despite Recent Tensions," *Washington Post*, January 2, 1995, p. A 2.

50. Michael Gordon, "G.I.s to Relieve Scandinavians for Bosnian Duty," *New York Times*, May 11, 1994, p. A 7; for a trenchant critique on the limitations of air power, see Eliot A. Cohen, "The Mystique of U.S. Air Power," *Foreign Affairs* 73, no. 1 (January 1994): pp. 109–24.

51. John Pomfret, "Hope Erodes for Muslims in Bosnia," *Washington Post*, November 28, 1994, p. A 1. Despite Perry's wise words, the myth of air power's efficacy lives on in the civilian community. See Albert Wohlstetter, "Bosnia: Air Power Not Peace Keepers," *Wall Street Journal*, December 9, 1994, p. A 9.

52. Laura Silber "International Call for Settlement in former Yugoslavia," *Financial Times*, November 29, 1994, p. 1; for an interesting essay on the need for international conciliators to work with the grain of Balkan society as the key component of bringing peace to that region, see Stjepan G. Mestrovic, *Habits of the Balkan Heart: Social Character and the Fall of Communism* (College Station, Texas: Texas A & M University Press, 1994).

53. Keith B. Richberg, "In War with Aideed, UN Battled Itself," *Washington Post*, December 6, 1994, p. A 1.

54. Keeley was quoted by Boyce Rensberger, "Anthropology: Violence is Nothing New," *Washington Post*, May 30, 1994, p. A 2.

Chapter 7
Diplomacy beyond Force

1. Shultz, *Triumph and Turmoil*, p. 688.
2. Brian Urquhart, "For A UN Volunteer Force," *New York Review of Books*, June 10, 1993, p. 3; UN Secretary General Boutros Boutros-Ghali later formally endorsed this plan. See Boutros Boutros-Ghali, *Supplement to the Agenda for Peace: Position Paper of the Secretary General on the Occasion of the Fiftieth Anniversary of the United Nations*, UN Document A/50/60 S/1995/1, January 3, 1995, pp. 1–24.
3. There is abundant official and academic material on NATO's search for a post–Cold War role and its relationship with European institutions. See, for example, Charles Glaser, "Why NATO is still the Best," *International Security* 18 (Summer 1993): p. 18; and Jeffrey Simon, "Does Eastern Europe belong in NATO?" *Orbis* 37 (Winter 1993): p. 21. A succinct overview may be found in David Haglund, S. Neil McFarlane, Joel J. Sokolsky, "NATO and the Quest for Ongoing Vitality," *Nato's Eastern Dilemma*, ed. David Haglund (Boulder, Colo.: Westview, 1994), pp. 11–36.
4. UN Secretary General Boutros Boutros-Ghali has written, "it is undeniable that the centuries old doctrine of absolute and exclusive sovereignty no longer applies. A major intellectual requirement of our time is to rethink the question of sovereignty." Boutros Boutros-Ghali, "Empowering the United Nations," *Foreign Affairs* 71, no. 5 (Winter 92/93): p. 98. The "law of democratic intervention" originates with France's Minister for Humanitarian Action, Bernard Kouchner. "The United Nations: Mr. Human Rights," *Economist*, December 26, 1992, pp. 57–60.
5. Boutros Boutros-Ghali, Commencement Speech at the Paul Nitze School of Advanced International Studies, Johns Hopkins University, Washington, D.C., May 26, 1994, UN Document S9/SM/5301, p. 2.
6. Professor Adam Roberts of Oxford University makes the point that the UN is suffering from severe overload. Roberts, "The United Nations and International Security" in *Ethnic Conflict and International Security*, ed. Michael Brown (Princeton, N.J.: Princeton University Press, 1993), pp. 210–12.
7. For a discussion of this risk, see "The Somali Specter," *Economist* 333, no. 7883 (October 1, 1994): p. 20.
8. John Chipman, "Managing the Politics of Parochialism," in *Ethnic Conflict*, ed. Brown, pp. 237–64.
9. Noel Malcolm, "Furiously in All Directions," *National Review*, March 7, 1994, p. 49; in arguing that the prime reason for invading

Haiti was to assert American "essential reliability," National Security Adviser Anthony Lake was putting forward the same institutional argument in favor of engagement. See Ann Devroy and John Goshko, "Lake says U.S. Reliability is at Stake," *Washington Post*, September 13, 1994, p. A 1.

10. The word "indispensability" comes from the communique of the Ministerial Meeting of the North Atlantic Council meeting in Istanbul, Turkey, on June 9, 1994. NATO Press Communique, M-NAC-1, (94), 46, p. 1. For an example of thinking that takes NATO's institutional survival as its starting point, see Zbigniew Brzezinski, "A Plan for Europe," *Foreign Affairs* 74, no. 1 (January/February 1995): pp. 26–42.

11. Boutros Boutros-Ghali, *An Agenda for Peace: Preventive Diplomacy, Peacemaking, and Peacekeeping*, UN Document A/47/277, June 17, 1992 (New York: The United Nations, 1992).

12. Jenonne Walker, "International Mediation of Ethnic Conflicts," in *Ethnic Conflict*, ed. Michael Brown, pp. 178–79; see also "Learning from Rwanda," *Economist* 332, no. 7877 (August 20, 1994): p. 13.

13. At the time, it was clear that both Bush and Baker, concerned about a possible uncontrolled disintegration of the Soviet Union, placed stability ahead of self-determination in their list of priorities for Eastern Europe. In a speech to the Supreme Soviet of the Ukrainian Soviet Socialist Republic on August 1, 1991, Bush warned of a "suicidal nationalism." In June, Baker had advocated the continuing territorial integrity of Yugoslavia. U.S. Department of State, *Dispatch* 2, no. 26 (July 1, 1991): p. 463.

14. Quoted in Johnson, *A History of the Modern World*, p. 341.

15. *Ibid.*, p. 281.

16. A cautionary word from an experienced African specialist may be found in James Murray, "Rwanda's Bloody Roots," *New York Times*, September 3, 1994, p. 19.

17. Morton Kaplan, *System and Process in International Politics* (New York: Wiley, 1957), pp. 50–2.

18. Marten van Heuven, "How Will NATO Adjust in the Coming Decade?" Rand Corporation N-3533-JS (Santa Monica, Calif.: Rand Corporation, 1992), pp. 6–7.

19. David E. Sanger, "North Korea Foils Efforts to Halt Nuclear Program," *New York Times*, May 29, 1994, p. 1.

20. See, for example, the diverse views that are to be found in Robert D. Kaplan, *Balkan Ghosts: A Journey through History* (New York: Vintage, 1993); Michael Ignatieff, *Blood and Belonging: Journeys in the New Nationalism* (New York: Farrar, Strauss & Giroux, 1994); Leonard Cohen, *Broken Bonds: the Disintegration of Yugoslavia* (Boulder, Colo.: Westview, 1993); Misha Glenny, *The Fall of Yugoslavia: The Third Balkan War* (New York: Penguin 1994); and, most especially, Alex Dragnich, *Serbs and Croats: the Struggle in Yugoslavia* (New York: Harcourt, Brace, Jovanovich, 1992).

21. Michael Krepon, ed., *A Handbook of Confidence-Building Measures*

for Regional Security (Washington, D.C.: Henry L. Stimson Center, 1993), pp. 11–15.

22. For an inside perspective on why fundamentalism is growing in the Middle East, see Robert D. Kaplan, "Eaten from Within," *Atlantic Monthly,* November 1994, pp. 26–44.

23. James Gow, *Legitimacy and the Military: the Yugoslav Crisis* (New York: St. Martin's Press, 1992)

24. Brian Hocking, *Localizing Foreign Policy: Non-Central Government and Multilayered Diplomacy* (New York: St. Martin's Press, 1993), pp. 31–69. For the application of localized foreign policy to the United States, see John M. Kline, "Managing Intergovernmental Tensions: Shaping a State and Local Role in U.S. Foreign Relations," *Foreign Relations and Federal States,* ed. Brian Hocking (Leicester, England: Leicester University Press, 1993), pp. 105–21.

25. Virginia Abernethy, *Population Policies: the Choice that Shapes Our Future* (New York: Insignia Books, 1993).

26. For an illustrative study of how the abundance or paucity of local associations respectively strengthens or inhibits the emergence of civil society, see R. D. Putnam, *Making Democracy Work: Civic Tradition in Modern Italy* (Princeton, N.J.: Princeton University Press, 1993).

27. Jay Rothman, "The Human Dimension in Israeli-Palestinian Negotiations," *The Jerusalem Journal of International Relations* 14, no. 3 (Fall 1992): pp. 69–81.

28. Bill Keller, "Zulu Party Ends Boycott of Vote in South Africa," *New York Times,* 20 April, 1994, p. A1; John Battersby, "Buthelezi Agrees to Join South African Election," *Christian Science Monitor,* April 20, 1994, p. 1.

29. David Buchan, "African Peacekeeping Force Has Moved Nearer," *Financial Times,* November 10, 1994, p. 6

Chapter 8
Whose National Interest Is It?

1. Henry Kissinger, "Global Realities: Risks and Opportunities," in *Leading the Global Enterprise,* ed. Theresa Brothers, Conference Board Report Number 1024, (New York: Conference Board, 1993), p. 10.

2. "In Clinton's Words: What U.S. Interests Are," *New York Times,* February 19, 1994, p. A 1. (emphasis added)

3. Philip Habib, "Looking at the Middle East," in *Thinking about America,* Annelise Anderson and Dennis L. Bark, eds., (Stanford, Calif.: Hoover Institution Press, 1988), p. 77 (emphasis added).

4. Charles A. Beard, *The Idea of National Interest* (Chicago: Quadrangle Books, 1934), p. 1.

5. Betty Glad, *Charles Evans Hughes and the Illusions of Innocence* (Urbana, Ill.: University of Illinois Press, 1966), p. 154.

6. For a realist's interpretation of Wilson's motivations, see Walter

Lippmann, *U.S. Foreign Policy: Shield of the Republic* (New York: Little, Brown, 1943), pp. 33–39; indeed the premise stated on page 1 of Smith's *America's Mission* that the prime objective of American diplomacy during the twentieth century was to "make the world safe for democracy" is based on a false reading of history.

7. Both Palmerston and de Gaulle are quoted in Joseph Frankel, *National Interest* (New York: Praeger, 1970), p. 18.

8. Thomas H. Etzold and John Lewis Gaddis, eds., *Containment: Documents on American Foreign Policy and Strategy* (New York: Columbia University Press, 1978), pp. 385–6.

9. This process is summarized in "The Road to War," *Foreign Affairs* 70, no. 1 (January 1991): pp. 1-4; see also, David Hoffmann, "Bush Denounces Saddam as Threat to Arabs, West," *Washington Post*, August 16, 1990, p. 1, for a catalogue of reasons for opposing Saddam.

10. Carnegie Endowment, *Changing our Ways* (Washington, D.C.: Carnegie Endowment for International Peace, 1992), p. 13.

11. Edwin J Feulner, Jr., *A Safe and Prosperous America*, Kim R. Holmes, ed., (Washington, D.C.: Heritage Foundation, 1994), p. 1.

12. Schlesinger, *Cycles*, p. 76; Barbara W. Tuchman, *The March of Folly* (New York: Ballantine, 1984), pp. 3–31.

13. Brookings Institution, *Major Problems in U.S. Foreign Policy: A Study Guide Prepared by the Staff of the International Studies Group* (Washington, D.C.: Brookings Institution, 1955), pp. 373–5.

14. George Kennan, *Around the Cragged Hill* (New York: W. W. Norton, 1993), p. 190.

15. Frankel, *National Interest*, p. 19.

16. Julien Benda, *The Treason of the Intellectuals* (New York: W. W. Norton, 1969), p. 15.

17. T. S. Eliot, "East Coker" (line 190), *The Four Quartets* (London: Faber and Faber, 1959), p. 31.

18. Michael Howard, "The World According to Henry: from Metternich to Me: Diplomacy by Henry Kissinger," book review in *Foreign Affairs* 73, no. 3 (May 1994): pp. 132–40.

Chapter 9
Sovereignty and the Coming
International Structures

1. Michael Mandelbaum, "The Reluctance to Intervene," *Foreign Policy* 95 (Summer 1994): pp. 3–17.

2. See Robert W. Tucker and David C. Hendrickson, "America and Bosnia," *National Interest* 33 (Fall 1993): pp. 14–27.

3. Adam Roberts, "Whither the UN?," *Oxford Today*, March 1993, p. 23.

4. John Chipman, "Third World Politics and Security in the 1990s: The World Forgetting, By the World Forgot?" in *U.S. Security in an Uncertain Era*, Brad Roberts, ed., (Cambridge, Mass.: MIT Press, 1993).

5. Roberts, "Whither the UN?" p. 25.

6. The future of the transatlantic security relationship is immensely complex. For an account of how intemperate attitudes have been struck by both Americans and Europeans, see "Marital Problems," *Economist*, 333, No. 7892 (December 3, 1994): pp. 15–6. The fact remains, however, that the two sides "need each other." Statesmanship will be required to steer a course through the mutual frustrations that inevitably lie ahead. See "UN Out of Bosnia," *The National Review* XLVI, No. 25 (December 31, 1994): p. 14.

7. The importance of the transatlantic relationship and the need for an integrated approach in reforming it is stressed in Jonathan Clarke, "Replacing NATO," *Foreign Policy* 93, (Winter 1993–94), pp. 22–40.

8. For an example of this approach, see Charles Krauthammer, "The Romance with Russia is Over," *Washington Post*, December 16, 1994, p. A 25.

9. For an example of this attitude, see Mark Almond, "Bear Hug," *National Review* XLVI, no. 25 (December 31, 1994): pp. 22–4.

10. Anthony DePalma, "U.S. Offers Billions to Mexico to Help Rescue the Peso," *New York Times*, January 3, 1995, p. A 6. The vital importance of Mexico to the United States is further attested by the fact that in early 1995 Mexico's need for immediate assistance prompted President Clinton to bypass congressional objections and provide large financial help on his own authority. (David E. Sanger, "Clinton Offers $20 Billion to Mexico for Peso Rescue: Action Sidesteps Congresss," *New York Times*, February 1, 1995, p. A 1.)

11. For a speculative look at some of the potential consequences of constitutional upheaval in Canada, see Lansing Lamont, *Breakup: The Coming End of Canada and the Stakes for America* (New York: W. W. Norton, 1994), pp. 227–45.

Chapter 10
Toward a New Public Consensus

1. Alexis de Tocqueville, *Democracy in America*, I, chapter viii.

2. Quoted in C. Vann Woodward, *The Future of the Past* (New York: Oxford University Press, 1989), p. 18.

3. Compare polls quoted in Janet Elder, "Ideas and Trends: Does this Jury Count?" *New York Times*, February 13, 1994, section 4, p. 3, and R. W. Apple, "Conflict in the Balkans," *New York Times*, February 8, 1994, p. A 1.

Notes

Notes   211

4. For an argument that the United States has lost its traditional prerogatives in Latin America, see Gaddis Smith, *The Last Years of the Monroe Doctrine* (New York: Hill and Wang, 1994), pp. 21–40. We are less sure that this interpretation is correct.

5. Ole R. Holsti, "Public Opinion and Foreign Policy," *International Studies Quarterly* 36, no. 4 (December 1992): p. 440.

6. In his various addresses at the time of the Haitian intervention, for example, President Clinton had to devote almost as much time to describing the minimal nature of the risks and the speed with which the U.S. troops would be withdrawn as to discussing the actual tasks that the troops would perform. See "Text of Clinton's Address," *Washington Post*, September 19, 1994, p. A 17; even when the intervention seemed to be going well, Congress's first instinct was to mandate a date for termination. The U.S. Commander in Haiti General Henry H. Shelton was repeatedly called on to defend the limited scope of his mission. See Larry Rohter, "U.S. Inaction on Gunmen Upsets Haitians," *New York Times*, October 19, 1994, p. A 3.

7. Holsti, "Public Opinion," pp. 439–66.

8. Daniel Yankelovich and I. M. Destler, eds., *Beyond the Beltway: Engaging the Public in United States Foreign Policy* (New York: W. W. Norton, 1994), p. 44. Though containing much interesting poll data, the book's failure to distinguish between domestic policy formation and that between sovereign states makes it a flawed guide for foreign policy.

9. Martin Kriesberg, "Dark Areas of Ignorance," *Public Opinion and Foreign Policy*, ed. Lester Markel (New York: Council on Foreign Relations, 1949), pp. 49–69.

10. Catherine McArdle Kelleher, "Security in the New Order: Presidents, Polls, and the Use of Force," *Beyond the Beltway*, ed. Yankelovich and Destler, pp. 225–52.

11. Nik Gowing, *Real Time Television Coverage of Armed Conflicts and Diplomatic Crises: Does it Pressure or Distort Foreign Policy Decisions?* (Cambridge, Mass.: Harvard University Press, John F Kennedy School of Government), pp. 16–20; public realization that TV images can be manipulated—or downright fabricated—may reinforce this sense of caution. For an account of the activities of public relations firms in the run-up to the Gulf War, see Jarol B. Manheim, *Strategic Public Diplomacy and American Foreign Policy: The Evolution of Influence* (New York: Oxford University Press, 1994), pp. 39–60. On this issue, the UN conclusion that the Bosnian Army shelled its own civilians in order to garner international support is relevant. See Chuck Sudetic, "Bosnian Army Said to Shell their Own Territory," *New York Times*, November 11, 1994, p. A 10. For a lucid presentation on the abuse of TV images for political purposes, see David Binder, "Anatomy of a Massacre," *Foreign Policy* no. 97 (Winter 1994–95): pp. 70–78.

12. Arnold Kanter, "Adapting the Executive Branch to the Post–Cold War World," *Beyond the Beltway*, ed. Yankelovich, p. 133.

13. Daniel Yankelovich and John Immerwahr, "The Rules of Public Engagement," in *Beyond the Beltway*, ed. Yankelovich, pp. 43–77. We disagree, however, with some of his suggestions of how this engagement is to be achieved. Foreign policy by "trial balloon" (p. 58), for example, is doomed to failure as foreign governments treat such devices as evidence of weakness and uncertainty.

14. Schlesinger, *The Cycles*, p. 300.

15. Abraham Lincoln, speech at Columbus, Ohio, September 16, 1859.

16. See Richard Morin, "Look in the Mirror Voters: The Trouble Starts with You," *Washington Post*, October 16, 1994, p. C 1.

17. "Voters, Blame Thyselves," *Economist*, 333, no. 7887 (October 29, 1994): pp. 17–8; Anthony Lewis, "Pie in the Sky," *New York Times*, October 31, 1994, p. A 19.

18. This should not lead us into the ahistorical error of thinking that Cold War policy was either obvious or uncontroversial. For an overview of the main points of view see Alastair Buchan, "United States Foreign Policy and the Future," in *America as an Ordinary Country*, ed. Richard Rosencrance (Ithaca, N.Y.: Cornell University Press, 1976), pp. 20–37. We should also not forget that actions that seem self-evident today, such as Truman's response to the Berlin blockade in 1948, were at the time bitterly disputed; see Stephen E. Ambrose, *Rise to Globalism* (New York: Penguin Books, 1985), p. 102.

19. *Beyond the Beltway*, ed. Yankelovich, p. 62. Incidentally, in a comic bow to political correctness, Yankelovich speaks only of the world's "police officer"!

20. The phrase belongs to the British journalist Peregrine Worsthorne, quoted by Ian Buruma in "Action Anglaise," *New York Review of Books* XLI, no. 17, (October 20, 1994): p. 67.

21. Bruce W. Jentleson, "The Pretty Prudent Public: Post Post-Vietnam American Public Opinion on the Use of Military Force," *International Studies Quarterly* 36, no. 1, (March 1992): pp. 49–77. Jentleson also served from 1993-94 in the State Department as a Clinton administration political appointee.

22. A wise reader's letter to the *New York Times*, October 25, 1994, p. A 20, pointed out that the average voter does not have a fax machine; Rich Lowery demonstrates unintentionally the artificiality of this kind of popular pressure in "Fax Populi," *National Review* XLVI, no. 21 (November 7, 1994): pp. 50–4.

23. Mort Rosenblum, *Who Stole the News?* (New York: Wiley, 1993).

24. On this point, see Owen Harries, "A State of Mind," *National Interest*, no. 38 (Winter 1994/95), pp. 111–2.

25. Remarks by Henry Kissinger at the National Press Club, Washington, D.C., on April 7, 1994.

26. Gary Wills, "What Makes a Good Leader?" *Atlantic Monthly* 273, no. 4 (April 1994): pp. 63–80.
27. "American Foreign Policy: Otherwise Engaged," *Economist* 329, no. 7835 (October 30, 1993): p. 24.
28. Godfrey Hodgson, *All Things to All Men* (London: Weidenfeld and Nicolson, 1980), pp. 13–49; Charles O. Jones, *The Presidency in a Separated System* (Washington, D.C.: The Brookings Institution, 1994), pp. 52–112.
29. See, for example, George F. Will, *Restoration: Congress, Term Limits, and the Recovery of Deliberative Democracy* (New York: The Free Press, 1992), pp. 73–91.

Chapter 11
Changing the Bureaucracy

1. Polling data in November 1994 showed that an overwhelming majority of Americans looked on government with disfavor. Quoted in editorial article in *Wall Street Journal*, November 10, 1994, p. A 16.
2. The Central Policy Review Staff review of the Foreign and Commonwealth Office (London: Her Majesty's Stationery Office, 1976) is the classic example of an exhaustive report that produced little result.
3. John Maynard Keynes, *The General Theory of Employment, Interest, and Money* (London: Macmillan, 1936), Chapter 24.
4. The citation derives from Douglas Hurd. See "A Battered Rolls Royce," *Economist* 330, no. 7854, (March 12, 1994): p. 68.
5. Ball, *Diplomacy,* p. 196.
6. Kennan, *Around the Cragged Hill,* p. 188.
7. *Ibid.,* p. 190.
8. *Ibid.,* p. 192.
9. Jim Hoagland, "The Unimperial Presidency," *Washington Post,* April 7, 1994, p. A 27.
10. According to press reports, CIA and State Department were playing these respective roles in U.S. assessments of Boris Yeltsin. See R. Jeffrey Smith, "U.S. Reluctant to Count Russian President Out," *Washington Post,* January 8, 1995, p. A 1.
11. David R. Mayhew, *Divided We Govern: Party Control, Lawmaking, and Investigations 1946-1990* (New Haven, Conn.: Yale University Press, 1991).
12. Mention has already been made of differences between the Pentagon and State Department over the use of air power in Bosnia; but these differences also extend (publicly) to major policy issues, such as the American attitude to a confederation between Serbia and the Bosnian Serbs. See Elaine Sciolino, "U.S. Policy Shift on Bosnia Creates a Muddle with Allies," *New York Times,* November 30, 1994, p. A 1.

13. For a sadly typical account of harmful bureaucratic turf wars between agencies to which national security should be their chief concern, see Mark Riebling, *The Secret War between the FBI and CIA* (New York: Knopf, 1994), pp. 454–60. Despite the book's title, this war has in fact been painfully public.

14. The city was Goradze. Michael Gordon, "Secretary of Defense Wins Few Points for Candor," *New York Times*, April 8, 1994, p. A 10; Peter Grier, "Perry's Remarks Muddle Bosnia Policy," *Christian Science Monitor*, April 11, 1994, p. 8.

15. "Top U.S. Officials Appear to Disagree on Haitian Leaders," *New York Times*, September 12, 1994, p. A 6.

16. Daniel Patrick Moynihan, *Pandaemonium: Ethnicity in International Politics* (New York: Oxford University Press, 1993).

17. John Tower et al., *The Tower Commission Report: The Full Text* (New York: Bantam, 1987).

18. Richard Challener, "The National Security Policy from Truman to Eisenhower" in *The National Security: Its Theory and Practice,* Norman A. Graebner, ed. (New York: Oxford University Press, 1980), pp. 44–5.

19. "Perrypatetic," *Economist* 331, no. 7858 (April 9, 1994): p. 32.

20. All too often this leads to counterproductive tensions. The Clinton administration is no exception. See Elaine Sciolino, "Two Key Advisers In a Bitter Duel on U.S. Policy," *New York Times*, September 23, 1994, p. A 1, and Elizabeth Drew, *On the Edge*, p. 431.

21. John Prados, *Keepers of the Keys: A History of the National Security Council from Truman to Bush* (New York: Morrow, 1991), p. 94.

Chapter 12
New Directions

1. *Exodus*, Chapter 20, Verse 5.

2. John McCain, "We Can't Show Weakness to North Korea," *New York Times*, May 28, 1994, p. A 14.

3. Michael Lind, "The Op-Ed History of America," *National Interest*, no. 37 (Fall 1994): pp. 16–23.

4. This point is made by J. Robinson West, "A Menacing Alliance in the Gulf," *Washington Post*, October 27, 1994, p. A 23.

5. For an example of this phenomenon with regard to Iran, see two (ludicrously juxtaposed) articles: Daniel Pipes, "Same Differences," and Peter W. Rodman, "Mullah Moola," *National Review* XLVI, no. 21 (November 7, 1994): pp. 61–69.

6. Leo Tolstoy, *War and Peace* (London: Penguin Books, 1957), p. 1400.

7. Ann Devroy, "President," *Washington Post*, January 6, 1994, p. A 1.

8. Daniel Williams, "U.S. Shifts Policy Focus to Russia Border States; Moscow's Troops, Ukraine are Emphasized," *Washington Post*, February 5, 1994, p. A 1.

9. Anthony Sampson, *New Anatomy of New Britain* (London: Hodder and Stoughton, 1971), p. 104.

10. See, for example, E. J. Dionne, "Out of the Box," *Washington Post*, September 20, 1994, p. A 21. This argument also omits the many-sided debate that produced the containment policy. The Truman Doctrine, for example, which now looks as though it was delivered on stone tablets, was greeted in its day by the British Foreign Office as a "panic measure." See Kenneth O. Morgan, *Labour in Power* (Oxford, England: Clarendon Press, 1984), p. 272.

11. Herbert Croly, *The Promise of American Life* (New York: Macmillan, 1909), p. 306.

12. George F. Kennan, "The Failure in our Success," *New York Times*, May 17, 1994, p. A 17.

13. Samuel Pufendorf's *De Systematibus* appeared in 1675; Campanella's *Discorsi* was published in 1624.

14. See, for example, Kevin Phillips, *Arrogant Capital*, (New York: Little, Brown, 1994), pp. 23–57.

15. Hedley Bull, *The Anarchical Society* (London: Macmillan, 1977), p. 121.

16. For an analysis of the potential for Theater Missile Defense, see Keith B. Payne, *Proliferation, Potential TMD Roles, Demarcation, and ABM Treaty Compatibility* (Washington, D.C.: Institute of Public Policy, 1994), pp. 1–5.

Chapter 13
The Roads Best Traveled

1. Lester Thurow, *Head-to-Head: The Coming Economic Battle Among Japan, Europe, and America* (New York: Morrow, 1992), pp. 27–66.

2. On some of the constant factors in international competition, see Donald Kagan, *On the Origins of War and the Preservation of Peace* (New York: Doubleday, 1995), pp. 6-9. Although competition between states may be natural, this does not necessarily imply conflict between them—as some have suggested. See John J. Mearsheimer, "Back to the Future: Instability in Europe after the Cold War," *International Security* 15, no. 1 (Summer 1990): p. 47.

3. Andrew Pollack, "Motorola Gaining Access to Japanese Markets," *New York Times*, March 11, 1994, p. D 1.

4. Unpublished telegram from Acting Secretary of State Lawrence Eagleburger to all U.S. ambassadors, cabled on September 14, 1992.

5. Winston Lord, State Department memorandum, April 1994.

6. For a later account of this episode, see Seymour Hersh, "On the Nuclear Edge," *New Yorker* 69, no. 6 (March 29, 1993): pp. 56–62.

7. Cited in *Japan Digest*, June 24, 1994, p. 5.

8. Barton Gellman, "Wider U.N. Police Role Supported: Foreigners Could Lead U.S. Troops," *Washington Post*, August 5, 1994, p. A 1; under the 1995 Post–Cold War Powers Act proposed by Senator Robert Dole, restrictions on the involvement of U.S. troops under UN command would grow even tighter. See, Elaine Sciolino, "Dole Offers Foreign Policy Initiatives," *New York Times*, January 5, 1995, p. A 3.

Index

Transcaucasus region, 124
Transdniester Republic, 22
Truman, Harry, 132; comments
on Eisenhower, 37; NSC and,
146; Truman doctrine, 103
Tuchman, Barbara, 104
Turkey: Cyprus and, 90; Iran
and, 90; United States and, 92;
Webster, Daniel and, 53

Ukraine, 19, 82, 176
Union of Soviet Socialist Republics (U.S.S.R.); Afghanistan
and, 24, 129; border disputes
in, 25; Cold War actions of,
vii, 21–22, 24–25, 43, 59, 104,
129–30, 150–54; Crimea and,
16; Czechoslovakia and, 129;
Europe and, 21, 41; fears of
disintegration in, 89; former
Soviet Union, 3, 19, 46, 127,
176; human rights and, 46;
Hungary and, 129; implications of demise of, vii, ix, xix,
xxii, 1–2, 7, 71, 82–83, 115,
154; Kissinger, Henry and,
163; national interest and, 104;
National Security Council and,
103, 146; nuclear weapons
and, 162, 175–76; OSCE and,
118; United States and, 43, 73,
83, 92, 154–55; Ukraine and,
82
unit veto system, 92
United Nations (UN): Angola
and, 112; Bosnia and, 31, 75,
80, 112; Cambodia and, 9, 91;
failed states and, 5–6, 10, 113,
116; Gulf War and, 97–98;
Haiti and, xxvi; Kashmir and,
112; Libya and, 112; military
force and, 79, 82; peacekeeping and, 79, 86–87, 93–95, 113;
Rwanda and, 91, 112; Security
Council, vii, 70, 87, 91–92, 97,
112, 181–82; Somalia and, 5,
82, 92; sovereignty and, 112–
22; Trusteeship Council, 6;
United States and, 81, 87, 186

United States: Asia and, 43, 47,
93, 117–20, 174, 178; balance
of power and, 54–55; Britain
and, 32–33, 52, 141–42; bureaucracy and, 139–50; Canada
and, 117, 120–22, 170, 179;
Chechnya and, 25, 82; China
and, 43, 46–47, 157, 165, 173,
185; Cold War and, 17, 43, 46,
59, 68, 121, 127, 162, 169; constitutional changes, 121; Cuba
and, 155; decline of, 4, 28–29,
36, 59; defense and, 15; defense of interests, xxx, 11;
defense spending, 69–70, 83;
empire and, 55–56; enemies of,
15, 23, 73, 75–76, 83, 129, 154–
55; Europe and, 56, 80, 88,
117–119, 156, 172, 175; excep-
tionalism of, 40–41; force and,
63, 65–60, 68–72, 75; foreign
affairs and, xiv; foreign aid
program, 35–36, 157; foreign
policy system in, xvi, 148–50,
151, 160–61, 164–67; GATT
and, 173, 179; global engagement of, xviii–xix, 4–6, 9, 52–
53, 56–57, 61–62, 88, 98, 152,
170; Haiti and, 29, 66, 68, 70,
80, 131, 153; historical memory and, 107–8, 131; Iran and,
66, 71, 154–55, 177; Iraq and,
66, 71, 154–55, 177; Islam and,
95, 176; Israel and, 185; Japan
and, 33, 36, 131, 155, 157, 172–
73, 182–85; leadership and, vii,
xiv, 28–29, 61–62, 94–95, 135;
Libya and, 85, 154; masterly
inactivity and, xxiv–xxv; Mexico and, 117, 120–22, 156, 170;
Middle East and, 25, 86, 102;
morality and, 41, 46, 56–58,
61; national interest and, 101–
9, 169; North Korea and, 23,
66, 71, 73, 80, 92, 94–95, 120,
150, 154–55, 166, 186; nuclear
weapons and, 168, 175–78;
peacekeeping and, 79; proposed agenda for, 8, 15, 73,

About the Authors

Jonathan Clarke is a former British diplomat. Specializing in international security issues, his assignments included Germany, Zimbabwe, and the United States. He is now a writer, lecturer, and commentator on foreign affairs with a regular syndicated column in the *Los Angeles Times*. Mr. Clarke graduated from Oxford and Hamburg Universities and now lives in Washington, D.C., with his wife and three children.

A former New Zealand diplomat and longtime foreign correspondent for the *Far Eastern Economic Review*, James Clad now lives with his wife and three children in Washington, D.C., where he writes and lectures about foreign policy. Beginning in mid-1995 he will be Research Professor of Southeast Asian Studies at Georgetown University. The recipient of fellowships at Harvard and Oxford Universities, Mr. Clad was born in New Haven, Connecticut, and grew up in California. His last book, *Behind the Myth: Business, Money & Power in Southeast Asia*, was published by HarperCollins in 1991.